# TESTIMONY AFTER CATASTROPHE

# Rethinking Theory

*GENERAL EDITOR*

Gary Saul Morson

*CONSULTING EDITORS*

Robert Alter
Frederick Crews
John M. Ellis
Caryl Emerson

# TESTIMONY AFTER CATASTROPHE

*Narrating the Traumas of
Political Violence*

Stevan Weine

Northwestern University Press
Evanston, Illinois

Northwestern University Press
www.nupress.northwestern.edu

Printed in the United States of America

10   9   8   7   6   5   4   3   2   1

ISBN 0-8101-2300-2 (cloth)
ISBN 0-8101-2301-0 (paper)

Library of Congress Cataloging-in-Publication Data

Weine, Stevan M., 1961–
     Testimony after catastrophe : narrating the traumas of political violence / Stevan Weine.
          p. cm. — (Rethinking theory)
     Includes bibliographical references and index.
     ISBN 0-8101-2301-0 (pbk. : alk. paper) — ISBN 0-8101-2300-2 (cloth : alk. paper)
     1. Torture victims—Rehabilitation. 2. Victims of state-sponsored terrorism—Mental health.
     3. Narration (Rhetoric) —Psychological aspects. 4. Dialogism (Literary analysis). 5. Bakhtin, M. M.
     (Mikhail Mikhailovich), 1895–1975—Criticism and interpretation. I. Title. II. Series.
     HV8593.W45 2006
     362.87—dc22

                                                                                  2005034756

To my father and mother

*We'll keep pushin' till it's understood*
*And these badlands start treating us good.*
　　　　—Bruce Springsteen, "Badlands"

# Contents

# Acknowledgments

Many persons helped me on the journey of writing this book. Mentors gave the gifts of their words, ideas, inspiration, and discipline. I am indebted to Ivan Pavkovic, Daniel Levinson, Tvrtko Kulenovic, Suzanne Feetham, Robert Jay Lifton, Allen Ginsberg, and Jerrold Maxmen.

I benefited from ongoing conversations with leading professionals and scholars on testimony, including Inger Agger, Soren Jensen, and Dori Laub, and on Bakhtin, including Caryl Emerson and Gary Saul Morson.

I greatly appreciate the support and guidance of Ferid Agani, Boris Astrachan, Ismet Ceric, Ralph Cintron, Alma Dzubur-Kulenovic, Vaughn Fayle, Joe Flaherty, Sander Gilman, Joop de Jong, Alma Klebic, Kathleen Knafl, Yasmina Kulauzovic, Karen Malpede, Mary Marshall Clark, Jerrold Post, John Rolland, Jack Saul, Bruce Shapiro, Amer Smajkic, Andrew Stone, Stephen Teich, Norma Ware, and Phillip Woollcott.

I enjoyed opportunities to share my work in professional and scholarly dialogues, and learned from the responses. I would like to thank the American Psychiatric Association, the International Congress for Southeast European Studies, the International Rhetoric Culture Conference, the International Society for Traumatic Stress Studies, the New York University International Trauma Studies Program, the Oral History Association, the University of Amsterdam, the University of Illinois at Chicago, the University of Prishtina, the University of Sarajevo, and World Relief. I would also like to thank the National Institute of Mental Health for its support of my research. I would especially like to thank my colleagues and students at the International Center on Responses to Catastrophes and the Kosovar Family Professional Education Collaborative.

I thank Nerina Muzurovic for her editorial work and Gary Saul Morson and Northwestern University Press for bringing this book to publication.

I could not have written this book without the music of Miles Davis, John Coltrane, Bob Dylan, Patti Smith, and Bruce Springsteen.

Lastly, I would like to thank my daughters and wife for putting up with a sometimes "too serious writing Dad." Their love makes my work possible and gives me a reason to believe. *Junbee.*

# Introduction

The survivors of political violence give testimonies in families and communities, trials and truth commissions, religious institutions, psychotherapies, newspapers, documentaries, artworks, and even in solitude. Through spoken, written, and visual languages, survivors' testimonies tell stories that may change history, politics, and life itself.

The testimonies that are the focus of this book have three defining characteristics: they are personal, truthful, and ethical. Personal: each testimony is a survivor's account of the events of political violence that they themselves have endured or witnessed. Truthful: the testimony consists of what the survivor believes is true; if they know that they are lying, then it is not testimony. Ethical: the testimony is linked with an obligation to redress the injustices of political violence.

I am a psychiatrist and scholar in the field of mental health and human rights. My work is providing community-based care for survivors and studying political violence in terms of its causes, consequences, and responses. Hope draws me to testimonies. Yes, hope. No matter what horrors and humiliations a person has endured, in testimony I hear the hope expressed that something good may come from that person's story. This hope propels me, and people from many walks of life, to better understand survivors' stories and what we should do with them. Thus I wrote this book not just for specialists in either literature or mental health and human rights, but for any readers with an interest in survivors' stories of political violence.

Because testimonies carry the power to change the meanings that people derive from their experience of political violence, many see testimonies as helpful. Others at times see them as problematic or even dangerous. Delivering on the hope that lies in testimonies is rarely straightforward and sometimes not at all possible. Multiple disciplines and institutions concerned with addressing the consequences of political violence claim that they believe in the value of testimony. Although their work may help survivors in important ways, all of us struggle over how to use what testimonies convey. Too often psychiatrists, lawyers, journalists, aid workers, historians, and politicians approach the testimony instrumentally; we use it as a source of information to be extracted, a task to be performed, or as a theory or ideology to be applied. We show little interest in the testimony as a story that is open to many alternatives, meanings, or responses. My concern is that when testimony is depersonalized, decontextualized, objectified, and reduced, it is not being used how it wants to be used—as a story. Such closed uses of testimony may have their benefits, but they also put at risk testimonies' legitimacy, resourcefulness, and power.

The central thesis of this book is that efforts to use testimony to address the consequences of political violence would be strengthened, though by no means guaranteed, if based upon a fuller acknowledgment of the personal, truthful, and ethical elements that are embodied in the narrative essence of testimony. This means we should especially learn from those who present artistic models that can help us to better regard testimony as a story. Literary artists and philosophers help us realize that although testimonies give accounts that are bound to what has been destroyed, lost, or damaged, testimonies remain—precisely because they are stories—a valued part of life as hopeful energies of living history.

## Testimony in Chile

On January 3, 2000, the *New York Times* ran a feature entitled "Pinochet Case Reviving Voices of the Tortured."[1] The belated arrest and detention of the accused general Augusto Pinochet in August 1998 in London had brought back the nightmare of torture for scores of Chileans. Between 40,000 and 100,000 citizens of the nation of Chile were victims of torture during the dreaded seventeen-year-long Pinochet regime, which ended in 1990. The *Times* reporter interviewed victims. He painted a picture of their lives: "The torturers are always inside of me . . . ," "The torture made me hate life . . . ," "People isolate you, and you can't find work."

With the arrest of Pinochet, the article recounted, their silence had been broken. More victims were seeking help. Chile's mental health professionals and human rights activists were again offering help, which some began decades ago. The journalist called it "therapy" and "treatment," but also reported that Chilean mental health workers were doing "testimony."

Two Chilean mental health professionals, Elizabeth Lira and Eugenia Weinstein, first introduced the "testimony of political repression as a therapeutic instrument" in a paper presented in 1980. This landmark paper not only marked the start of the "Latin American testimony school" but also defined the contemporary field of mental health and human rights.[2]

Testimonies courageously recorded and smuggled out of Chile in the 1970s were instrumental in first informing the world about the Pinochet regime's crimes and in galvanizing the international human rights movement in support of torture victims. In 2000 the *New York Times* reported that testimonies were again being gathered by Chilean human rights organizations, such as the Group of the Families of the Disappeared. Human rights lawyers in London and Madrid were gathering testimonies too, for it was anticipated that Pinochet might soon be tried in a court of law for crimes against humanity.

Then, a few weeks later, in February 2000, the *New York Times* reported that Pinochet was declared too frail to stand trial.[3] So these testimonies wouldn't go to court this time, but did they somehow help anyway? I note that in the *New York Times* article on torture, belief in the testimonies had soared. Many believed that testimonies bore the truth, that testimony would help, that testimony would bring legal justice, and that testimony would set things right.

The stories people told the journalist did not allow for much hope. Many Chileans' testimonies had been gathered by mental health professionals and human rights activists in the 1970s, '80s, and '90s. It must have seemed like the right thing to do, but was it possible to know what good it actually did? If there was convincing evidence to affirm those testimonies' contribution, the *New York Times* journalist did not find it. Did testimony significantly ease the victims' suffering? Did it make their lives any better? Did it affect either the government's or the international community's ability to bring the perpetrators to justice? Did it help Chile to "move on"? Answers to these questions were not available. Much of what was being claimed by the mental health and human rights field about testimony—beginning with the basic claim that testimony is helpful—appeared to be based upon an intuitive grasp of the testimony and its unique energetics. Testimony just seemed right.

Even if we wanted to believe that testimony was helpful, it would be impossible to forget all that testimony does not address. The journalist himself named many problems for which testimony had no answers. He heard survivors speak of their grave and lasting difficulties. Their lives were ruined by unemployment, poverty, alcoholism, suffering, loneliness, and crime. It is somewhat surprising, then, that in this article written by a sympathetic journalist, testimony was not at all condemned or even questioned: not by the survivors, the mental health professionals, or the human rights activists. Rather, it appeared that the opposite was true: more people spoke of testimonies being gathered and affirmed the role of testimony. And testimony was certainly not condemned by the journalist, who in his article facilitated testimony work. He received survivors' stories, and in one day's news article, transmitted them to the world.

It is remarkable how the belief that something good can come of testimony is so persistent and so outweighs concerns about the testimonies' obvious limitations. This was the case not only in Chile but also in other situations of political violence, where we likewise find the imperative to give testimony and the sense that giving testimony is helpful. It finds expression in the fifteen countries that have conducted truth commissions, most recently in South Africa.[4] It is also present in the notion— commonly expressed in recent years by aid workers and trauma mental health professionals in the Balkans, Rwanda, and East Timor—that survivors should tell their stories because something good will result. More recently, following the events of September 11, 2001, New Yorkers also called for the gathering of survivors' stories. Oral historians gathered survivors' stories, and artists, including the American rocker Bruce Springsteen, turned survivors' stories into art.[5] The Bush administration's manipulation of 9/11 fears to support the war on Iraq was itself the focus of

Michael Moore's film *Fahrenheit 9/11*, which featured the voices of soldiers and their working-class families from Flint, Michigan. When Saddam Hussein's regime fell after the U.S. attack on Iraq, even Secretary of Defense Rumsfeld wanted testimonies; he urged ordinary Iraqis to go to journalists and tell their stories to the world. Given the various ways that survivors' stories have appeared, it is all the more important to enumerate some difficult questions concerning the uses to which people are putting this belief in testimony. Who is talking and who is listening? Who or what is helped by testimony? By what means? Toward what ends?

In this book, the term "testimony" is used to signify the stories told by survivors of political violence, including torture, genocide, and war. Not always, but often enough, some survivors really want to tell their stories. There is no one reason for telling, nor one way of telling or listening, nor one type of story. Nor does the giving of testimony promise any simple resolution. Sometimes it may satisfy the aim for which it was attempted, but there is not always a clear aim. Testimonies are often given because it is believed that they will bring good. People believe that a restorative power resides in them for individuals, families, communities, nations, and for humanity. At the same time, there may also be the fear that testimonies may make matters worse. If people give testimony, it could make them suffer more or even retraumatize them. Rather than establishing the truth of historical events, it might only further confuse and introduce falsehoods or outright lies. It might not dissipate hatreds, but could actually fan those flames.

It is likely that telling the story raises unanswerable questions and irresolvable feelings or promotes unwanted actions. If giving testimony is like opening a Pandora's box, then in a time of war or genocide, civil unrest or social transition, this is not always desirable, and sometimes not at all indicated. Yet not even this is enough to stop the desire to tell, which is a persistent feature of humankind. Where there is political violence, testimonies are going to be spoken by survivors and witnesses, creating areas of considerable struggle across many institutions and disciplines concerning what to do with their stories. This book aims to explore those struggles. This will involve coming to a better understanding of what draws people so compellingly to testimony and what difficulties that attraction poses. How might we make good on the belief in testimony while managing the difficulties?

## Clinical Testimony

In the late twentieth and early twenty-first centuries, testimony narratives given by survivors of political violence found a niche in the psychiatric province of trauma mental health. This I call "clinical testimony." Clinical testimony is an approach to testimony that is dependent upon clinical theory and methodology from the fields of trauma mental health, psychiatry, psychology, or psychoanalysis. Although it may sometimes utilize nonclinical theories and methods, the clinical testimony approach regards testimony as a therapeutic intervention for the traumatic mental health consequences of political violence. Clinical testimony is especially associated with cognitive approaches to mental illness and treatment that are bedrock assumptions in the traumatic stress theory of the trauma mental health field. Clinical testimony approaches are applied in both clinical and nonclinical situations. In this book, I consider how many different players in the field of mental health and human rights and related fields have applied the clinical testimony approach to address suffering, peace and reconciliation, and historical documentation.

The topic of testimony is a relatively recent concern in the field of mental health. The Danish mental health professionals Inger Agger and Soren Jensen described "the testimony method" (first derived by the Chileans) in their 1996 book *Trauma and Healing Under State Terrorism* and in several prior journal articles. Inger Agger also authored *The Blue Room: Trauma and Testimony Among Refugee Women* (1992), based upon testimonies she conducted with women refugee survivors of trauma and torture. These works are widely read and cited by humanitarian workers and scholars concerned with political violence.[6]

Testimony work has been central to work with Holocaust survivors, producing a genre within a genre of "Holocaust testimony," which includes "survivor testimony" but also "testimonial literature" and "video testimony."[7] In 1992 the psychiatrist and psychoanalyst Dori Laub and the literary scholar Shoshana Felman used the concept of testimony in their book *Testimony: Crises of Witnessing in Literature, Psychoanalysis, and History,* which combined literary criticism and psychoanalysis.[8] Their writings are key texts for Holocaust studies and trauma work with survivors of the Shoah and other forms of political violence.

Mental health professionals' involvement in testimony is not surprising. They were among the initial few to listen to the stories, both in humanitarian emergencies and in resettlement countries. After all, these are stories of the extremities of suffering, horror, and even madness. The stories called for professional approaches to assess and treat survivors, and these professional approaches shaped the various forms of clinical testimony that Agger, Jensen, and Laub initially described and that others have extended and applied in the field. However, I note that even the proponents of clinical testimony recognized that testimonies were not only cognitions (as traumatic stress theory underlines) but also stories, and that there was a need to grapple with such narrative concerns as voice, meaning, and imagination. Indeed, clinical testimony writings often turn toward literature and literary theory in order to understand and engage with the testimony. For example, in *The Blue Room* Agger wrote: "One of the most important elements in a healing process is to come to possess *your* own story and thereby create your own narrative. Poets have always known this" (BR 5).

Although intellectually broad in certain respects, clinical testimony also presents some important limitations. When professionals in trauma mental health delineate the theory and practice of clinical testimony, something of concern happens; the ideas may become rigid as the boundaries of specialization are drawn. In the field testimonies may come to be regarded, by mental health professionals and by other intervenors who are influenced by mental health professionals, as if they are one-dimensional clinical trauma stories; they may become closed and isolated from the broader expanse of human experience and interaction to which they truly belong. The notion of clinical testimony may also do little to help broaden other important but potentially narrowing approaches to testimony, such as the human rights focus upon testimony as a source of legal evidence.

Many people have considerable difficulty with the medicalization of trauma stories. I don't think that the nature of this difficulty with respect to the testimonies of political violence has been sufficiently articulated, however. Nor has there been an adequate discussion of what may be done to better address (or contest) the issue of the clinical claim over testimony. In this book I contend that with the clinical, testimony finds itself in a blind, though not irredeemable, alley. One problem with clinical testimony is that it does not grasp the fundamental properties of testimony as a story—an energetic and unfinalized story—and therefore may respond in ways that end up betraying or degrading an essential nature of testimonies. Is this the ruin of testimony, or does it have a future? I do not know. But what I want to do in this book is to help point testimony work in a more promising direction.

## Intuition and Imagination

I propose that a key to moving in this new direction is attending to the testimony as a story of living history, which is how testimonies truly want to be used. This must involve finding new ways of moving with what intuition tells us about the testimony as a storied source of considerable energy. Intuition says that testimonies are not a rarefied, professional-technical practice evacuated from life, but instead belong to a broader understanding of human meaning and communication, embedded in life itself, and engaged with history, culture, and suffering.

Dori Laub, Inger Agger, and Soren Jensen saw testimony in a broader context. I know because I was fortunate enough to learn about testimony directly from each of them. One day in New Haven in 1993, I showed Dori Laub the Chileans' landmark papers. Another day in Zagreb, Croatia, two years later, I introduced Inger Agger and Soren Jensen to Dori Laub's writings. It is interesting that two groups working in different sociohistorical contexts would both use testimony, yet in such distinct ways. It is necessary not only to understand how their two works compare, but also to rethink clinical testimony from a broader perspective involving stories, speech, and language. In comparison with the multiple dimensions of the word "testimony" represented in the *Oxford English Dictionary*'s definition, testimony in the clinical framework, as articulated by Laub, Agger, and Jensen is a more restricted proposition.[9] For example, the *New Shorter Oxford English Dictionary* lists the following definitions and phrases for "testimony":

> Evidence, proof, esp. . . . evidence given in court, an oral or written statement given under oath or affirmation . . . Declaration or statement of fact . . . (An) open acknowledgment or profession, esp. of religious faith or experience . . . A written certificate, a testimonial.

I am concerned about the limitations of clinical testimony for mental health professionals and for other intervenors from human rights, journalism, law, oral history, and politics who also look at survivors' testimonies through the lens of clinical testimony. I want to explore testimony from a broader perspective that is focused on its narrative dimensions.

We owe Agger, Jensen, and Laub recognition for taking new paths in the work with survivors of political violence. I find in their writings (as I found in conversations with them) a recognition that clinical perspectives are valuable, but not enough. And I find that they made attempts to go beyond the clinical framework. I learned from their works and used what they taught as a perch for achieving new understandings. This is what I believe needs to be done to get testimony out from that blind alley—to advance a narrative-focused understanding of testimony that improves its capacity for engaging in the living worlds of survivors.

Too much of testimony work has been left to intuition. That includes how testimony is spoken, received, documented, interpreted, retransmitted, and understood. It is not necessarily bad to be rooted in intuition, but it is necessary to know if there is any discernible shape to that intuition. Are there some structures that can be identified, and would it help to do so? The role of intuition in testimony must be approached with caution, as suggested by Karl Popper in the 1982 preface to *The Open Universe*:

> I regard intuition and imagination as immensely important: We need them to invent theory. But intuition, just because it may persuade and convince us of the truth of what we have intuited, may badly mislead us: It is an invaluable helper, but also a dangerous helper, for it tends to make us uncritical. We must always meet it with respect, with gratitude, and with an effort to be severely critical of it.[10]

Precisely this must be a concern in exploring testimony. To begin, we must listen when intuition tells us to be concerned with the stories that survivors tell of their journeys through history. In psychiatry and psychology, the systems that are employed (and the organizations that employ mental health professionals and workers) are often oriented in directions other than the historical and the narrative. Traumatic stress theory, which dominates trauma and refugee mental health, has been criticized for taking history and historical crimes and making them into a clinical disorder.[11] Nonetheless, as a physician I believe that we must respect the obligation to address suffering through clinical, preventive, and psychosocial approaches. But we should also trust our intuition that steers us toward history, because it is an essential element for understanding and helping survivors, their communities, and nations.

Karl Popper suggested that it is essential to turn to the imagination. In literature there are remarkably imaginative forms of testimony. In novels, poetry, plays, short stories, and essays far too numerous to name, there is a dexterity with the linguistic and narrative aspects of testimony that strict memoirists or "objective" observers from the clinical and social sciences often fail to capture. In literature, evocations of the psychological, the ethical, or the historical are less dependent upon ideology or theory and in that way are perhaps closer to life. Given that so many texts have plumbed the depths of human suffering and injustice, a vast literature pertaining to testimony exists. It is far more than I could cover in this book. But I will read from several literary works and use them to reread the clinical testimony texts and to offer a storied approach to testimony.

For example, in his masterful novels *The Radetzky March* and *The Emperor's Tomb*, the Austro-Hungarian Jewish novelist Joseph Roth depicted a struggle over memory that is closely related to that of families from Bosnia-Herzegovina. In Roth's tale, several generations of a family's men live and die under the spell of a painting of a soldier who once saved the life of the emperor. The futility of knowing how to act in these circumstances is brilliantly articulated by Roth: "The old revolver that Herr von Trotta had taken along pressed in his back pocket. What good was a revolver? They saw no bears and no wolves in the borderland. All they saw was the collapse of the world."[12]

Roth's characters move in the dark. How can you read the signs in a collapsing world? How exactly do you protect yourself? For what do you live? It took a brilliant literary imagination to depict the struggles over historical memory in the life of a family marked by wars. It so happens that the persons from Bosnia-Herzegovina who gave testimony in Chicago and Sarajevo struggled with memories in their lives in ways that are not so unlike those in Roth's novels. They gave testimonies that were driven by personal and historical experience, and which in turn demonstrated the power of these stories to shape life and history. Although these survivors were not novelists, sometimes their testimonies have the narrative power that I find in Joseph Roth's novels. How is that possible?

Those persons whose work addresses the consequences of political violence, for example, aid workers or journalists, sometimes ask: What kinds of stories are these? Though some of these professionals may appreciate the literary strength of these narratives, their approaches to testimony production and transmission often depend more upon fact and cognition than on story and imagination. The challenge that they face is not only getting survivors to tell their stories of pain, degradation, humiliation, and evil, but also getting others to listen to these awful stories. Some turn away. Some look back. Does anyone know how to really work with these stories in ways that convert their narrative power into something consequential and good?

In the hope that survivors' stories can teach us something about life, many people gather, share, and study them. They believe that survivors' stories and the memories they carry are not simply the human residue of a machinated history. They regard testimonies as a source of collective identity that shapes social life and the making of history. It is thus no surprise to find struggles over these stories in many different corners of cultures.

But who is gathering, interpreting, framing, and communicating these stories? Often the memories themselves are contested. It is no exaggeration to say that in the contemporary era, where memory drives history, the struggle for the future is to a significant degree a struggle over these stories. But are those elements of society that watch over testimony adequately prepared for the challenges of these struggles? I fear not.

The recognition of this intense, many-sided, and complex conversation on testimony stands opposed to the claim that testimony is one large, diffuse, reducible thing like clinical testimony. This claim has issued from the field of trauma mental health and works to uphold its own claims of legitimacy. Understandably, professional disciplines have their commitments, and we need to be aware of them. But because I believe these can also become impediments, I propose an alternative view of testimony as a heterogeneous space, a space containing many particular, distinct universes of testimony that are in multidimensional relationship with one another.

## Universes of Testimony

Testimony concerning political violence exists in several spaces and has acquired the shape of several movements. The spaces best described in the testimony literature of the West are torture testimony and Holocaust testimony, and more recently testimonies from Bosnia-Herzegovina. Other newer spaces have emerged, such as Partition in South Asia, apartheid testimony, Kosovar testimony, and survivors of September 11 and other terrorist acts. Older spaces defined by a particular group's survivor experiences are also being reclaimed as testimony. In the United States, for example, these include Vietnam combat veterans, African slaves in America, and Native Americans. Several different movements are committed to testimony, including human rights, trauma mental health, present history, creative arts bearing witness, and peace education. I believe that we stand to gain more by recognizing and embracing, rather than rejecting and erasing, the dilemmas presented by acknowledging this heterogeneity of voices and histories. For that reason, this book will explore testimony in several (although by no means all available) different spaces.[13]

Yet there is a risk in seeing testimony as many separate and unrelated fragments. What are some of the major strands that hold the discourse on testimony together? Is it possible to articulate a framework of understanding that supports testimonies' engagement across many different settings, and in the shape of numerous different movements, without being excessively reductionist? This book looks at testimony in relation to three basic concerns of human development that stem from the consequences of political violence in post-conflict societies and diasporic communities: How to relieve suffering? How to create cultures of peace and reconciliation? How to document histories? These questions have emerged from a rethinking of testimony across several settings where survivors of political violence live. They are questions not only for any one discipline, but also for any and all disciplines that seek to approach the phenomenon of testimony. They are also questions that may be relevant to other groups of trauma survivors, where political violence is not necessarily the cause (for example, natural disasters), although that will not be the focus of this book.

*Testimony After Catastrophe* offers a new view on mental health and human rights. It claims that, by focusing on cognitive and legal processes, the mental health and human rights field has tended to take too narrow an approach to the universes of testimony. Mental health and human rights work should be grounded in testimony— but where that testimony is truly a story. Only when the testimony is a story do we really learn the perspective of the survivor, the subjective experience of political violence, the survivor's analysis of his or her situation, and the moral position of the survivor.

One way to address this level of complexity is through meaningful and substantive multidisciplinary dialogue and inquiry that includes the humanities as well as the clinical and social sciences. This depends on a far better articulation of how testimonies function as stories amid troubled social contexts. Specifically, part 1 of this book explores testimonies in four different sociohistorical spaces: torture testimonies (chapter 1), Holocaust testimonies (chapter 2), testimonies from wartime Bosnia-Herzegovina (chapter 3), and Kosovar testimonies (chapter 4). This part traces a trajectory of time that goes from testimony subgenres that were produced years ago and are relatively more completed to those that were produced more recently and are still very incomplete. In each context, literary testimony is introduced and is read alongside clinical testimony. As the narrative of this book proceeds, the different testimony spaces are encouraged to speak to one another, though without forgetting that they also belong to different universes. I aim to articulate the central dilemmas of testimony within each space, and the roles of intuition and imagination. I want to better understand how testimony work has been structured and why.

The concept of the "dialogic" as explored by the twentieth-century Russian literary theorist Mikhail Bakhtin in a lifetime of writings provides a helpful means of exploring testimony's relationship to the aforementioned three questions about human development. Ironically, Bakhtin never wrote about testimony nor gave testimony, although he experienced political oppression and suffered from a debilitating chronic bone disease. Bakhtin's literary philosophy is valuable because it can help us to explore testimony and human development in a way that is based upon intuition and imagination and yet is also disciplined. The second part of this book will use Bakhtin's approach to "dialogic work" and related Bakhtinian concepts (as contained in his writings and as interpreted by the scholars Gary Saul Morson and Caryl Emerson) and apply these ideas to testimony.

I find that Bakhtin offers what is needed for testimony and human development because he is so able to balance structure and freedom. To make testimony work freer, we need to build new structures, but those structures must have the capacity for openness. Testimony needs dialogism, but because dialogism requires "depth and duration," testimony does not promise that healing, peace, or remembrance will come easily or at all. Testimony work is difficult, and dialogism is neither a shortcut nor a means of safe passage, but it offers a way of taking an intuitive grasp of testimony's energetics and then envisioning and taking steps toward positive changes. Part 2 of this book envisions testimony as dialogic work that takes shape around three critical imperatives for survivors and their societies. These three imperatives are relieving suffering (chapter 6), creating cultures of peace and reconciliation (chapter 7), and documenting histories (chapter 8).

Although in this book I sometimes openly state my disagreements with others, including my professional colleagues, *Testimony After Catastrophe* is not a polemic. I try to let the testimonies and those who work with testimonies have their say before applauding, questioning, challenging, and negotiating with them. This book is intended for a new generation of multidisciplinary professionals, paraprofessionals, scholars, writers, artists, activists, and survivors who find hope in testimony and want to help deliver on testimony's promise. I seek to contribute to dialogues and collaborations on testimony for this growing community of helpers and thinkers.

# TESTIMONY AFTER CATASTROPHE

# PART I

## Testimonies in Four Spaces

*In all the faculties, do-gooders are now trying to listen their way back into the past (like me), but the problem has always been our ears, not their voices.*
> —Breyten Breytenbach, *Dog Heart*

# 1

# Torture Testimonies

Efforts to end the use of torture worldwide have been a primary focus of the mental health and human rights movement since the 1980s. This movement has established a body of practice, a clinical literature, and service institutions that have used the survivor's testimony for individual healing and advocacy. Torture testimony is regarded as a modified form of brief individual psychotherapy for survivors, but questions remain about whether testimony is able to ameliorate the mental health consequences of torture. Torture testimony is also used as a means of human rights documentation; however, this is complicated by concerns over the testimonies' truthfulness. In literature, torture testimony may be incorporated into literary testimony, which has opened up additional communicative channels for the documentation, exploration, and condemnation of torture.

## Death and the Maiden

Living in exile in the brutal years when Pinochet's military dictatorship still ruled over Chile, Ariel Dorfman wrote a "dramatic situation." "As I began to write I found the characters trying to figure out the sort of questions that so many Chileans were asking themselves privately, but that hardly anyone seemed interested in posing in public" (DM 73).[1] Dorfman returned to Chile several years later in the time of transition to democracy. Upon his return, he then completed writing the play *Death and the Maiden*. It seems important, if not mandatory, that Dorfman wrote at some margin of distance from the state of terror, in the safer and calmer situations afforded at first by exile and then by democratic transition. The writing was completed in a post-Pinochet society in transition where communication was not only possible, but in a way, necessary. There were fears and many questions concerning what the dictatorship had meant for Chileans and a hunger for answers.

Dorfman's drama takes place in a Latin American country after dictatorship, in an unnamed place that could be Chile. A woman who has survived kidnapping, torture, and rape, Paulina, has an accidental encounter with a man whom she immediately believes was her torturer and rapist. Her husband Gerardo, a lawyer, is the newly appointed head of the country's Truth and Reconciliation Commission. Gerardo brings this stranger into their home after the man rescues Gerardo from a flat tire on a remote road near the seaside. When Paulina realizes that it is him, she takes this man, Roberto Miranda, a doctor, binds and gags him, and holds him at gunpoint. Miranda claims to be innocent. Gerardo sides with Miranda, not his wife.

An outraged Paulina insists that Dr. Miranda had tortured and raped her while she was held in detention by government forces. Gerardo hears her speak of these events for the very first time. The eeriness of this fact is not lost on Paulina: "Isn't this bizarre, that I should be telling you all this as if you were my confessor, when these are things I've never told Gerardo, or my sister, certainly not my mother" (DM 29).

Strange are the conditions that Dorfman creates in which truth-telling finally becomes possible, after fifteen years of strained family and public silence. Strange that it is not her family members or loved ones who provoke Paulina's agonizing confession, but the man who allegedly brutalized her. After saying some of these things to the men, she suddenly reverses course—she ceases her telling, and demands that Miranda himself now do the confessing.

She turns on a tape recorder and asks for his testimony. "You should know, Doctor, that everything you say will be recorded here" (DM 31).

Gerardo protests: "What are you trying to do, woman, with these insane acts?"

Gerardo is asking: What good can come of this? We too wonder: Why did she suddenly insist that Miranda speak instead of her? What is she trying to accomplish?

Paulina: "I already told you—put him on trial."

Gerardo does not like this. "What are you going to—and all this because fifteen years ago someone . . ."

"Someone what? . . . what did they do to me, Gerardo. Say it" (DM 34).

At this crucial moment it is not Miranda, the alleged perpetrator, or Paulina, the survivor, who assumes the position of confessor. Instead it is Gerardo. Paulina now demands that he tell all. She prods him to say yes, she was tortured, yes, she was raped.

Why is it that Gerardo has to be the one to say these things? Why is it that Gerardo is not trying to help Paulina to talk? After all, it is she who is the survivor and she who has lived in silence with those memories of torture for fifteen years. Does she make Gerardo say it because she believes that he was complicit in her silence? Or could it be that there is something else she wants to hear from her husband?

Dorfman effects another strong reversal by having the lawyer, usually in command of the courtroom, instead occupy the position of the witness under interrogation. What's even more fantastical is the irony that the head of the Truth and Reconciliation Commission has been living and sleeping with a torture story for years but did not know and still does not want to know about it. Public role crosses with personal experience and with pillow talk. It is too much, and he is not prepared to give Paulina what she wants and what to her is so clearly deserved.

Paulina's problem is not that she does not believe what happened. We are given the impression that the memories that she lives with are all too real for her. She wants desperately to do something with the memories to help her to move on. But what can she possibly do that would be helpful to her or to others? This is the dilemma that Dorfman presents.

At first she wants to rape the doctor. Then she changes her mind. "I want him to confess. I want him to sit in front of that cassette recorder and tell me what he did—not just to me, everything, to everybody—and have him write it out in his own handwriting and sign it and I would keep a copy forever—with all the information, the names and data, all the details. That's what I want" (*DM* 41).

Then comes another reversal. Gerardo wants Paulina to say everything into the tape recorder. He is worried about what this mess will mean for his important new role at the commission. His very important new role. He fears that it is they who will be accused of kidnapping. Gerardo wants to get Paulina out of the mess that she has caused. If she tells the whole story, then maybe it can be used to protect them. For the moment, Gerardo gets his way.

Paulina begins by telling the story of her kidnapping on the street corner, with the gun in the back, the words, the garlic breath, and then meeting Dr. Miranda in the prison. But Dorfman never lets her finish her testimony. Just as the story comes to the brink, Paulina says, "when your body is falling apart, when . . ." (*DM* 58). Paulina's telling is cut off.

Instead, Dorfman replaces her voice with Dr. Miranda confessing to what he did as a doctor in the prison where Paulina and others were held. Dr. Miranda tells how it came to pass that he became a torturer and a rapist. He concludes, "I ask forgiveness" (*DM* 60). Paulina asks him to sign a statement that his confession is true. But then Dr. Miranda insists that he only said what Gerardo had told him to say, and that in truth he is innocent. Paulina says that she knows he is lying. She knows because he did not stick with the multiple errors that she had fed him by several intentional misstatements she had made to Gerardo. Paulina insists Dr. Miranda corrected them in his account because he was drawing upon the actual experiences of being the torturer and rapist. It is him after all. Now Paulina wants to kill Dr. Miranda.

But at the play's conclusion in a concert hall, the outcome of these events is left open. The music that fills this public space, Schubert's *Death and the Maiden*, is the same that was played in the very different spaces, the ones of the torture and rape in prison, and the place of the testimonies in the house by the beach. Dorfman ends the play with us not knowing if Paulina killed Dr. Miranda or if she let him go. She was convinced of the truthfulness of her testimony, but we do not know if Gerardo or others were ever convinced, or whether she bore that truth alone.

In *Death and the Maiden* a survivor has a story she wants to tell. Testimony in the play is not the straightforward recounting of a factual given. Dorfman does not present testimony as the survivor giving a completed story. The matter gets very complicated as the truthfulness of testimony is shown to be shaped by context, motivation, ideology, politics, and interpersonal factors. Any potential unity, wholeness, or resolution of the testimony is transgressed by reversals in who is doing the telling, and the standpoint from which they speak. Three persons' voices embody several critically different, interrelated positions with respect to torture: those of the survivor, the perpetrator, the family, the lawyer, and the activist. Testimony here is characterized by many-sided relationships between these positions. No sooner does one person start to tell than they stop, or are stopped. Another begins, only to stop or be stopped, for another to start again. The characters are carrying the testimony along through twists and turns that are surprising to the reader. Stated otherwise, in *Death and the Maiden* Dorfman envisioned and made a world where testimony is able to occur only through the surprising interpersonal interactions of his characters. Again and again Dorfman has his protagonists rescue the fragile testimony from silence, and struggles ensue over its truthfulness.

Here testimony is both private and public. Gerardo calls it a "private trial." In a sense he is right. Paulina is taking justice into her own hands. She wants to get over what was done to her, in her own way. But Gerardo is biased, given that he is the head of what is to be a state alternative to a trial. Even if we do not consider the issue of a Truth and Reconciliation Commission, there are innumerable ways in which Paulina's torture testimony is public. Her private life was violated by crimes committed by the regime. Her testimony is situated in a complex web of public events, roles, and relationships over which she, as a private person, has had little or no control.

All these complications of testimony that Dorfman has introduced come as no surprise, given the difficult conditions in the unnamed country where the testimony occurred. The Truth and Reconciliation Commission to be headed by her husband apparently does not offer Paulina a safe space for private and public truth-telling. Nor is there any other such space in public life. There is no acceptable space for this story to be told in her private life either. Where can Paulina turn?

The space that Dorfman gives Paulina is accidental, risky, and highly traumatic. Neither she nor the two men are safe. She has to decide then and there if Dr. Miranda is the one, if he is guilty, and if so then how she will sentence and punish him. Her memory has prepared her for this confrontation. It is all in her hands. All of a sudden, it is as if nothing has prepared her for this moment of truth-telling. She does not find that space. She wants to tell. She wants others to know. She wants it to make a difference in her life and in the lives of other victims of torture, in her torturer's life, in history. But in the presence of these confusing conditions, the right connections are not made. She does not complete her production of a testimony.

What Dorfman has Paulina wanting from testimony is what any survivor would want: truth, justice, and healing. But what is it that separates truth and lies, healing and retraumatization, justice and vengeance? In testimony, not much, and this haunts both the givers and the receivers of testimony. They want it to be simpler, but in the world of Dorfman's play it never is. Of course, the limited choices of Dorfman's world reflect actual social conditions that many survivors face and that offer little opportunity for justice or healing. We are also left wondering if Paulina's giving of testimony with Miranda and Gerardo in the house by the sea is answerable to the experience of sexual torture. Or if any testimony could ever be.

Now, I will step into another world of torture testimony with this question: What if Paulina, this survivor of torture from Dorfman's imagination, is not alone in this dangerous space, but together with another, in a special place created just for truth-telling after torture? Would that make it go any better?

## Testimony in Chile

Several years before I happened to meet Inger Agger and Soren Jensen in Zagreb, Croatia, these two Danish mental health professionals had visited Chile. They went to conduct an inquiry into the psychological and social consequences of torture and political violence. Equipped with the tools of psychology and ethnography, they went to listen, to look, and to learn from people who survived and from professionals who did mental health work with the victims.

Agger and Jensen wrote a book about Chile called *Trauma and Healing Under State Terrorism*. It described political violence and its consequences in Chile and put forth a theoretical model of trauma and healing under state terrorism. This model attempted to explain the aims of repressive political strategies at the individual, family, and group levels. It detailed what was done to families, such as when family members were "disappeared." The model described the nature of the trauma at different phenomenological levels and the "therapeutic strategies," which included clinical work and community-based work by survivor groups and humanitarian organizations, for dealing with it. Lastly, the authors called for attention to "issues of social reparation." Agger and Jensen's model came to occupy a leading place in the field of mental health and human rights.

Although testimony itself was not Agger and Jensen's stated primary focus, it was central to their concerns. They even wrote that the text of their book became their testimony. Through listening to survivors' testimonies, they were able to formulate answers to their questions of concern: How are people able to develop psychological weapons of self-defense to protect their human rights? How do they heal the psychological traumas caused by violations of their basic rights?

These would have been salient, but perhaps not the most urgent, questions to ask about Paulina, preferably years before her alleged torturer reentered her life. It is possible to imagine that investigating these questions might have helped to protect and heal her. But would she ever have agreed to give testimony, and tell her story to one of the psychiatrists? It seems unlikely to me. When Agger and Jensen went to Chile, they found some survivors who were willing to give testimony. (Is it that they were willing to be subject to an inquiry, or that they were willing to get treatment?) Agger and Jensen gathered some testimonies and read the testimonies that Chilean mental health professionals had themselves done. These testimonies spoke to their central concerns and became a component of their inquiry on mental health and human rights.

Several passages in their book gave evidence of the specific meanings of testimony for Agger and Jensen. The authors placed special emphasis on the "case story" of Julia: "Seventy-five interviews later we realize that it was Julia who gave us the most detailed and eye-opening description of the world of torture" (*TH* 82). Julia's story was one of those produced by the "testimonial type" interviews that Agger and Jensen conducted. It is printed at length in their book (with some editing, I presume).

Julia was a psychiatrist who gave her story of kidnapping and torture. She was arrested at her hospital, then brought to a secret detention center. She was interrogated, tortured with electric shocks, and then imprisoned in solitary confinement. She told Agger and Jensen her story and they wrote it down. "Together with Julia, we have been in the world of torture—the world in which silence and speech take on new meanings, and you are caught in the impossible choice between physical life and psychological death" (*TH* 87).

Based on the case story of Julia, it is possible to make inferences about what Agger and Jensen hoped to find in testimony. Agger and Jensen wanted detailed knowledge of the torture experience itself. They wanted to know exactly what the perpetrator had done to the victim in the torture chamber. For the mental health professional, taking testimony was akin to taking a thorough history of any patient or client: the person tells you all that happened leading up to their present condition. It's just that here the conditions happened to be caused by a crime against human rights.

Agger and Jensen also wanted to know the victim's inner experience of undergoing torture. The ideal testimony for Agger and Jensen was one in which they found out not only what events happened but also what were the psychological and existential contours of the world defined by torture. This history was more than just an accounting of events. It had to include the person's subjective experiencing of those events. By asking about attitudes, feelings, thoughts, perspectives, and changes, Agger and Jensen's inquiry broached new phenomenological dimensions, but did it make testimony any more answerable to the experience of torture? To know, we could have asked Paulina: Would it make any difference for you, who had chosen silence?

Julia had a chance to tell that Paulina never had. Agger and Jensen concluded from Julia's testimony:

In the meeting with Julia, we enter a world in which silence and speech take on new qualities. To be silent or to speak may constitute the difference between life and death. The life that comes from speaking, the life that comes from being silent; the death that comes from speaking, the death that comes from being silent. (*TH* 82)

Agger and Jensen learned from Julia that speaking offered hope and that silence did not.

They also sought out the Chilean professionals who used testimony as a healing intervention. Agger and Jensen described the testimony method as a "psychotherapeutic process" (*TH* 108), which doctors associated with FASIC, the Social Aid Foundation of the Christian Churches in Chile, originally developed. They discussed the Chileans' writings, interviewed the innovators of this technique, and asked them to reflect upon their work with testimony. They quoted one of the Chilean doctors, Elizabeth Lira, who told them how they conducted testimony:

You propose that the affected people record on a tape-recorder what has happened to them in order to make a documentary proof of the illegal acts and the violence which have been perpetrated against them. You point out to them that this detailed reconstruction can be painful but that it will permit them to understand the emotions, contradictions and ambivalence associated with this traumatic experience . . . You also include the complete life-story from early childhood, because this contributes to the integration of the traumatic experience into the entire life of the subject. (*TH* 106)

Like Paulina in the vacation house, the Chilean mental health professionals used a tape recorder to get every word down. On the basis of their clinical observations, the Chileans claimed that testimony was healing. Their explanation for why it worked was that testimony made the survivor's traumatic memories less powerful. Agger and Jensen endorsed this claim, and added that testimony also healed by being a narrative. Testimony enabled the survivor to build connections of meaning between their trauma story and the other parts of their life story, especially those that were not directly concerned with trauma.

Agger and Jensen further explained that testimony addressed potentially destructive responses to the experience of being tortured: "Some of the aggression which the torture has created in the survivor can be channeled and elaborated in a socially constructive manner, thus changing the self-destructive spiral" (*TH* 106).

Agger and Jensen made smaller mention of how testimony functioned in healing at the level of the community. Several times they described community groups that collected large numbers of testimonies. But they did not describe what was done with them, or how the testimonies were received, communicated, or interpreted. However, Agger and Jensen made the general claim that "to remember the violence is one of the most powerful tools of prevention" (*TH* 217).

Agger and Jensen claimed that testimony played a central role in the psychological and social processes of remembrance. They believed that this worked at three levels: private, professional, and political. But how did remembrance function at each of these levels, and in interactions between the levels? How did remembering work as prevention? Precisely what was being prevented and how? To me, their claims for what testimony could achieve appear to overreach both their conceptual rationale and their recognition of the limitations and difficulties of testimony.

For example, the perpetrator was not a part of Agger and Jensen's framework. Neither Agger and Jensen nor the Chilean mental health professionals were asking what motivated the perpetrators, the Roberto Mirandas. However, they did want to describe the aim of the perpetrators' torture with considerable precision. It was clear to them, as it is to the reader, that they were taking the victims' sides. But then how could they presume to know how to prevent torture in the perpetrators? How could they use the testimonies as "a political and legal weapon against the aggressors"? (*TH* 106) They were not looking to prosecute, punish, or rehabilitate the perpetrators of torture, as would a war crimes tribunal. The torture testimonies did not provide any kind of elaboration of the perpetrators as persons, or the processes by which they became torturers, unlike the play with its Dr. Miranda giving his confession. Their testimonies did not come close to gathering enough evidence to be used in an actual trial in which a Gerardo might try a Miranda. Instead, they sought to prevent the traumatic sequelae of the survivors that they believed could interfere with reconciliation and peace.

The Chileans and Danes were aware that testimony itself could be retraumatizing. As in Dorfman's play, it could even feel like torture. Dorfman's play took this possibility to a literal extreme, where the actual revisitation of the torturer coincided with the survivor's first real attempt at testimony.

Agger and Jensen, on the other hand, discussed the problem of retraumatization with an emphasis upon the situation of the "wounded healer" (*TH* 114–16). Julia was a psychiatrist. Agger and Jensen's interest in her, and in other physicians who were victims, focused on their becoming activists. Agger and Jensen regarded physicians' political transformations as an inspirational and exemplary way to cope and heal after torture.

Agger and Jensen were also concerned that the traumas of political violence could lead to problems for the healers. They were specifically concerned with what might happen to the quality of their professional listening to other survivors. Agger and Jensen described what has since come to be called "vicarious traumatization" or "compassion fatigue" in the traumatic stress field.[2] As they described these problems, it was also clear that they were identifying themselves with survivors and borrowing the moral authority that was uniquely linked with survivors' experiences. Agger and Jensen did not seem bothered by one drawback of focusing on the problems of professional listeners: this highly selective sample is not generalizable to most survivors on the community level and thus has little public mental health significance.

Overall, Agger and Jensen were less concerned with evaluating the effectiveness of testimony work than with explaining how they imagined it could work. They did ask Elizabeth Lira to tell them her ideas about the results of the testimony work that she and others had done in Chile. Lira believed that the basic aims of testimony held up over time: "To me the most important thing was to confirm the reality and also to avoid people having to tell the same story again and again" (*TH* 108).

Lira's comments indicated that the aims of testimony were focused upon individual survivors. She also made the point that the purpose of testimony dramatically changed in Chile over time: "This method was useful when you needed to confirm a reality as a reality lived and experienced by a lot of people, and you needed also to communicate feelings, facts and a lot of things, and to give it into the hands of the people, of the person, as an instrument that could be used, if he or she needed it" (*TH* 107). Over time, Lira believed that the testimony became more and more like any other psychotherapy. She expressed some doubts about how well testimony engaged with history: "When you ask about the testimony, I begin to think that we need to reflect more about it. Because we used this method in a certain historical situation, and we lost it" (*TH* 108). Lira asked an important question about the relationship between testimony and historical time: *Did the practice of testimony lose its fit as the historical era changed?* Yes it did, said Lira, the Chilean doctor. But the visiting international professionals, Agger and Jensen, answered from another perspective; after all, they were building global models of mental health and human rights. Whereas the Chileans sounded a note of skepticism, Agger and Jensen offered an affirmation; but it came from their use of testimony in another universe: "It is our experience in therapeutic work with refugees in Denmark that the testimony method has proved valuable as a transcultural therapeutic tool" (*TH* 108).

Agger and Jensen emphasized the potential applicability of testimony as a method of psychological healing across many historical and social spaces. However, their belief was based upon testimony work that came from the very different geographical and socio-cultural-historico-political space of refuge in Denmark. Agger and Jensen shifted the focus away from Chile to work that they, and especially Agger herself, had completed years earlier, in a far different context.

## Testimony in the Blue Room

So what did I do? I attempted to create a ritual space which I have called "the Blue Room." The Blue Room was the domain of my work. It was in this space my field work was carried out; it was here the women told me their stories; and it was here I wrote my narrative. It is both a totally real room in my apartment, with blue walls, but it also symbolizes the healing space in which two people, two cultures, two worlds meet. Here I met the 40 women who came from ten different countries, and here they gave their testimony. (BR 4)

In her earlier book, *The Blue Room,* Inger Agger was in a position quite different from the one she and Soren Jensen held in *Trauma and Healing Under State Terrorism.* The testimony work that she described in *The Blue Room* is another example of the clinical testimony approach that is widely recognized in the field of mental health and human rights. Here she functioned more like the Chilean mental health professionals in the sense that she herself was the mental health professional receiving individual survivors' testimonies. However, unlike testimony in Chile, these survivors were living in exile in Europe. But we do not know some important facts: Was their exile temporary or permanent? Were they alone or with their families? Did their stories stay in exile or did they go home? From the outset Agger intended to gather these testimonies and to write a narrative. Agger was the book's sole author and left no doubt that this narrative was to a great extent hers.

Agger said that in using the testimony method in Copenhagen, she tried to work similarly to the Chileans in Chile. She considered herself a "researcher/therapist" who endeavored both to understand and to use the testimonies as an opportunity for healing. The Chileans believed that the aims of testimony were simultaneously "documentation," "purification," and "de-privatization." In this project, Inger Agger clearly emphasized the latter two over the former. Objective documentation of torture was far less of a concern for Agger than was a focus on the women's lives and the consequences of political violence.

Agger claimed that in the Blue Room, when the survivor "told her private story about a common oppression," it "nurtured the feeling of fellowship, or communitas" (BR 115). I doubt that Paulina ever felt that way about her testimony in the summer house. Her testimony was not only accidental and traumatic but also was done in the presence of her husband, who had become implicated in her years of silence. By contrast, testimony with Agger in the Blue Room was intentional and healing. She linked it with the transcultural practice of "purification rituals that rid one of inner evil by bearing witness in the presence of a socially recognized person or the whole society in a culturally recognized context" (BR 115). Agger noted that the impulse of "bearing witness" was also present in the culture of recovery movements and self-help groups found in Western cultures.

In the experiential space of a Blue Room in Denmark, Inger Agger transformed the aims of testimony. She was less interested in proving that torture happened over there (in history), and more interested in describing what of that experience lived on over here (in women's lives): "They are stories about daily life in exile. Thus, it is not my purpose here to prove what 'really' happened" (BR 5).

Unlike the Chileans, she did not focus on describing the enterprise of torture nor the national politics behind it, but rather the socio-cultural-political processes centering upon gender that may oppress and sometimes brutalize women:

> Through their testimonies I tried to understand how the disciplinary punishment of politically active women is connected with the surrounding sexual and political power structure and with the historically transmitted definitions of "the shameful" and "the unclean." This could, I thought, add to the understanding of the problem of complicity. (*BR* 10)

Agger presented a detailed description and exploration of "the female world of exile." A predominant theme experienced by many women from different cultures was the risk of expanding yourself beyond societal boundaries against women and becoming "a dangerous woman." Isn't this what happened to Paulina? The refugee women who came to the Blue Room brought stories of their "first blood" of menstruation and defloration, of violated sexual boundaries, of "disgracing women's bodies" with the "technology of torture," and of ruined family lives. Far more was known about that prototypical one woman in the Blue Room than about Paulina, who never gave a completed testimony in Dorfman's text. But if Paulina ever had a chance to be in that Blue Room, then the story she would have told would probably have had much in common with the forty women.

In compiling her narrative, Agger believed it necessary to find an innovative writing style. She wrote that she did not want her text to succumb to the dissociations which trauma engendered. Her text was written using "metaphorical language," in which each chapter was a new space: "The Daughter's Room," "The Father's Room," "The Cell," "The Mother's Room," "The Living Room," "On the Veranda." These were chosen to represent essential spaces in the lives of contemporary women in exile. It was an aestheticized writing solution, where she followed the women's "one testimony" on this map of a new territory but gave it contours conferred by variations in individual and cultural experiences. Each chapter contains powerful testimony excerpts amid Agger's compelling interpretive, metaphorical narrative. Most impressive was the way that she got the stories and the theories on trauma and women to talk to one another.

Testimony was not only what was received from the women but also what Inger Agger produced in the form of the book *The Blue Room*. After listening she said, "It was now up to me to write my narrative and my testimony of what I had seen, heard, thought and felt" (*BR* 6). It could not be her testimony in the sense of being a survivor, because she did not personally endure political violence like the forty women, or like Paulina. But she claimed that it was her testimony in the sense that she was there, in the Blue Room, and shared in the experience of the telling. She could offer her confession of what she heard and saw and felt. "It is my narrative in the sense that through my presence in the room, I influence what is told. I am present, as woman, therapist, researcher and witness; the choice of voices is influenced by my personal, professional, and ideological background. I also choose the theoretical sources used in reframing the stories" (BR 18).

But perhaps her narrative was testimony in another sense. Through writing her narrative she has joined with the women survivors in producing testimonies that achieved a kind of completion. If it weren't for Inger Agger and her Blue Room, would these stories have ever been told? At most there could be something like what happened to Paulina. Each time in Paulina's story where we noted a reversal, the telling could have ceased. In *The Blue Room* Agger has absorbed and contained all these potential disruptions into her one inclusive and overarching narrative. Thus, the testimony is certainly not Agger's alone, but the shared creation of Agger and the forty women. They needed each other in order to complete the testimonies to the point at which they could be told and retold.

What Inger Agger has essentially done is to intuitively and imaginatively make a narrative testimony whole out of the received testimonies of the forty women, which I presume were somewhat less whole. The Blue Room was far from Gerardo and Paulina's beach house, and the conditions were presumably far safer and more relaxed. Yet isn't it safe to assume that the women's actual testimonies came out less whole than the narrative whole that is Inger Agger's book?

Agger has a theoretical explanation for her approach to testimony inquiry. She says that she was trying to overcome dissociation and fragmentation in her use of an innovative narrative style. Agger's use of the language of trauma mental health reflects her assumption that the primary obstacles to the survivors' telling are dissociative and traumatic stress symptoms. But in the language of narratology, Agger has internalized the mechanics of testimony production, interpretation, and re-expression. However, this was not Agger's way of describing herself in *The Blue Room*. Instead, she utilized the technical descriptive terminology of trauma psychiatry to justify an aesthetic solution that appeared to be more driven by intuition and imagination. If the language of trauma psychiatry cannot explain how Agger's intuition and imagination have shaped testimony, I wondered, then what language could?

*The Blue Room* also introduces a significant breach in the integrity of the boundary that demarcates the testimony as a narrative. Now, testimony does not necessarily have to come from survivors directly and exclusively. Survivors and a listening other can indirectly and conjointly construct it. In my opinion, this is a constitutive moment in testimony work because here testimony stops belonging exclusively to survivors. Now it also belongs to the receiver as theirs to claim, to shape, to interpret, to transmit, and to perform. Yes, the survivor goes along for the ride; but the receiver now sits in the driver's seat, guided by intuition, imagination, discipline, and obligation. In clinical testimony, that receiver is guided to a significant degree by core assumptions of trauma clinical theory and practice.

When testimony is in that other driver's hands, in what directions and just how far will the testimony be asked to travel? To what extent will motives, ideas, or methods extrinsic to the testimony be allowed to shape testimony work? How far can testimony stray from the survivor and what she or he wants? Through this breach, testimony is transformed. It can now become that which it never was because of the desire, will, ideas, and activities of the receiver. Who are those who receive? How do they understand their obligations to the testimony and to the truth? Do they believe that what they produce—theory, method, practice—is responding to the testimony? What do they think testimony is for? What keeps them honest?

## The Torture Treatment Movement

In Europe in the 1970s, the human rights organization Amnesty International began organizing doctors and health care professionals to provide care for torture survivors. Those who listened to the torture survivors' stories knew: here was suffering in need of professional mental health treatment. A new medical subspecialty and an international health and human rights movement were both born from torture testimony.[3] We have a treatment center here in Chicago, called the Marjorie Kovler Center for the Rehabilitation of Torture Survivors, which used to be down the hall from the refugee mental health program where I once worked with refugees from Bosnia-Herzegovina.

The Rehabilitation and Research Centre for Torture Victims was founded in Copenhagen in 1982. Later its sister International Rehabilitation Council for Torture Victims (IRCT) was founded to sponsor the global development of other such centers. Today this movement boasts a worldwide network of nearly 200 institutions that provide specialized clinical services to torture survivors. In the 1990s the United States government sponsored a multimillion dollar torture victim rehabilitation act that gave money to these torture treatment and rehabilitation centers. The torture treatment movement is also anchored in human rights laws, including the United Nations Declaration of Human Rights and the UN Declaration Against Torture.[4]

The torture treatment movement is not only an offspring of torture testimony, but is now also one of the testimonies' prime keepers. Blue Rooms the world over? Not quite. Inger Agger's *Blue Room* reads as her individually driven response to testimony, set apart from the IRCT's institutionalization of torture treatment. The Blue Room allows a lot more space for intuition and imagination than the torture treatment center, which is primarily about providing clinical, rehabilitative, and legal psychiatric services. By contrast, the torture treatment movement is run largely by health professionals and is located at health institutions. Thus, it is more like doctors' white coats in a psychiatric treatment room in hospitals bearing the Red Cross. This movement more resembles what Ian Hacking has called "the liberal solution": take victims of a crime and make them someone to care for.[5]

Torture testimony performed outside of Agger's Blue Room and in the universe of the psychiatric treatment room acquires new shapes. How well is clinical psychiatry able to contain, explain, and maintain what the testimonies offer and demand?

In the psychiatric treatment room, the torture testimony becomes a psychotherapy narrative of clinical testimony. The advocates for this movement say that treatment is needed to address the "devastation" of torture upon the individual and their family. The psychotherapy narratives of clinical testimony emphasize the major themes of trauma mental health. The field's individually focused constructs of "torture," "post-traumatic stress disorder," "personality change," and "psychotherapy" are placed in the foreground, and practically all else is relegated to the distant background. Therapeutic achievements are indeed possible. But what is at risk of being left out is also immensely important: history, politics, family, community, culture, meaning, morality, social suffering, peace, and justice.

Clinical testimony is also used in the courtroom, where it becomes legal evidence. It may be a refugee's claim for asylum, where the refugee must prove that they survived torture, and that if they return it will be far worse for them (either they will be killed, or their condition will significantly worsen). Or it may be a victim's statement for the prosecution of a war criminal. If the victim must testify to the criminal guilt of the alleged perpetrator in a war crimes trial, then torture testimony becomes subject to cross-examination by the defense, which may attack the victim and the truthfulness of their statement. Because of the likelihood that testimony would fail as legal testimony, there are truth commissions to complement or substitute for criminal trials. In a truth commission, the torture testimony is allowed to stand without cross-examination. Even then, the bottom-line concern is still: Is the survivor's testimony true?

In the court of public opinion the torture testimony becomes a condemnation of human rights abusers. Public knowledge of the crimes is cited as a priority. President Clinton said upon signing the Torture Victims Relief Act of 1998: "The United States will continue its efforts to shine a spotlight on this horrible practice wherever it occurs, and we will do all we can to bring it to an end."[6] The late senator Paul Wellstone, an advocate for torture treatment policy, said: "Providing treatment for torture survivors is one of the best ways we can show our commitment to fighting human rights abuses around the world."[7] Critics say that spending money on torture treatment is an easy way for governments to act on behalf of human rights without being compelled to commit to political positions or political acts, which is far more risky. Although torture testimony has its inadequacies, it might also be helping the torture treatment movement by keeping it in contact with the survivors' perspectives, struggles, and real lives.

What the torture testimony still embodies is the heroic voice of the survivor. Testimonies often bear as much or more courage and resilience as devastation and distress. They are the records of crucial life struggles, not just passive victimhood.

As one advocate said, "I have spoken to countless victims of human rights abuses, and I have come to think of them not as 'victims' deserving of our pity, but as heroes and heroines, real people with names, faces, families, and histories, their own griefs and their own hopes. When I think of them, I think less of the weight of their suffering than of the awe-inspiring resilience of their human spirit." At a collective level, torture testimony is also a people and its culture and history speaking: perhaps speaking out of pride and out of joy in the spirit of resistance and persistence. I am concerned that testimonies' receivers often do not sufficiently acknowledge survivors' strengths and broader contexts. But when survivors speak in testimony these elements are almost always present.

Yet it is really not up to survivors and their testimonies to protect and strengthen the torture treatment movement. This matter appears to be largely out of their hands. It is left up to those leaders, professionals, and intellectuals who receive, gather, interpret, and present testimonies. What is next for the movement? Will it be more openings or further closings? This will have a lot to do with how well torture and trauma mental health relates to the testimonies themselves. As the keepers of testimonies, the health and mental health professionals of the torture treatment movement have taken on an obligation. Its success as a movement may depend on how well they do in honoring what testimonies demand of their receivers.

## Where Psychotherapy Meets Cruelty

Torture testimony began as a means for survivors of political violence to seek justice, but it became understood more and more as a clinical treatment that derived its legitimacy from trauma psychiatry. Torture testimony moved psychotherapy from the mainstream into mental health and human rights, where the testimony was asked to address human cruelty as a modified form of brief individual psychotherapy. I will further discuss several complications in the use of torture testimony as a clinical treatment.

The readings of torture testimony claim that the suffering of victims of torture is intense, persistent, destructive, and difficult to address. Without wanting to question the seriousness of the crimes or the veritable existence of suffering, there are still several serious reasons to question the generalizability of this grand claim. First, the evidence for it is based on select cases, not on actual ethnographic or epidemiologic studies of populations. Second, the cases most discussed in the literature were often self-selected. Third, the movement finds it in its own interests to heighten the awareness of suffering, even at the risk of exaggeration, because this may help it to obtain support, money, and legitimacy. Fourth, the identification of psychological suffering of any form is taken as sufficient justification for the framework of understanding of trauma mental health. But there is a lot more to being a survivor or a refugee than trauma and torture. There is poverty, bad jobs, crime, drugs, HIV/AIDS, and troubled schools. Furthermore, not all survivors are psychologically devastated. Only a small minority will accept psychotherapy, treatment, or testimony.

And yet, if Paulina had given her testimony earlier to Lira or to Agger and Jensen, would she have had a better life? The advocates of clinical testimony suggest that the answer is yes. Some victims of torture are fortunate enough to have the chance to give testimony in a psychotherapeutic context. The testimony literature offers reasonable evidence leading me to believe that Paulina would have benefited from giving testimony. If this were so, it would only be partial and preliminary evidence that still falls far short of scientific proof that torture testimony is an effective intervention with individual torture survivors. As a researcher, I believe that there need to be studies comparing testimony to other treatments, or to a control condition. Research needs to investigate who benefits from testimony and under what conditions. What are the limitations of testimony? What characteristics are associated with no benefit from it? What are the potential risks? We should also acknowledge that the chances that Paulina would have ever gotten to see Lira or Weinstein, Agger or Jensen would have to be incredibly low. Therefore, it is also necessary to investigate the matter of access to testimony and how to improve it.

It is also a priority, though a very challenging one, to think of testimony as a public health project and to approach the question of how testimony might address the social suffering of a people.[8] There is, as of yet, no scientific evidence that torture testimony has worked on a public health level to reduce suffering or to change attitudes or meanings. There are reasons to think that it might, but these too have to be investigated. To think that testimony could function as prevention at a social level would require a far greater appreciation of what exactly a post-trauma public prevention effort means, something that has not yet been sufficiently addressed in trauma mental health.

Torture testimony has barely begun to anticipate the challenges of public health problems. Like many other aspects of contemporary trauma mental health, it is closely linked to the individually oriented approaches of psychoanalysis and psychodynamic psychiatry. I believe that one reason for this linkage is that "torture" as a frame of reference may have greater appeal to some mental health professionals than more public and collective frames of understanding. The torture paradigm is focused on what one individual does to another, and this fits in with the mental health field's dyadic frame of understanding. As such, trauma mental health is oriented toward a relatively small number of individuals and to the healing of damaged selves. Torture testimony imagines that for every torture survivor there is a story to be told. But is it realistic to think that it would ever be possible for all or enough survivors to give testimony in order to have a public health impact? The people who participated in torture testimony in Chile were a highly select group of intellectuals, professionals, or activists. Like Paulina, these were the elite. Testimony was a part of a life with a beach house by the sea that very few were able to enjoy. If torture testimony aspires to be something public and social, then it will have to find ways to be more a part of many other people's lives. Issues of who is selected, why they are selected, and who does the selecting are crucial.

Another problem is that torture testimony has been far more concerned with the production of testimonies than with their transmission, interpretation, and reception. The space in Dorfman's play was less than ideal. Yet the primary concern was how to get the testimony told. Agger devised a healing space to produce testimonies. Furthermore, both Agger and Jensen argued that a prime challenge for societies that have suffered state terrorism was to find more ways to create such spaces where testimonies could be produced. All parties agree that producing testimonies is of the highest priority. They recognize testimonies as an essential ingredient in healing after torture, in preventing more torture, and in moving on. But there is far more emphasis on getting survivors to give testimonies than there is upon what will happen next to the stories.

Consider the attention these texts pay to the question of what will happen to the testimonies once they have been produced. *Death and the Maiden* presented a testimony that was having great trouble being born, in part because of the uncertainties and problems associated with what would then happen to it. There was the sense that neither the survivor nor the others were able to control the circumstances of transmission and reception (not to mention production). Inger Agger, on the other hand, seemed to have total control over these processes, given that she had internalized them in *The Blue Room*'s narrative and testimony. Agger and Jensen saw the place for testimony work in the larger social context and theorized on the need for testimonies to be part of a larger process of "social reparation," but they did not specify how that could be done in a post-conflict context.

All these examples suggest that producing testimonies and addressing the consequences of political violence have to involve governmental, transgovernmental, or nongovernmental institutions. For Dorfman, it was the newly established Truth and Reconciliation Committee. For Agger and Jensen, it was a constellation of governmental and nongovernmental organizations that existed on the public-private boundary. Inger Agger in *The Blue Room* was much less concerned with institutions. Instead she intuitively and imaginatively devised a space that represented a merger of private and public, domestic and political, in the form of the Blue Room. Mental health professionals may find this Blue Room compatible with the idea of the healing space in psychotherapy or psychoanalysis, which is an institution of a kind, but not one necessarily generalizable to community or societal levels. Dorfman was not writing in relation to any body of mental health theory or practice. In that sense his vision of testimony seemed the closest to lived experience. In his drama, which

I presume accurately reflects the difficulties of life in Chile, there was not the logic of a model or program as there was in Agger and Jensen's writings, which carried the burden of articulating a theoretical model. Dorfman's literary text better anticipates the challenges and obstacles to finding a safe space for testimony in a post-conflict society.

Although torture testimonies are narrative constructions of memories, the writings on torture testimony show remarkably little interest in thinking about the complexities of memory, especially traumatic memory. Agger and Jensen's Chilean testimonies never lie. Agger honestly conceded that she did not know the truth of the events in these testimonies, but she then left it at that, and proceeded to interpret them as if they were true. A central tension in Dorfman's drama was whether or not what Paulina claimed was true. How can one reconcile her narrative with the bystanders and the alleged perpetrators? Reading these works provokes questions for which there are no answers. How do you tell if the testimony is true? Will testimonies change over time? Is there more than one truth? Does it matter? There is little sense about what survivors or receivers can do to better manage problems concerning the truthfulness of testimonies.

Torture testimony, as represented by Agger, Jensen, and the torture treatment movement, has instead focused on other questions that are centered on psychotherapeutic healing. These questions include: What feelings are documented? What are the signs of damage to the self? What are the signs of healing of the self? These are important questions for healing, but the focus on feelings cannot make up for the lack of focus about historical facts in torture testimony. In torture testimony, the question of documentation is perceived not as the documentation of crimes, but as documentation that there was an event that could have produced trauma. But given that the events in question were possibly criminal events, and even crimes against humanity, testimony should not be understood only in a mental health frame. Testimony crosses into the realm of human rights. But there too testimony encounters complications.

Torture testimony, as noted earlier, has roots in the international human rights movement and its assumptions that there are universal human rights. Torture testimony is able to offer reasonably credible evidence of the occurrence of human rights crimes. It produces stories, not just ideas or slogans, which have the power to move the listener and to compel one to action, such as protest against the practice of torture. The victim is able to give a truthful account of human rights violations in a dignified, humane, and consequential way. After the degradation and humiliation of torture, there is goodness in being able to tell one's own story, and in believing that you are being believed. But there is no guarantee that the stories will generate a response that the survivors feel really answers their concerns. This depends upon how testimony functions as a human rights intervention.

In trying to serve human rights, torture testimony has become implicated in the many difficult problems of the human rights movement. There are, for example, multiple and different agendas of human rights which are under the influence of particular political cultures: religious or secularist ones; ethnic identities and nationalisms; liberalism, socialism, and fundamentalism. The global human rights movement struggles to contain and address all such differences, country by country. I am afraid that testimony has partial answers, or none at all, for these challenges to the human rights movement. It is naive to believe that simply giving testimony is enough to stop human rights violations. Testimony has no choice but to deal with local conditions, which often stand in the way of human rights. Testimony is bound to the given history, culture, politics, and complexities of a particular social context; these are the frames within which testimony will be produced, received, transmitted, interpreted, and believed, or not.

Of all the texts on torture testimony that I considered, it is Dorfman, writing from inside one local context, who most compellingly engages the problems of local conditions. He wrote his play in order to make the meanings of political violence addressable at the level of Chilean society. Torture testimony, as a mental health and human rights intervention, has not shown itself so well prepared to engage the complexities presented by local peoples and local organizations, local understandings and local beliefs. It is able to show, though not prove, that torture happened, and that it caused emotional suffering. Whether torture testimony, as an international mental health and human rights practice, can contribute to making changes on an individual clinical or collective political level in particular locations is not yet clear. Chileans still wait.

It is also important to note that torture testimony does not conceive of itself as legal testimony, and thus does not constitute a legal fact. This means that torture testimony cannot work through the legal system in a way that renders existing laws enforceable. Torture testimony may work through adjunctive, paralegal structures—such as a truth and reconciliation commission—that have been tried in Chile and in several other societies.[9] Of course, these work differently in different contexts. The investigative journalist Tina Rosenberg wrote that they work better in societies where government is too small than in places where government has had an inflated role in society.[10] Timothy Garton Ash said that it is more complicated, that you need to ask: When? How Much? What? Why?[11] Michael Humphrey has critiqued the very belief that "revealing is healing."[12] I do regard torture testimony as a legitimate intervention, but I believe that as a human rights intervention it must engage these questions far more so than it yet has.

Torture testimony has not adequately anticipated the needs of legal testimony that would be required for prosecuting war criminals. Neither Agger and Jensen nor Agger herself ever speak of legal testimony in their texts. There is little written in the field of torture testimony that would be of help to the prosecuting attorney facing that task. The feminist legal scholar Catherine MacKinnon has insisted on the straightforward truth of the testimony of women who survived rape.[13] Because the women claimed it to be so, it would be possible to prove that it was a war crime. Later she and others who tried to bring these cases to trial found out how difficult they were to prosecute.

*Death and the Maiden* was the only one of the texts discussed in this chapter that considered the problem of legal testimony. Gerardo knew what it took to prosecute a case, and he claimed that Paulina did not have what was required. A believable story was necessary, but not enough. You needed proof beyond a reasonable doubt. He could simply not accept that Dr. Miranda was the perpetrator based only upon Paulina's story. Gerardo insisted that Dr. Miranda was innocent until proven guilty, and he became Miranda's defense attorney (Miranda's name refers to the Miranda clauses against self-incrimination). Gerardo insisted that the only way to determine the truth was through a legal trial, and he tried to orchestrate one in their beach house. Paulina did not want to submit herself, her story, or the matter of her justice to the courts. I believe that she would have accepted the court's justice if she felt that she could get it, but she did not believe that it was possible. So she went outside the legal system. She would do it on her own. She became a one-woman truth commission. She could go to the newspapers and try her case in the court of public opinion.

Does Dorfman really believe that the legal channel is the only way for testimonies to render social or cultural change? I do not think so, because the play itself is an example of what I call "literary testimony" and thereby works through other communication channels for public expression and condemnation. Literary testimony may include the literary reworking of true testimonies and also the imagined representation of testimonies that do not actually exist. Literary testimonies offer access to the human experience of traumas of political violence that are otherwise inaccessible. What is remarkable about some literary testimonies, of which *Death and the Maiden* is a strong example, is not just that they can accomplish as true a rendering of the situation of torture as can be found; it is also that literary testimony overcomes the limitations of torture's degrading and horrific traumas through artistic form. How so? By bringing Paulina face-to-face with Miranda and Gerardo, making them negotiate with one another and getting the testimony out, Dorfman offers us more than we would otherwise know about the meanings of torture in a post-conflict society. In doing so, literary testimonies also remind us that there is so much we do not know about how testimonies can and cannot be used to intervene in the real-life contexts that they so poignantly illuminate.

# 2

# *Holocaust Testimonies*

Holocaust testimonies have retrieved and shared the silenced memories of those who personally endured the Nazi genocide. In conveying these experiences, Holocaust testimonies have sometimes depended upon visualizing survivors telling their stories. Led by the figure of the knowing, suffering, and courageous survivor telling a personal and family story, Holocaust testimonies have helped to render the Nazi genocide and its aftermath more knowable, especially for succeeding generations. Holocaust testimonies have emphasized how that history and its traumatic consequences live on in survivors' lives long after the Holocaust, a theme that has also been of concern to psychoanalysis and psychiatry. As the genre of Holocaust testimony continues to grow and evolve, it struggles to find adequate means for representation, to address the suffering of survivors and their families, and to bear the burdens of institutionalization.

### Maus

*"I still want to draw that book about you"* (M 12).[1]

Art Spiegelman, a veteran of the American underground comic book scene of the 1970s and '80s, created a memoir in a comic strip of his father Vladek, a survivor of the Holocaust. The Holocaust theme had never before appeared so explicitly in his work. Years before, he had created the strip "Prisoner on Hell Planet: A Case History" about his mother's suicide. She, too, survived the Holocaust, but she took her life when the artist, Art Spiegelman, was age twenty. One panel in the earlier strip includes the claim "HITLER DID IT!" but even that claim is sandwiched between the lines "MENOPAUSAL DEPRESSION," "MOMMY!" and "BITCH" (M 103). This strip was not explicitly about history. But the question I have is: Should there be a comic strip about Holocaust testimony?

This early "Hell Planet" strip appears inserted in a two-book-length comic strip that is explicitly about the Holocaust—*Maus* and *Maus II*, published in 1986 and 1991, respectively. It consists of 1,500 drawings in a comic grid form, with most of its nearly 300 pages in eight panels. Black-and-white drawings present the Jews as mice and the Nazis as cats; amazingly enough, it comes across without any pretensions. In the first *Maus*, Artie's father, Vladek, is seen having found his son's "Hell Planet" strip and being shocked by what he sees. But Art Spiegelman's *Maus* comics do much more than shock. They turn incredulity inside out and offer a new and invigorating visual remembrance of the Holocaust and of one family of survivors.

The *Maus* books are a product of the stories that Artie heard from his father after years of estrangement. He asked his father to do some interviews; the son tape-recorded the father talking about the family's Holocaust odyssey. Over eight years, from 1972 to 1979, Art recorded many reels containing scores of hours, eventually constituting several hundred pages of text. Later he transcribed those tapes word for word, and then started setting the story to a comic strip that he called "picture writing" and "sign language." A fascinating exhibit at the Museum of Modern Art in 1992 presented all the materials side by side: the tapes of the testimony interviews could be heard with a headset; under glass sat the typewritten transcription of the testimonies; and on the gallery walls were doodles, drafts, and several of the remarkable final drawings which comprise the *Maus* books.[2] Several years later came the *Maus* CD-ROM, which brought together all these materials and more, an invaluable source for this discussion.

Spiegelman presents two stories in *Maus*. One is the story that Vladek tells about his and his wife Anja's experiences in being sent to Auschwitz. Both were lucky and clever enough to survive, and then decided to emigrate to the United States. The other story is about life with Vladek forty years later in New York City, the Catskills, and Florida. Taken together, we see that Vladek was an extraordinary pain to live with, but one hell of a storyteller. In the first *Maus*, Vladek told the story up to their capture and deportation to Auschwitz. *Maus II* entered Auschwitz. Throughout the texts Spiegelman preserved his father's language, his broken Central European English and its humorously frustrating rough edges. (Spiegelman said that when working on the translations for international publication, he had difficulty finding translators to translate Vladek's broken English back into Polish and into Hebrew.) When Vladek was remembering the horrors, the artist's rendering broke the "usual eight-frame grid" in extraordinarily evocative ways; he merged frames and crossed boundaries, as if to say that ordinary structures could not contain the memories, the pain, and the misery. "I found myself violating that grid constantly," recalled Art Spiegelman (CM).

*Maus* is not only a book of the survivor telling about Auschwitz or of the son's retelling of his father's stories. It is a book that is at least as much about Art and his struggles as it is about Vladek. Spiegelman's comic presents the son in dialogue with himself and with his father about the prospect of telling the stories and writing the book. *Maus* is the story of the relationship that they share, which includes the telling and receiving of the survivor's story and much, much more. Here Vladek and Art talk about what to do with Vladek's story:

> "It would take many books, my life, and no one wants anyway to hear such stories."
>
> "I want to hear it. Start with Mom. Tell me how you met."
>
> "Better you should spend your time to make drawings what will bring you some money . . . But if you want, I can tell you . . ." (M 12).

When Vladek speaks, it is as if Art has pressed a button that activates remembrances that have long been present but unspoken.

Vladek tells of many aspects of camp life, of life before the war, and of the time after. Nevertheless, in Vladek's testimony there are no revelations to either Vladek or Art. No heretofore unrecalled events or unimagined aspects. No reconstructions and no surprises. Vladek knew in advance all that he would say. He had always known it and always would. These memories appear to be as stubborn and invulnerable to change as Vladek himself.

Art coaxes the story from Vladek because he wants to hear about his lost mother. "Start with Mom. Tell me how you met," he begins. Vladek tells the story of their first meeting and their subsequent engagement. Art tries to structure the story the way that he wants to hear it. When Vladek jumps ahead, he interrupts, "Please Dad, if you don't keep your story chronological I'll never get it straight" (M 82). Again and again Art has to bring Vladek back to talking about his mother. In a later interview, Spiegelman reported that he recognized that he had a choice: "to deal with the telling as [Vladek] told it," with all its "drifting" into a "scattershot approach," or to impose a chronological order (CM). Spiegelman chose the latter, but he also made sure to show the reader that this approach required considerable discipline. The reader of *Maus* takes in the story chronologically, but also appreciates that "people's memories are not chronological," as Spiegelman said (CM).

Why did Vladek give his testimony? The concrete answer is because Art kept demanding it. Art had to cajole and bribe Vladek to get him to talk of the past. Once Art mentions something he had read the night before. Another time Art says that he will put the storm windows in if Vladek tells him what happened to Anja. Several times Vladek wants to stop, and true to life, *Maus* shows him doing just that. Sitting at his drawing table, Art turns on the tape recorder and finds his father groveling about his second wife's will. "Let's get back to Auschwitz," the son reminds the father on tape (M 47).

Art Spiegelman has noted that Vladek was "not reluctant to bear witness," but felt "no specific need to bear witness" (CM). From what Spiegelman said, it did not appear to help Vladek one bit to tell his story. Nevertheless, Vladek accepted Art's claim about the book he wanted to write. It sounded important. It did shock Vladek to read Art's comic strip about his wife and his life on "hell planet" at first. Later on, however, Vladek acknowledged that Art's writing and drawing might somehow help his son, if not himself. Vladek said: "It's good you got it outside your system. But for me it brought in my mind so much memories of Anja . . . of course I'm thinking only about her anyway" (CM).

Vladek drowns in the same memories for which Art feels a great thirst. Art desperately wants to evoke Anja, to rekindle her memory, to see what she saw, and to feel what she felt. What Vladek wants is to forget.

Art says: "I wish I got Mom's story while she was alive. She was more sensitive" (M 132). More sensitive than Vladek. Art trusts her memories over his. But she is not there. Art keeps asking Vladek about her diaries. He will need them for the book. Vladek keeps putting Art off, then finally confesses, "All these things I destroyed. These papers had too many memories. So I burned them" (M 159).

"You—You Murderer!" Art rages at Vladek (M 159). Vladek had been delivering Art indirectly to the memories of his mother. In burning her diaries, however, he was also the one who had taken her direct remembrances away forever. Who could blame Vladek for wanting to push those memories away? Sometimes they broke through: "Oh Anja, Anja, my Anja" (M 136). These memories of Anja were too much to bear. But were her diaries his to destroy? Vladek annihilated memories as readily as he transmitted them.

The missing diaries could never be replaced. Nevertheless, in the wake of this literary loss, not to speak of all the immense human losses and miseries of the Holocaust, Art could still make his *Maus* books. Spiegelman drew upon the redemptive power of art and the specific legacy of survivors' drawings, including the famous children's drawings from the concentration camp at Terezin.[3] He took a personal story that was completely untellable and unlistenable, and opened it up with his imaginative drawings. A person who was so infuriating became an understandable, almost lovable character. To Vladek's words Art brought the sensitivity missing in life. For those turned off by Holocaust stories, he drew a book that was a bridge. Even crusty old Vladek became involved in the idea of a comic strip testimony: "I know already my story by heart and even I am interested" (M 133).

*Maus* is a family story through and through. First there is Art and Vladek, father and son. Next there are the couples: Art and Francoise, Vladek and Anja, Vladek and his second wife. Then there are the generational ties binding them, heightened by the anticipation of Art and Francoise's yet-unborn child. The *Maus* saga is that of a family torn asunder by the Nazi genocide and aged on decades of misery, but still with some glimmers of hope for the young and unborn. The intergenerational family relationships, rendered with psychological nuance and depth, are what make *Maus* great, and an archetypal document of Holocaust testimony. A survivor father tells his Holocaust story to his son, a story of his lost wife and son. *Maus* represents a larger thread in Holocaust testimony in which the testimony is essentially a portrayal of a personal and a family story that centers on the knowing, suffering survivor.

The psychological struggles that this family story illustrates are also the stuff of therapy. So it is not surprising that in *Maus II* Art goes to see his psychotherapist, a Czech Jew named Pavel. Pavel is also a survivor of Auschwitz. Art tells him that he can't work: "I am totally blocked" (*MII* 43). He is bothered too much by interviewers and business propositions that came as a result of the first *Maus* book. His relationship with his father hasn't gotten any better. Pavel tries to help Art understand his relationship with his father, and the difficult bind of being in a relationship with Holocaust memories and of doing a book about them. This moment in *Maus* represents another important theme in Holocaust testimony: psychoanalysis and psychotherapy become involved in an attempt to interpret the meanings and to address the suffering in survivors and their families.

In *Maus II*, walking home after a psychotherapy session, Art says to himself: "Gee. I don't understand exactly why . . . but these sessions with Pavel somehow make me feel better . . ." (*MII* 46). We are struck that Vladek would never say the same about telling his story to Art (let alone that Vladek would never tell his story to a therapist).

At a Catskills resort, when Art asks his father if he can find out more about Auschwitz, Vladek replies: "Of course, darling, to me you can ask anything!" (*MII* 24). And the strip has Vladek launching straight into the part of the story that Art asked about. But after giving a lengthy account, Vladek suddenly yells, "STOP." He takes Art by the hand and insists that the two of them sneak into a neighboring resort to snatch some free food. Art is tiring of Vladek's epic cheapness. At one point, we see him listening to Vladek's taped voice going on and on about money, and then we see Art screaming at the tape recorder, "Enough! Tell me about Auschwitz" (*MII* 47).

Vladek's own sense of his problems was more about money than about memories. The bottom line, not history, was on his mind. Art explains to Francoise: "Since gas is included in the rent, he leaves a burner lit all day to save on matches" (*MII* 23). Vladek's constant kvetching over money drives Art to distraction, as it would anyone. Its place in the scheme of the book is in part to offer some comic relief, which is badly needed. But it also underlines the important point that not all survivors or survivor families buy into the psychologization of the Holocaust experience.

*Maus II* concludes with Vladek telling the story of liberation and his reunification with Anja. "More I don't need to tell you. We were both very happy and lived happy, happy ever after. So . . . Let's stop, please, your tape recorder . . . I'm tired from talking, Richieu, and it's enough stories for now . . ." (*MII* 136).

Now Vladek will rest. But did he really live "happy, happy ever after"? Nothing that we know about Vladek tells us so. If Vladek wanted to see it that way, then so be it. He needed a rest from those stories, those memories, that life. As impossible as his life was, when he managed to get a rest, things were all right. Still, we notice that he called Art "Richieu," the name of his lost son and Art's "ghost brother" (*MII* 15). Those memories of loss were still undeniably present. How wonderful it is that Art does not respond, and allows Vladek to say that. *Maus* also lets Vladek's closing statement stand uncorrected, and say all that it does say about memory, loss, and survival in families.

Vladek is Vladek, from beginning to end. His personality was transformed by the Holocaust to withstand and overpower any further attempt to change it. Hearing his father's story and drawing from it does, however, change Art. He feels possessed by a thirst for these stories that he can't quite explain. As a second-generation survivor, there is some desire to explicitly know that which was palpable, but hidden, for much of his life: "My father's ghost still hangs over me" (*MII* 43). "I can't visualize it clearly and I can't BEGIN to imagine what it felt like" (*MII* 46).

*Maus II* concludes with a rendering of a tombstone for Vladek and Anja. Death, not insight, is the text's end point. The drama that has taken place in *Maus* is not that of Vladek's strained psyche undergoing personality change. No, it takes place in a family across the generational boundary that both separates and binds father and son. The action here is a transmission across those generations in the Spiegelman family, as in so many other survivor families.

The *Maus* books are deservedly reported to be a new kind of literature. Spiegelman has merged the genre of avant-garde comics with the genre of Holocaust documentary literature. Like many works of literary testimony on the Holocaust, Spiegelman's work contains testimony, is about testimony, and is testimony. But it happens to do so in a wonderfully alive way, through intuition and imagination, which is a lot to say about a subject so deadly. In particular, the use of the comic book visual medium fits very well with Spiegelman's effort to tell two stories—the family story and the Holocaust story—simultaneously. Spiegelman's use of imagery and the animal characters enable him to give each story its necessary coherence and also to show how they penetrate one another. Spiegelman, the creative artist, found in his comic art what it takes to depict and share the human consequences of annihilation. Just being open to survivors and their stories is not enough; representation and communication of testimonies requires the appropriate frameworks of understanding, the methodological tools to craft a response, and the capacity to imagine the unimaginable.

It is also important to note that Vladek's testimony is thoroughly apolitical. This testimony is neither about social justice nor human rights. Spiegelman said that "*Maus* was never intended as a history lesson." He claimed that it is "only when a real life is portrayed in some kind of historical context that something rich can be found" (*CM*). The testimony in *Maus* is fundamentally concerned with imagining what the Holocaust felt like for those who were not there. That same aim can be recognized across the genre of Holocaust testimony, which has felt a great obligation to find the images by which the unrepresentable and unimaginable can be seen.

In Holocaust testimony, there is a different relationship between family and testimony than there is in torture testimony. Paulina's testimony contained the knowledge of torture that had been silenced by Gerardo's unwillingness to listen and to acknowledge it. When that knowledge came out, it precipitated a crisis that threatened to shatter their already shaky marriage. In *The Blue Room*, the family was approached from the point of view of women oppressed and violated in and through their families. In *Maus* the family is the primary context, and family to Spiegelman means something different. Art loves Vladek and loved Anja. By finally having the story told and documented as a young adult on the brink of parenthood, Art is ready to fill in the silences that haunted their family life and his youth. Part of why he wanted the story was that he thought it would help him to be a better son, husband, and father. The young man stimulated and received the transmission of memories across the generations. He believed that this transmission of memories was needed for his family and indeed for the culture of the Jewish people to persist.

Lovingly and doggedly, Art got his survivor father to tell the story. If Paulina ever has children, perhaps they will do this one day. That is unlikely, though, as long as Gerardo does not acknowledge or accept what a government physician did to her womanhood. The important point is that testimony is linked to hope for the future in families through the younger generation. Because we have hope for a better future, we give and receive testimonies. If there is no ground for hope, then there is little reason to submit to testimony.

Furthermore, the total portrait of testimony in *Maus* is not restricted to remembrances of the Holocaust and especially not only to remembrances of the concentration camp. This portrait encompasses the entire family odyssey: from home life into evil and death and then out again. Spiegelman gives family life before and after the traumas equal weight to the remembrances of traumatic events, conveying that each is a part of what must be considered with respect to the meaning of the Holocaust.

Holocaust testimony often centers on members of the older generation retrieving silenced memories and transmitting them to the younger generations before their passing. In life, as in *Maus*, survivors age, move on, and live their lives. They cross the ocean and make new lives in big cities, where some become writers or artists and some become health care workers, even psychiatrists and psychoanalysts. They, too, come to face the testimony, and feel the obligation to respond. Someone in Vladek's generation *could* find himself sitting before a psychoanalyst survivor and telling his story.

## Testimony in New Haven

New Haven, Connecticut, is a small city with a famous university. It has a rich legacy of collaboration between psychiatry, the social sciences, and the humanities. Such collaborations are a powerful attraction to persons with interdisciplinary leanings like myself. I arrived there in 1987 to do a psychiatry residency. Before long I found myself in the professional and intellectual circle that formed around the concept of testimony as it was employed in work with Holocaust survivors (a circle which included the scholars Kaï Erikson, Cathy Caruth, and Geoffrey Hartman). I participated in a faculty seminar on testimony taught by the literary critic Shoshana Felman and the psychoanalyst Dori Laub. It was the year before they published their book *Testimony: Crises of Witnessing in Literature, Psychoanalysis, and History* (1992), which became a key text in the field of trauma mental health and a classic on the subject of testimony.

This book represented a culmination of the interdisciplinary and psychiatric work that centered on the Fortunoff Video Archives for Holocaust Testimonies at Yale University. Laub authored chapters 2 and 3 of *Testimony*: "Bearing Witness, of the Vicissitudes of Listening," and "An Event Without a Witness: Truth, Testimony and Survival." The other five chapters were written by Shoshana Felman. The central focus for both authors was testimony, but each approached it from a different vantage point and addressed different sorts of materials. Shoshana Felman wrote about teaching the Holocaust, about the writings of Albert Camus, Paul Celan, Fyodor Dostoevsky, and Sigmund Freud, about Claude Lanzman's film *Shoah*, and about the controversy regarding the wartime writings of Paul de Man. She explored concerns about writing and survival that Inger Agger pointed to in *The Blue Room*. In his two chapters, Dori Laub wrote about his work as a psychoanalyst with Holocaust survivors and described a psychological approach to testimony work.

Like Agger in Copenhagen, Laub in New Haven defined himself as a professional occupying a unique space. Psychoanalysis was the major determinant of his theoretical approach and his pattern of practice. He also drew from the literatures of survival, but not from anthropology, sociology, philosophy, narratology, or history as did Agger. Laub reported that he operated in two spaces, described as more similar than different: the psychoanalytic consulting room and the Holocaust video testimony project. Laub also presented himself as an actual survivor, whereas Agger did not (although she did make the claim that her text was testimony).

In Dori Laub's chapters, the focus was less upon the survivors themselves and more upon the listener to testimony. The listener faced supreme challenges, needing to grasp the ungraspable, endeavoring to know, to understand, to feel, to explain, to find meaning. The major drama of testimony was happening for the listener who had a survivor in his proximity. This listener was "a participant and co-owner" of the truth. Without the listener there would be no truth, for it was the listener who "is a party to the creation of knowledge de novo" (*T* 57). This is not so unlike the claims made by Agger that she was an essential part of the making of the testimonies. She explained that this was because of the way in which traumas induce dissociation and silencing, thereby complicating any attempts at remembrance. What Laub offered was a lopsided exaggeration of Bakhtin's dialogic scenario: *Not only he, but me, instead of us*. Laub's writings expressed an important and controversial theme in Holocaust testimony and testimony in general: the person who listened to and received testimony was in an authoritative position.

Laub's theorizing stretched this last point so far that he claimed that the very definition of Holocaust trauma was that it "has not truly been witnessed yet" (*T* 57). It was inherent in the nature of the traumatic event that the experience of it was unknowable to those who passed through it. Laub was making two claims here. One was that the historical event was to be defined by survivors' retrospective subjective experiencing of the event. The other was that the survivor needed the listener in order to fully achieve a remembrance. Both of these claims were implicit in Agger's *The Blue Room*, but Laub made them more explicit.

The idea that testimony must be co-created by a survivor and an authoritative listener does resonate with *Maus*: a book on a survivor's testimony that was not written by that survivor but by another who was a creative artist. In this regard, it is also interesting to note Agger and Jensen's claim that the "best result" they had from testimony was from Julia, who was a professional. This begs the question: Does testimony require a survivor who is a professional, who is synchronous with the intellectual level and value system of the authoritative listener, to make it work really well? With respect to *Maus*, Vladek's experience had never before been witnessed in the way that Art, the downtown intellectual hipster, would then render it. In testimony, the listener takes something from the survivor and adds something to make it anew. Agger took forty women's voices that she heard, and through the metaphor of the Blue Room, made them into one refugee woman's experience. What did Laub do in his testimony work?

Laub's two chapters introduced several survivors. In chapter 2, Laub wrote about "a woman in her late sixties" (*T* 59). We are told some small facts about her physical presence and her tone of voice, but nothing of her life, her family, or her community. She is primarily known to us as the woman who made the claim that in Auschwitz "we saw four chimneys going up in flames, exploding" (*T* 59). Laub emphasized that although what she saw was historically inaccurate, it was of value because it represented the subjective point of view that the Nazi death machine could be opposed. What country, city, or village was she from? What was her life like? We are not given those kinds of details, which Agger and Jensen provided for the psychiatrist Julia, from Chile. The text does not give the sense that Laub wanted to know of them. It seems contradictory to not give historical facts about survivors and then to claim that those survivors can provide access to historical truths. In

Laub's perspective on testimony, history was not a focus. The focus was on a psychology of the inner experience of surviving trauma.

Laub's chapter 3 gave more highly detailed portraits of survivors. The story was told of a "little boy of about five years old" from Poland who survived the war and later became an officer in the Israeli army (*T* 86). We see photos of him with his mother, as a young boy, and as a grown man. Even then, this does not approach a biographical level of detail. Nor is there an attempt to detail the sociohistorical experiences in which he was trapped. Contrast this with Agger and Jensen's narrative on dictatorship in Chile and with Agger's extensive consideration of the actual events of the torture of women.

Dori Laub introduced a limited number of details about himself. He confessed to his "autobiographical awareness as a child survivor" (*T* 75), which he characterized as "almost like the remembrances of another child, removed, yet connected to me in a complex way" (*T* 76). He noted the unusual strength, intensity, and accuracy of these memories. Laub's presentation of himself is as ahistorical and unbiographical as his presentation of survivors. Laub was not interested in the reader developing a picture of him, nor of any other survivors, as lives lived in the presence of history. Compared to Vladek or to Paulina, Laub wrote far less about the survivors' lives. Instead, what comes through in Laub's portraits of survivors is a focus on some psychoanalytic or psychiatric facets of the survivor experience. What fascinated Laub was the "eeriness" of those memories and the struggle of living in their presence.

This is not surprising in light of Dori Laub's statement that for him, testimony was like psychoanalytic practice. In his schema of testimony, testimony was a psychoanalytic event and the psychoanalyst was its Lord. The essential processes were psychoanalytic, psychodynamic, and psychological. More generally, this reflected how Holocaust testimony has been closely linked with psychoanalysis and psychiatry.

In Laub's testimony work, the listener actually knew more than the survivor. The survivor had memories, but they were fragmented until the listener was able to make a unity of them. The survivor was lost in silence until the listener was able to give the survivor his or her voice. The survivor was in the possession of a subjectivity which gained authoritativeness only with the endorsement of the listener. It went even further. The survivor had no story until he or she had a listener, given that "the absence of an addressable other . . . annihilates the story" (*T* 68). When the survivor did tell, there was the possibility for some kind of individual healing.

Laub located this healing in a clinical context but left many questions regarding that context undefined. We do not know who is telling to whom, where, and why. We do not know if there is any community context for the healing and the telling. Laub did write that not just any listener in any circumstances could garner these achievements for the survivor. It takes a special kind of listener, claimed Laub: "I make myself known as one who knows" (*T* 63). Contrast this with Agger. The

Blue Room that she created was like an empty vessel, into which the survivor poured her testimony. You go there because it is a caring place, because other women have, and because it is a place to find community with other women, although you will never actually meet them. You go to Laub because he knows what you experienced before you even told him what it was. What does he know, and on what basis does he know it?

Laub knew because of his experience as a child survivor. He could say that he was "there" during the Holocaust, "there" being a concentration camp (although for some, this claim may be uncomfortably wide open). He could say that he was there, having been part of a family of survivors. Laub's ability to communicate the sense that he was "there" was part of his appeal as a healer and a teacher. It drew many of us young mental health professionals in New Haven to him, searching for a humanity we could not find in more biomedical psychiatric approaches to trauma mental health. Dori Laub was a skilled listener and he taught many of us what it takes to listen to trauma stories. These same qualities also functioned as a draw for Bosnian survivors when Laub and I were doing that work together in New Haven. The Bosnians would be reassured to have him there as one who claimed to have experienced something close to that which they had experienced. I believe that Laub used his personal experience as a child survivor to establish his authority vis-à-vis testimony. But overall, Laub tended to emphasize the psychoanalytic part of his role more than he did the worlds of the survivor.

Laub claimed that testimony required not just a survivor and a listener, but a psychoanalytic listener. That listener must have a keen understanding of how trauma shatters the self and entraps it in a world of fragmented knowing. That knowing comes in part through the experience of having heard these stories before from other survivors, and having lived with them for so long that they become a part of you. The listener must be firmly convinced of the value of individual subjectivity over empirical accuracy; of lived experience over institutionally brokered reality. The listener must believe in the transformative power of one's own narrative about the saga of the survivor's life and be skilled in the reconstruction of life narratives.

Laub never said that testimony was identical to orthodox psychoanalysis, but he did associate testimony with the psychoanalytic process, and with Freud. So did Shoshana Felman in her writings on Freud in *Testimony*. Turning to Freud, she addressed testimony in relation to the famous Irma dream from the *Interpretation of Dreams*. Freud wrote about his dream of his patient Irma, whom he failed to cure. Felman found in Freud's insights on the "interchangeability between doctor and patient" what she likened to the very discovery of the psychoanalytic dialogue (*T* 15). Felman took note of "an unprecedented kind of dialogue in which the doctor's testimony does not substitute itself for the patient's testimony, but resonates with it, because, as Freud discovers, it takes two to witness the unconscious" (*T* 15).

Dori Laub believed that it took two to make a testimony and that he, the psychoanalyst/survivor, had what it took to listen to survivors. Although he down-played the survivors' part, I believe it was more important than he cared to admit. Because he had been there, he knew. His story resonated with the survivors. They knew, too. Art Spiegelman was there, too. He was born in a refugee camp. His parents were there. His mother took her life as a consequence. Spiegelman was a sur-vivor of that family life, what is called a "second-generation" survivor. He, too, did not emphasize how that helped him to listen to Vladek. Looking again at *Maus* and Laub's writing, we can see how important "being there" was in creating the figure of a listener in relation to the survivor. But we do not really know enough about what constitutes "being there" in testimony listening. Is this "being there" an actual direct experiencing of the event, or an indirect experiencing through the family?

The issue of the authority of the listener/receiver also has implications regard-ing the credibility of the survivors' testimony. That testimony is dependent in part on the credibility of the one who received, transmitted, and interpreted it. Laub and Spiegelman have very different approaches. Dori Laub established his author-ity as the one who knows through being both a psychoanalyst and a survivor. His credibility rested on his being on the inside of the experience of trauma. By con-trast, Spiegelman rested his authority on not having been there (although he really was) and upon really wanting to know. It also helps Spiegelman that in *Maus* the reader gets to know Vladek directly, not just through Art's interpretation. We even get the exact words Vladek spoke to Art on the tape recorder, which we see Art dutifully transcribing. Contrast this with Dori Laub, who conforms to the psychoanalytic/ psychiatric approach in case study writing, which presents the patient as under-stood by the professional, not as a person knowable in his or her own right.

Vladek would have never drawn a comic strip. This is inconceivable and ridicu-lous. In making a comic strip Art demarcated it as his activity, his preoccupation, his struggle, and his endeavor in a way that surely wouldn't have been as clear had it been a literary memoir. We do not resent Art for what he did with that story, es-pecially given that he did such a fine job of presenting Vladek to us.

In his text, Dori Laub did not do as good a job of presenting survivors as fully rendered persons despite the fact that Laub could claim, with even greater author-ity than Art Spiegelman, that he had been there. Is it important that although they are both children of survivors, a generational difference separates them? Laub is closer to the world of our fathers, those psychoanalysts with grey beards, than to the hipsters making underground comics in New York and San Francisco. Or is it that Spiegelman was born after the war, but Laub was actually a child in the camps? It must also be that Spiegelman is an artist, whereas Laub is a doctor. Something about his art enabled Spiegelman to represent survivors without establishing him-self as the all-knowing authority—an occupational hazard for us physicians.

The adult Dori Laub would claim to be as remote from that child experience as was Spiegelman, who was not a child survivor. But associated with that remoteness was a persistent intensity, which claimed: I was there, and therefore I know. Dori Laub married this sense with the psychoanalytic approach and its claims to authority over human experience. He also invested it with the claims of authority that are beholden to the professions of psychoanalysis, psychiatry, and medicine. This is a complicated burden to bear. There is the insight, based upon Freud, that the psychoanalyst's knowing and not knowing is of equal or higher primacy than that of the patient's. There is also the risk of arrogance that accompanies these professions, which says that *we, not you, know the truth.* If you take seriously the psychoanalytic insights, then you are not bothered by the arrogance. But if you don't, then Laub is in danger of losing the credibility that underlies his argument.

There is no way for me to be completely objective about Dori Laub and Holocaust testimony. But there is probably no need to be, either. *Maus* embodied the claim that Holocaust testimony is all about relationships, including that of fathers and sons. For several years when I was at Yale, Dori Laub was my mentor. I would go to his office, or he would come to see me in the clinic, or we would meet at his house and sip tea in the family room. We enjoyed conversations that eventually became the texts we coauthored on testimony with Bosnian survivors of ethnic cleansing.

What is not written in the texts, but was part of those conversations, and many others in New Haven, can further illuminate the vision of Dori Laub. In those years, I was part of a group organized by Laub that shared a mission. Laub wanted to build an international, interdisciplinary trauma center which was to be an institutional home for the kind of work that he described with survivors. Something much larger than a Blue Room. A place for scholarship, research, teaching, and training. A place for an ongoing, all-encompassing dialogue that would actually match the silence which the Holocaust had generated.

Without this vision of a center, there is no doubt our work with Bosnians would have been diminished. And yet there was a tension between this grand vision and the actual work with survivors from Bosnia-Herzegovina who had recently resettled in Connecticut. Part of that tension had to do with the gap between the psychoanalytic posture that guided Laub's approach to testimony and the need to address the real lives and actual histories of the Bosnian survivors. Still, what Laub offered was in many respects a better vision than the mainstream psychiatric approach to trauma that the Yale psychiatry department was imposing upon me, and that I was at risk of imposing upon the refugees. Laub had the capacity to imagine the unimaginable in the Balkans. Laub believed that listening to the survivors' stories was essential, and he was committed to the stories as a basis for helping the survivors to heal and to tell their history.

Retrospectively, I recognized that to honor their stories and their lives, which were as rich aş Spiegelman's *Maus*, we needed better frameworks and tools to do testimony work. When the necessary concepts and methodologies are lacking, the promises of testimony are diminished. The hope of survivors' stories may then become captive to limitations that are neither recognized nor understood, including those associated with psychiatry and psychoanalysis. Dori Laub was right that scholarship, research, teaching, and training were necessary.

## Holocaust Video Testimony

In 1979 Dori Laub and his colleagues began a "Holocaust Survivors Film Project." By 1982 this innovation in testimony work became the Video Archives for Holocaust Testimonies at Yale. One participant in that project, the Yale literary scholar Geoffrey Hartman, has written extensively about the Holocaust, including his book *The Longest Shadow: In the Aftermath of the Holocaust* (1996).[4] There he examined the advent of video testimony work with Holocaust survivors.

Hartman explained that there were several reasons for choosing to do testimonies on video. Holocaust video testimony was provoked most directly by the video event of the 1979 television special *Holocaust.* This video event disappointed and angered many by its Hollywoodization of the Holocaust. Yet it demonstrated that video offered certain advantages "because of the immediacy and evidentiality it added," "the 'embodiment' of the survivors, their gestures and bearing" (*LS* 144). Furthermore, it seemed that video, and not audio, was the educational medium of the future. The possibility of video testimony was never discussed by the Chileans or by Inger Agger and Soren Jensen. Was this a matter of the availability of the technology, or did it say something more fundamental about differences in their approaches to testimony? Video would seem to invalidate the milieu of safety and trust that Agger endeavored to establish in the Blue Room. But wouldn't it also threaten the psychoanalytic approach that Laub advocated? Then again, refugee women of torture exiled in Europe would probably feel a lot more vulnerable than Holocaust survivors forty years later, by then well established in their lives in the United States, Europe, or Israel.

Explicitly centered upon education, the Yale video testimony project had a different aim than the Chileans' or Agger and Jensen's work. In his description of testimony, Hartman placed a substantial emphasis upon teaching the Holocaust. One of Hartman's central concerns was: How can we teach younger and future generations about the Holocaust so it will never again recur? Hartman waded through many ideas voiced by other Holocaust scholars that the issue was not only about sharing information but about what the adequate form of representation was for transmission.[5] He noted that the mass of writing and research on the Holocaust has often not succeeded because it had not found a form of representation that was adequate for the extreme nature of the topic. Holocaust survivors' testimonies, he argued, came close to embodying the desired form. Holocaust testimonies avoided being solely a "chamber of horrors." They did not only speak of the ultimates of death and destruction, but of the smaller details of a way of life that once was but is no more. Hartman quoted Czeslaw Milosz's poem "Song About the Porcelain": "Of all things broken and lost / The porcelain troubles me most" (*LS* 131).[6] Testimonies are a place where there is often a lot of consideration about the porcelain.

Holocaust video testimonies give a personal and intimate, rather than an institutionalized and distant, view of history. There is one person telling his or her story, rather than presenting information removed from life and experience. Video testimony perfectly captures the figure of the survivor. A Holocaust video testimony is one person speaking with another, and with the viewer. It is a kind of storytelling that stimulates responses. Hartman claimed that this fit with the desired result: "Dialogue, not paralysis or secondary trauma, should be the result" (*LS* 140).

Yet Hartman also identified some of the difficulties and limitations inherent in video testimony. In response to critiques of the complexities of memory, he wrote:

> Survivors' testimonies recorded long after the event do not excel in providing *verites de fait* or positivistic history. They can be a source for historical information or confirmation, yet their real strength lies in recording the psychological and emotional milieu of the struggle for survival, not only then but also now. (*LS* 142)

To achieve this, how were the video testimonies to be done? Hartman described the quality of the interviewing. It was "non-directive," "encouraging spontaneity," "intuitive," left open to chance. There was an implicit faith in the "welling up of memories" and "the flow of memory . . . so strong" to get the story told (*LS* 142, 144, 145). In a good interview the initiative remained with the person interviewed. The survivor's readiness was all, together with a conviction about the importance of giving public testimony and trust in the group that was providing the occasion. Explicit in Hartman's argument is that the survivor was volunteering to give testimony. He or she must really want to tell. If the survivor's motivation to tell his or her story was not there, then testimony would not work.

Hartman also made a demarcation similar to what Claude Lanzman held to in the making of *Shoah*: there should be a sharp boundary between book knowledge and survivors' stories of the Holocaust.

> Personal testimony has long been a significant part of both religious and secular literature, and is usually considered a type of autobiography. Videotaped oral testimony, however, is partly a creation of a modern technology and so has a chance of influencing that environment. As history it seeks to convey information, but as oral witness it is an act of remembrance. (*LS* 109)

Video testimony works through compiling many individual life stories to-gether into an archive to form a "group biography." What comes together is a "col-lective memory" (LS 142). Hartman saw in these testimonies the possibility of some other kind of knowledge and some other kind of community. Dori Laub believed in that community, but was probably too bound by individually oriented psycho-analytic theory to describe it. The Chileans, Agger and Jensen, and Agger herself, working in a mental health and human rights framework, went further in describ-ing how changes in collective memory could be linked to reconciliation and to fur-ther changes in political culture and structures. Hartman, the literary scholar, was less focused on video testimony as a psychosocial or human rights intervention and more on the cultural products it would yield. However, Hartman did say that it would be better if survivors of more recent episodes of political violence (Bosnia, for example) did not have to wait decades to give their testimony, and he did ex-press concern about the important roles of states and national movements in shap-ing the testimony narratives for political purposes.

Neither the Chileans nor the Danes nor Laub wrote that anything bad could come of survivors' remembrances. They trusted survivors more so than they did anyone else who would claim to have authoritative knowledge of traumatic expe-rience. They did not attend to the problems of memory. Hartman, the literary scholar, was the only one to consider that in the inaccuracies of memory lay po-tential dangers. Hartman wrote of the possibilities for a "falsified memory" (LS 141). It could come from politicians, especially ethno-religious-nationalists, who might utilize remembrances, selective and exaggerated, in order to get people to feel ha-tred and to commit violence on behalf of a political idea. In fact, Art Spiegelman said that one of the reasons he rejected the idea of Maus as historical writing was because of the abuses of memory that have been perpetrated upon Holocaust vic-tims and survivors. The appeal of a video testimony project is that individual sur-vivors have a chance to convey the heterogeneity of personal experiences and that video testimony is less vulnerable to being shaped or distorted by controlling au-thorities.

It is impossible to speak of Holocaust video testimonies without mentioning the Shoah Foundation's video testimony work, which was driven and supported by Steven Spielberg with profits earned by his Holocaust film Schindler's List (LS 82-98). Quantitatively, this video testimony project is far and away the most massive Holo-caust testimony undertaking of all time, consisting of nearly 52,000 testimonies. Consider the story behind this mammoth undertaking. A man who is a filmmaker and a Jew made a phenomenally successful movie about the Holocaust. He decided that a percentage of the profits of the movie should go to preserving the memories of the Holocaust. Not surprisingly, the filmmaker stuck with what he knew, deploy-ing the technology of filmmaking to do videotaped interviews with survivors. The project trained interviewers to do one-time, one-to-two-hour, semistructured interviews with the survivors. The technology available to Spielberg also enabled him to handle these individual videotapes in ways not imagined by the earlier generation of Holocaust video testimony projects. The information was digitized, moved onto a hard disk, coded for keywords, and then accessed through highly sophisticated computer technology. Today it is possible to sit at a computer terminal at one of many educational institutions worldwide, type in a specific keyword entry, and have all the testimonies brought up which address the selected point. A student may have instant access to the database of tens of thousands of video testimonies.

The aim was that access to these survivors' stories should be as easy as access to books and journals. This would be a practical fulfillment of some of Hartman's aims for testimonies to be used in education. The technologically mediated possibilities are even more awesome than anticipated by Hartman's writings. Something as ambitious and massive as the Spielberg project provokes strong reactions.

The criticism one hears from mental health professionals accustomed to either the Laub notion of testimony or to literary testimonies is that the Shoah project's method is structured to render sound bites, not meaningful narratives. I believe that this critique needs to be qualified, given that proponents of psychoanalytic psychotherapy are prone to say this about anything associated with brevity in treatment. Nonetheless, this is a valid criticism of Spielberg's video testimony project. Despite its awesome financial backing, the project still had to make basic compromises about what could be accomplished, and so it chose to fix the length of the interviews.

It doesn't take a psychoanalyst to know that the brief time of the interviews will limit what is said in them. One hour does not seem like a lot of time to allow for the welling-up of memories. Nor does it necessarily allow for the establishment of a safe place, as in the Blue Room. On the other hand, the psychoanalyst cannot make 30,000 testimonies. This reflects a basic problem for testimony work done on a societal or global level, as was the Shoah project, and as was also done in truth and reconciliation commissions such as in South Africa. There are always more stories than can be recorded. The stories could go on for much longer than time permits. Limits have to be set when choices are being made about who is in and who is out. This introduces boundaries and exclusions that conflict with the openness and freedom that testimony work values.

Is the idea of the Spielberg video testimonies an accidental or an integral extension of the genre of Holocaust testimony? I suppose it is accidental in the sense that Spielberg happened to be a Jew, to earn tons of money, and to put it behind the idea of video testimony. But this does not seem any more or less accidental than the other works that have been discussed with respect to Holocaust and torture testimony. Certainly no more accidental than the entirely unpredictable *Maus*. I regard video testimony as a product of a Holocaust testimony genre that is highly oriented to visual representation.[7]

*Maus*, which seems so outrageously exceptional in its form and approach, was prescient in assuming a visual approach: to see what could hardly be imagined. There is perhaps no one better suited than a filmmaker to do that work, and perhaps none better than Spielberg. He had already done his Holocaust film, an unprecedented look into the world of the Holocaust, and had obviously seen other Holocaust films, including Claude Lanzman's *Shoah*.

Video testimonies of actual survivors would do something that a feature film could not. These were not actors, but actual people who were not getting any younger. Spielberg had the financing, the technology, and the know-how to preserve their faces, voices, and speech. Just like Spiegelman, he wanted to record his elders' accounts for all eternity. The very idea of producing such a massive video documentary of testimony was itself innovative and imaginative. Spielberg was not after insight or understanding, but documentation and transmission. He put the project in the hands of documentarians and gave them technological innovations that made the recording, storing, and diffusing of these images possible. The achievement of Spielberg's project was to put more testimonies into more people's hands than ever before. It was then up to the receivers to respond as they saw fit with new aims, ideas, and methods that would keep Holocaust testimonies alive as times changed.

## Achievements and Complications

The political scientist Herbert Hirsch noted that there are more papers written on the Holocaust than on any other single historical subject.[8] In comparison, there are only a few texts on torture and its survivors. Because the field of Holocaust studies is far more voluminous and developed than torture studies, Holocaust testimony cannot be compared with torture testimony. But it is useful to keep the achievements and challenges of torture testimony in mind when reflecting upon Holocaust testimony. Holocaust testimony, with a far greater surplus of murders, survivors, institutional investment, and time to grow, has faced some different types of challenges concerning representation, suffering, and institutionalization.

The story that I have been telling about Holocaust testimony is one of growth and transformation. Holocaust testimony began with the modest efforts of a few survivors and writers, artists, and psychoanalysts. Over successive decades, the achievements of their small projects accumulated and led to bigger and more ambitious and technically sophisticated projects. Underlying these efforts of Holocaust testimony was a special urgency to get the testimonies recorded before the generation of survivors passed on. It is necessary to consider the achievements but also the complications associated with this proliferation of Holocaust testimonies.

Holocaust testimonies have struggled to find the most appropriate means of representation. In this chapter I have noted that these testimonies have uniquely depended upon compiling visual records of survivors telling their stories. I regard this as an innovative response to the problem of how to document and transmit the experiences of genocide and its aftermath so that it might have a healing and restorative function. As Susan Sontag noted in *Regarding the Pain of Others*, narratives and photographs work differently upon the human capacity to imagine the suffering of others. Sontag wrote: "Narratives can make us understand. Photographs do something else. They haunt us."[9] Holocaust testimonies have effectively combined visual with narrative approaches by focusing upon the figure of the knowing, suffering, and courageous survivor telling a personal and family story. The words and images of Holocaust testimonies say: this is a voice of the history of genocide; history is present in this individual and family, body and soul; this is the mark which history has left; and this is a history which is still living. Seeing the image of the survivor spontaneously giving his or her testimony sends the message that history belongs to survivors themselves. This has been a powerful legacy of Holocaust testimony and a valuable contribution to the arts and to history. One hopes that as Holocaust testimony remains open to innovations concerning representation, it remains true to this achievement.

The choice to focus Holocaust testimonies upon the survivor has gone hand in hand with psychoanalysis having had a much larger presence in Holocaust testimony than in torture testimony. This may in part be a consequence of all the survivors (like Pavel) or children of survivors who became psychoanalysts or psychoanalytically oriented mental health professionals. Psychoanalytic investigators have been at the forefront of Holocaust mental health research; they include Bruno Bettelheim, Henry Krystal, and Dori Laub, as well as the psychoanalytically influenced scholars Robert Jay Lifton and Lawrence Langer. Even the filmmaker Claude Lanzman, who owed nothing to psychoanalysis, was claimed to have made a psychoanalytic film.[10]

Psychoanalysis and Holocaust testimony share concerns with narration, remembrance, reconstruction, identity, meaning, and truth. They especially share concerns regarding the suffering of survivors or family members and the persistence of silenced traumatic memories. The psychoanalytic frame of listening has been helpful to Holocaust testimony in promoting open listening and in understanding inner experiences with a high degree of subtlety. The psychoanalytic influence is also reflected in the kinds of questions that receivers and interpreters of Holocaust testimony often raise in response to it, questions such as: What is the survivor's subjective experience of an event? What are the ways in which the survivor does not know or acknowledge his or her memories? Is the telling of the story part of a healing process for the survivor? What does the telling of the story add to our knowledge of the collective experience of the event?

These are all important questions. But as I noted earlier, my concern is that the psychoanalytic framework also brought to the experience of the Holocaust an ideology and a methodology that has at times been too constricting. I find this present in psychoanalysts and other mental health professionals, like Dori Laub, who have attempted to define the testimony and survivor experience as a psychoanalytic or psychiatric phenomenon. Holocaust testimony, in attaching such great importance to the figure of the survivor, has in a way encouraged psychoanalysts and other mental health professionals to assert their authority and to professionalize the experience of testimony.

All in all, I find that there are both advantages and disadvantages to the professionalization of testimonies by mental health professionals. Holocaust testimony has brought attention, but not necessarily clarity, to the suffering of survivors and their families. For example, there is a long-standing general disagreement between clinical case writings, which emphasize the mental health problems of survivors and families, and epidemiologic studies, which fail to find systematic evidence of mental health problems.[11] Many of the clinical psychiatric and psychoanalytic writings on Holocaust survivors have argued that they need treatment and support. I have no doubt that some do, but these writings are limited by many of the same problems as the clinical literature on torture survivors. They are making generalized assumptions about the larger population of survivors on the basis of work with a few individuals who self-selected for mental health treatment. The question of the effectiveness of testimony as a clinical or preventive intervention among Holocaust survivors has not been adequately addressed through scientific research. Nor has my concern about the obstacles to testimony as a therapeutic intervention been so addressed. In these senses, Holocaust testimony has not helped all that much to advance the science regarding testimony and trauma.

Given the aging of survivors and the presence of new generations, the focus of Holocaust therapeutics has turned more to the second- and third-generation survivors and to the oft-mentioned phrase, "the intergenerational transmission of traumatic memory."[12] Holocaust testimony is believed to facilitate the transmission of memories within families across the generations. I regard the focus upon whole families as a context for remembering as a fascinating one; it is a return to the origins of testimony in Oscar Lewis's family approach, where each family member was asked to tell his or her story.[13] However, I am again concerned that there is often a clinical bias in Holocaust testimony literature toward seeing families as a source of problems, deficits, and dysfunction, and not recognizing family strengths and resilience. Further research is needed to better understand what possible beneficial effects testimony has upon the younger generations. Some Holocaust testimony work has taken an interest in the stories as told by each and every family member, and has tried to understand the family as a context for remembrance. In my opinion, this is a promising direction for the future of Holocaust testimony work.

Holocaust testimonies' high level of interest in the survivors' subjectivity is accompanied by a high level of interest in the complexities of memory in Holocaust testimony (high in comparison with torture testimony). In between the traumatic experience and the survivor's account lie several decades full of exile, acculturation, family life, and work life, not to mention aging and historical changes, all of which can shape and reshape remembrances. There has been a lot of attention focused on the "internal" facets of memory, and there has not been enough on the "external" facets of memory. By this I mean that more attention is needed to remembrances in different familial, cultural, historical, political, and social contexts. For example, the collapse of Soviet communism and the breakup of Yugoslavia made it apparent that there were vast differences in how memories of prior aggression were being dealt with in different ethno-political contexts—something that is only beginning to be addressed sufficiently in the existing Holocaust testimony literature.[14]

Far more attention has been paid to the reception of Holocaust testimonies than to testimonies of torture. This could be because the Holocaust was such an unprecedentedly great evil on a global scale. There is by now a phenomenal number of Holocaust testimony materials, both in texts and in videos. It may also be that there are several readily defined constituencies for Holocaust testimony, including of course, Jewish communities and the state of Israel. There are museums, synagogues, and many other organizations, mechanisms, and channels in place for communicating the Holocaust experience to wider groups. There are well-funded university programs and majors in Holocaust studies that produce stunning documentary and scholarly materials. Testimonies are used in religion, education, artworks, politics, and histories. But the fact that we have all these testimonies does not make it clear how and for what purposes they should be used. Many of the aforementioned institutions continue to struggle over these questions.

An overall presumption behind many of the efforts to transmit the testimonies is that if we remember the Holocaust, then it will help us to prevent other genocides. The idea is that what we learn from survivors will help us to not become perpetrators ourselves, and to resist or oppose the appeals and activities of other perpetrators. Never again a Holocaust, many say. But how will this amassing of data from one event in the past help us to prevent other genocides against other peoples in wholly different circumstances in the future?

This has burdened Holocaust testimonies with obligations that are sometimes difficult to reconcile with the testimonies themselves. For example, testimonies and writings on testimony often state that the genocide itself is both inexplicable and fateful. The political scientist Daniel Goldhagen has pointed out in his controversial book *Hitler's Willing Executioners* that we have actually known very little about what makes people perpetrators in these types of events.[15] How, then, does it make sense for institutions to claim that retelling the stories will prevent further genocide if the stories themselves are used to basically disallow any kind of understanding of genocide? How can we prevent something that we don't understand?

Holocaust testimony work should be more bothered by this contradiction than it often is. It is one thing to say that events should be remembered, as opposed to forgotten, or that they should be remembered truthfully, as opposed to being replaced by revisionist lies. All that is understandable. But it is quite another thing to insist that one knows what these memories will do for the teller, listener, or for humanity. Holocaust testimony has at times come under the pressures of professions, institutions, and politicians who want to use testimony for specific purposes. At worst, they have blindly followed the dictate that retelling is healing and preventive, and they have made not forgetting a cottage industry.

In my opinion, it is not acceptable for those in the field of Holocaust testimony to say that remembering is enough. I believe that we need to learn more about whether and how Holocaust memories may change attitudes, opinions, and culture. Given that the work of sharing and interpreting Holocaust testimonies is going to continue, it seems important that the institutions that are responsible for doing testimony work also take up the challenge of advancing the art, science, and practice that pertain to the transmission of testimonies. I believe this challenge requires new conceptual frameworks for understanding testimonies that build upon the legacy of Holocaust testimonies as an open and honest communication about the survivor in history.

# 3

# Testimonies from Wartime Bosnia-Herzegovina

Testimonies were used in responding to the ethno-political violence in Bosnia-Herzegovina between 1992 and 1995, years marked by the Serbian nationalists' ethnic cleansing campaigns and their siege of Sarajevo, as well as by the formation of a new independent state of Bosnia-Herzegovina and by an enlarging Bosnian diaspora.[1] At first, Bosnians and Herzegovians gave testimonies to bear witness to genocide in the hope of provoking military and political interventions from international powers that could have put a stop to it. When they saw that those powers were not stopping the aggressors, this aim became suspect in the eyes of many Bosnians and Herzegovians, although they did continue to support international efforts to gather evidence for a possible war crimes tribunal.

Testimonies were also used to address other concerns related to the immense individual and collective consequences of the traumas of political violence: to facilitate reconciliation; to help survivors recover; and to reconsider Bosnian identity. Each of these uses of testimony was connected with concerns over historical memory, especially for Bosnian Muslims, who were addressing memories of recent and past political violence with considerable ambivalence over what kind of society those memories would obligate them to pursue. This stretched testimony in new and challenging directions toward the political, traumatic, and ethno-cultural—and it was all happening contemporaneously with fundamental political, social, cultural, and historical transitions. Not surprisingly, given such a highly turbulent field of human experience, testimonies from wartime Bosnia-Herzegovina often did not resolve these concerns. Nonetheless, many survivors believed that testimonies still offered valid and creative ways of addressing the traumas of political violence.

## Literature and Art Involving Testimonies

During the ethnic cleansing and sieges that devastated villages and cities in Bosnia-Herzegovina, Bosnians produced a number of literary and artistic works that involved testimonies. Memoirs, poems, short stories, essays, plays, and screenplays were written by survivors of, and bystanders to, this European catastrophe of the late twentieth century. Some even gained global fame; yet when I compare these works to the texts of Ariel Dorfman and Art Spiegelman, it often appears that something is missing from the works of literary or artistic testimony that were produced during the years of ongoing political violence in Bosnia-Herzegovina. Why is that?

*Maus* was the product of stories held silent, then passed to a new generation, then laboriously recorded, drawn, and redrawn—a forty-year project in its entirety. *Death and the Maiden* was written some fifteen years after Pinochet, through the prism of more than a decade of survival in exile, followed by reunification under democratization. By comparison, during the recent genocide and aggression in Bosnia-Herzegovina, the experiences of ethnic cleansing and siege were still far too raw and unmediated; the remembrances had not had enough time to settle into the fabric of private or public life; the forms of representation that art depends upon had not yet had time to emerge organically from artists in the context of their society and culture. During the genocide and aggression, testimony addressed multiple priorities other than remembrance, namely survival. Testimony was given to document the aggression in the hope that it would lead to international military intervention to stop the genocide. Testimony was given at a moment of tremendous urgency and at a time when the survival of the teller, the family, and the nation was in doubt. These differences did not stop artists and writers from incorporating testimony into their works, even while the siege of Sarajevo raged, or from making art that came directly from enduring genocide. In my travels from Connecticut and New York to Chicago and Bosnia-Herzegovina during and after the war, I got to know some of these artists, and I wrote of a photographer, a painter, and a writer in my first book. Here I discuss several others who impressed me because their works show what was being asked of testimony during wartime.

Mandy Jacobson's 1996 documentary film, *Calling the Ghosts: A Story About Rape, War and Women,* tells the story of two Bosnian women, Jadranka Cigelj and Nusreta Sivac, who survived rapes. Mandy Jacobson is a South African documentary filmmaker who was based in New York while making her film. We visited at her lower Manhattan apartment while she was busy filming and editing. Here I am interested in how Jacobson used the idea of testimony as an organizing idea in her film.

When *Calling the Ghosts* presents the two women's testimonies, their words are superimposed over stark black-and-white video shots of the Omarska concentration camp where they were imprisoned. Simply telling their stories would not suffice; instead, the narrative had to be visually supplemented with images to concretize the stories in the specific location where the atrocities had occurred. This reinforces the idea that the film is presenting actual testimonies and it makes their testimonies the film's centerpiece.

Jadranka and Nusreta were themselves using the testimony method to document the experience of rape. They are seen going to visit other women, using tape recorders, listening, and recording the stories. Jadranka and Nusreta gathered testimonies, we are told, because they wanted to help other women and because they needed to do so for their own survival. Jacobson presents activism and altruism as their therapies. The film asks us to believe that giving their testimonies and gathering testimonies from others were necessary for social justice and were good for healing.

I can't help but wonder, what if Paulina from *Death and the Maiden* had had that chance? Perhaps the tape recorder she used for Dr. Miranda would have been used instead with other women. Might that have been a more productive use of her efforts than to take aim directly at the alleged perpetrator? I imagine Paulina actually doing that as the topic of another film—a film that could explore the double-edged struggles of survivor and witness, teller and listener, linked through testimony. As much as they believe in testimonies, all parties likely also have their doubts about whether telling the story is a truthful and beneficial response to the experience. Roman Polanski's film of *Death and the Maiden* is not really this film that I imagine; it is more or less true to the play, which is essentially set in a chamber, Gerardo and Paulina's summer house by the sea. Nor is *Calling the Ghosts* that film. It presents a view of testimony in Bosnia-Herzegovina where the purposes are straightforward and the ambivalence is removed; testimony is a certain vehicle toward healing and justice.

*Calling the Ghosts* is also no *Shoah;* it points toward resolutions through testimony, especially before the International Criminal Tribunal for the Former Yugoslavia, as the way of addressing the crime of mass rape. The primary role it sees for survivors' testimonies is as evidence of the mass rape of women. The film does not consider the complexities and challenges involved in using testimonies as legal evidence for a war crimes tribunal (or the possibilities of other quasi-legal mechanisms, such as a truth commission). Would the testimonies be believed? Or would they be torn to shreds as Gerardo did to Paulina's claims? Would they make for personal or societal healing? What if a woman did not want to tell? What if telling made things worse? How would the family, the community, and the mosque respond to testimonies of rape?

*Calling the Ghosts* wants testimony to be something very large and powerful. But it offers a reduced interpretation of testimony that cannot fully live up to the enormity of the contextual challenges that these givers of testimony face. This approach to testimony is rather typical of the use of testimony in human rights advocacy, which serves the important purposes of documentation and prosecution, but which is far removed from the challenges of remembrance in the daily lives of survivors and their communities.[2]

Next I want to consider the writings of the Bosnian teenager Zlata Filipovic, who kept a diary of her experiences in Sarajevo before and during the siege. During the years of ethnic cleansing, *Zlata's Diary* (1994) was probably the most widely read text about Bosnia-Herzegovina, certainly more so than Zlatko Dizdarevic's *Sarajevo: A War Journal*, a searing and more politically incisive memoir of the same time and place. *Zlata's Diary* has been derided for offering a sentimentalized and unpoliticized view of Bosnia-Herzegovina that pandered to the American public's dehistoricized view of the Balkans. For example, critics note that in her text she did not specify for the reader who was dying and why, who was murdering and why.[3]

*Zlata's Diary* capitalized on the analogy of Zlata as an Anne Frank for the 1990s, an analogy that even Zlata was reluctant to accept.[4] She did not picture herself being deported and gassed. But she promoted the Anne Frank analogy in her text by writing to "Dear Mimmy" and by not filling out the narrative with enough detail to locate it in the historical present of Bosnia-Herzegovina in the early 1990s. I agree with others who have written that Zlata, a child, cannot be blamed for this.[5] In my opinion, Zlata deserves credit for being perceptive enough to recognize the contradictions being played out in the global media phenomenon that swirled around her diary. She wrote:

> Tonight the world will be looking at me (and that, you know, is because of you, Mimmy). Meanwhile I'm looking at the candle, and all around me is darkness. I'm looking in the dark.
>
> Can that outside world see the darkness I see? Just as I can't see myself on TV tonight, so the rest of the world probably can't see the darkness I'm looking at. We're at two ends of the world. Our lives are so different. Theirs is a bright one. Ours is darkness.[6]

Testimony is supposed to help close the gap between those standing inside the experience of political violence and those standing outside. The former should be less isolated; the latter more informed and engaged. But in the middle of the siege of Sarajevo it did not work that way, Zlata was saying, especially when the mass media got involved. As a consequence of her testimony going global, Zlata felt as degraded as many Bosnians came to feel about the onslaught of visits of Western journalists, politicians, and humanitarian organizations. In Sarajevo I heard many persons call them "safaris." It is to Zlata's credit that her testimony built upon her own self-doubt and awareness of the limitations of testimony, rather than pushing them aside.

For a great many young readers that I have talked with, there was never a problem of doubt. They either were not exposed to the media phenomenon that *Zlata's Diary* generated or were not bothered by it. Even if they didn't really understand what the fighting was about in Bosnia-Herzegovina, or why Bosnia's survival mattered, they saw an actual young girl engaged in a truth-telling that was courageous and rare. They believed her testimony and accepted her as a young survivor hero.

All over the world, *Zlata's Diary* earned a spot on many reading lists for young people on the topics of the Balkans, ethnic violence, and genocide. In a similar manner, a wide majority of Bosnian girls whom I have since met in Bosnia-Herzegovina and in the diaspora have read *Zlata's Diary*. They were able to identify with Zlata's hopes and fears. Her testimony addressed them in a truthful and inspiring way. Unlike the young American readers, who were more distant from the war and the political situation in Bosnia-Herzegovina, Bosnian and Herzegovian girls were able to fill in the politics. Furthermore, many young Bosnian and Herzegovian girls came away with the idea that they too had a testimony story to tell, and dreamed of telling it. And I wonder, in the long run, how many of these girls will actually decide to act upon this idea by telling their stories?[7]

I now want to turn to Aleksander Hemon, who is one of the most outstanding literary talents to have thus far emerged in the Bosnian diaspora. Hemon's "A Coin," a short story in his collection *The Question of Bruno* (2001), is a profound work of literary testimony. Two voices speak: the protagonist, who is living in exile in Chicago; and his friend Aida, trapped in Sarajevo, who sends him letters from within the besieged city.

> I open my mailbox—a long tunnel dead-ending with a dark square—and find Aida's letters, I shiver with dread. What terrifies me is that, as I rip the exhausted envelope, she may be dead. She may have vanished, may have already become a ghost, a nothing—a fictitious character, so to speak—and I'm reading her letter as if she were alive, her voice ringing in my brain, her visions projected before my eyes, her hand shaping curved letters. I fear to communicate with a creature of my memory, with a dead person. I dread the fact that life is always slower than death and I have been chosen, despite my weakness, against my will, to witness the discrepancy. (*QB* 120)[8]

The text alternates Aida's letters with the protagonist's reflections upon the dilemmas, if not the impossibility, of receiving her testimony by mail. The story derives its power from the intense but fragile connection between Aida's position, inside, and the protagonist's position, outside. Perhaps it helped Hemon that he himself had some measure of distance from the experience itself. Hemon left Bosnia-Herzegovina in 1992 and was outside during the siege, living in Chicago, leading a refugee life that he would later chronicle in his second book, *Nowhere Man*.[9] As I hypothesized earlier with regard to Dorfman and Spiegelman, a particular amount and type of distance appears to help the creators of literary testimonies.

Like many English-speaking, educated young adults in Sarajevo under siege, Aida finds some work with international journalists covering the siege of Sarajevo. Her job is to compile video shots of the most recent atrocities and to pass them on to the international networks for possible broadcasting.

At the beginning, I was trying to choose the most telling images, with as much blood and bowels, stumps and child corpses as possible. I was trying to induce some compassion or understanding or pain or whatever, although the one-two minutes that I would later recognize as having been cut by me would contain only mildly horrific images. (QB 122)

Her obligation to document the most grotesque evidence of war crimes is countered by an obligation that she feels to the living. Eventually, Aida's strategy changed.

I cut all that out and put it on a separate tape. From then on I was cutting out everything that was as horrid. I put it all on one tape, which I hoarded underneath my pillow made of clothes. There once was that corny idiotic movie *Cinema Paradiso*, where the projectionist kept all the kisses from films censored by a priest. Hence I christened the tape *Cinema Inferno*. I haven't watched it entirely, yet. Someday I will, paying particular attention to the cuts, to see how the montage of death attraction works. (QB 123)

Aida's witnessing was transformed from a focus directly upon atrocity to a focus on the living that included the marks of atrocity. The process of separating the most horrid images of war that she described is in some ways analogous to the mind of the traumatized person, which works to sequester the traumatic images into nightmares and flashbacks. This act, which embodies psychologically and ethically precise behavior, ascribes to her a human, not a heroic, dimension in Hemon's text. This human quality is characteristic of Hemon's literary testimony.

The protagonist, for example, came to have trouble trusting words. "I used to believe that words can convey and contain everything, but not anymore, not anymore" (QB 124). Words were not adequate for him to express how he thought and felt, being in a new country, receiving words from home about his endangered friend, loved ones, and city.

Aida, in turn, doubts the adequacy of the witness she sees being produced by the international media. She takes an American video photographer, Kevin, as a lover. The story contrasts the engaged witnessing of Aida, through letters, with the detached witnessing of Kevin. Aida says, "I liked him because he was so detached. He said it was the 'cameraman syndrome,' always being a gaze away from the world."

Aida hates him for that. She could never have loved him. "We just share stories, becoming a story along the way. And the story may end at any moment" (QB 125).

Eventually all the Kevins would leave Bosnia-Herzegovina, and eventually this Kevin did too, after Aida got pregnant. Neither Aida nor the protagonist had the luxury of such capacity for distancing. She wrote to her friend in Chicago about her Aunt Fatima's death. During the siege they couldn't bury her body; it was eventually devoured by a pack of roving dogs. Meanwhile in Chicago, her friend sat in his evacuated apartment, slicing cockroaches in half with his knife and taking pictures "to explore my absence." He read her letters about running from Point A to Point B exposed to snipers:

> I saw bloodstreams spouting out of surprised children, and they look at you as if they'd done something wrong—broken a vial of expensive perfume or something. But once you get to Point B everything is quickly gone, as if it never happened. (*QB* 134)

Through conveying the experiences of living under siege and being in exile, telling a testimony story and listening to the stories of others, finding the words and not having the words, Hemon represents testimony as a layered, nuanced, and complex phenomenon of the survivor's life. It is remarkable that he did so even without the benefit of very much time, which Spiegelman and Dorfman had, and while living in the difficult situation of refuge, still in sufficient proximity to the horrific events in Bosnia-Herzegovina. It is a testament to his artistry, but also a literary example of what is possible for testimony during wartime, for artists and for others as well.

These are some examples from a range of various artworks from Bosnia-Herzegovina that involved testimony. All reflected a sense of urgency—testimony had to be done now—as well as a sense of hope that the testimony could make a positive difference in the outcome of events. Compared to Holocaust testimony, this introduced new burdens and obligations into testimony work that proved highly difficult to address, especially under the adverse conditions of ethnic cleansing and siege. The examples of artistic representation of testimonies from Bosnia-Herzegovina that I have shared show how hard it could be to meet these challenges; but they also show that creativity was possible, if not necessary. I will now consider some examples from real life that show the failures to achieve the promises of testimony during the years of ethnic cleansing, siege, nation-building, and diaspora. But once again, that did not stop some people from trying to testify.

## Testimonies Everywhere in a Time of Genocide

In the time of genocide and aggression in Bosnia-Herzegovina, testimonies were used by journalists, human rights workers, diplomats, politicians, and lawyers; they asked testimony to do what it had done before—to bear witness to genocide and war crimes and to process the private and public consequences of traumas. The context, however, was new. In Bosnia-Herzegovina, testimony was being asked to play a role contemporaneous with the genocide and aggression, not afterward. It so happened that genocide in Bosnia-Herzegovina coincided with a hyperbolic growth in global communications due to an expansion of mass media coverage and the use of the Internet, thus providing new outlets for the sharing of testimonies. There was also a growth in the global governmental and nongovernmental capacities for monitoring and intervening in human rights and humanitarian crises. As a consequence of these changes, far more was expected of testimony in Bosnia-Herzegovina. I will focus on several examples that illustrate the new demands upon testimony, and I will consider how well testimony fared. Specifically, I will consider testimonies in relation to journalistic coverage of genocide and aggression, human rights monitoring, and an international tribunal for war crimes.

Internationally, genocide in Bosnia-Herzegovina was heavily chronicled in the newspapers and covered on television. One group of journalists wrote: "The Final Solution to the Bosnian Question was covered by CNN. The pictures were everywhere, including the east wing of the White House. There was knowledge and there was belief."[10] Never before had genocide received such contemporaneous media attention. (It probably helped that the genocide was occurring in Europe; although it did not help that the victims were mostly Muslim.) Journalists covering the story in Bosnia-Herzegovina, and also in the Bosnian diaspora, needed survivors' faces, voices, and stories to make it more real. Naturally, they sought the direct testimonies of survivors. This began with Roy Gutman's groundbreaking story revealing the existence of Serbian-run concentration camps in Bosnia-Herzegovina and continued for four years of ethnic cleansing and siege, punctuated by certain key events, including the market massacre in Sarajevo and the slaughter of thousands in Srebrenica.[11] In journalistic reports, testimonies appeared as background, as a few select quotes, or as a more extensive narrative. Bosnian journalists and writers also reported and wrote for international media outlets and wrote essays and memoirs of their own.[12]

As a consequence of all these journalistic testimony activities, nobody could claim that the story of genocide in Bosnia-Herzegovina was insufficiently covered. For example, writers from the *New Republic* noted: "Since 1992, and the editorial entitled 'Rescue Bosnia,' Bosnia has been an obsession of the *New Republic*."[13] Mainstream news outlets, such as the *ABC Evening News with Peter Jennings*, also showed the same commitment to telling the story, and that meant including many testimonies. Americans could read and see testimonies practically every day.

Troublingly, the *New Republic* writers continued: "And yet there was no action." Cushman and Mestorivic's *This Time We Knew*, an edited volume of essays, discussed the issue of Western media responses to the genocide in Bosnia-Herzegovina in the context of this larger failure of decisive and timely political and military action.[14] They argued that testimonies were not heard because there were problems in how testimonies were presented by the mass media. The French critic Jean Baudrillard claimed that the public suffered from knowing "too much," and that this lead to apathy.[15] Another point made by Cushman and Mestorivic and some of their other contributors is that although there were many stories, they were framed in historically inaccurate ways, emphasizing "Balkan wars" and ancient ethnic hatreds, or reflecting pro-Serbian and anti-Muslim and anti-Croatian biases; these were distortions which justified inaction on the part of international powers. But in *A Problem from Hell: America and the Age of Genocide*, Samantha Powers argued that the American government has never been committed to stopping genocide, and that in Bosnia-Herzegovina the American government did more to stop genocide than it had previously done anywhere else.

The Bosnian journalist and author Zlatko Dizdarevic wrote and published many first-person accounts during the genocide, and he often commented about the fundamental problems of journalistic testimony for Bosnians. For example, he wrote:

> "It isn't easy trying to explain [the necessity to testify] to people who think that the only aim in life is to fill your stomach and your pockets, and that you can be happy as a cow in five square meters of living space as long as you have your mercy provisions—the gift of a 'landlord' or humanitarian organization."[16]

Dizdarevic expressed withering criticism of the West's non-solutions and self-congratulatory and patronizing attitudes, as embedded in its failing humanitarian policies. America and the West falsely represented the events in Bosnia-Herzegovina as a humanitarian crisis and not as genocide. Dizdarevic's criticism may be extended to the promises embedded in journalistic testimony: "It's slightly more difficult to sell this story to those in Sarajevo who are still using their own heads to think with, something that, apparently, may constitute this disobedient city's gravest sin."[17]

Eventually Bosnians, and especially Sarajevans, learned to lower their expectations of giving testimony to internationals. At first they thought that giving testimony would help them; then they came to believe that testimony was not going to yield changes and that they were being used as freakish entertainment for a distant audience.

From the moment when testimonies were first being distributed in the West through the mass media, serious questions were raised in the public discourse: Is this really genocide or is it civil war? Hasn't this kind of fighting been going on for centuries? Aren't all sides guilty of war crimes? For Bosnians, the answers given could determine their future. The Western public looked to institutions that monitored human rights, such as Human Rights Watch or Amnesty International. These institutions were responsible for answering these questions on the basis of a balanced view of the evidence and for advocating on behalf of the victims of violations of human rights. I was interested to learn how they approached the testimonies.

"We visit the site of abuses to interview victims, witnesses and others." Human Rights Watch had this to say about its methodology:

Documenting abuses is inherently a preventive strategy. When we investigate and expose past human rights violations, we seek to hold their authors accountable, both politically and judicially. We shame abusers, seek to cut off their aid, and promote their prosecution. Our aim is to increase the price of human rights abuses. The more reliably this can be done, the more would-be abusers will think twice before committing future human rights violations.[18]

In Bosnia-Herzegovina this approach was very necessary. From the beginning of the conflict in 1992, human rights organizations were monitoring human rights abuses and violations and pressuring the United Nations Security Council to take decisive action. For example, Human Rights Watch published two volumes in 1992 and 1993, *War Crimes in Bosnia-Herzegovina*, which "documented the appalling brutality inflicted on the civilian populations" with "weighty evidence" of "genocide," and strongly condemned the UN and its member nations. The emphasis, in these and other reports, was upon "fact-finding investigations," which were then published with the intent of "generating extensive coverage in local and international media" in order to "embarrass abusive governments in the eyes of their citizens and the world."[19]

Human rights organizations depend upon eyewitness sources: persons who have directly experienced or directly witnessed criminal acts. The credibility of these organizations and their reports depends entirely on the quality of their reports. "The hallmark and pride of Human Rights Watch is the even-handedness and accuracy of our reporting."[20] If they are too one-sided, passionate, or subjective, then they risk being dismissed as partisan. That is why the only people they quote are those who actually experienced or directly saw an event. Word of mouth doesn't count. The focus is on crimes against persons and upon certainty of fact. More abstract notions of crimes against culture might be included, but only when they too can be concretized, as in the desecration of monuments or structures of cultural significance.

Concerning Bosnia-Herzegovina, human rights organizations used testimony to make the fundamental point that this was not simply a humanitarian emergency that required aid, but a genocide that required a military and political solution; something that the UN, the United States, and other Western powers reluctantly came to accept after several years of ethnic cleansing and sieges.

Although the international powers were highly ambivalent about stopping the crimes from being committed, from the beginning of the conflict in Bosnia-Herzegovina, their efforts to indict and prosecute those accused of crimes against humanity in Bosnia-Herzegovina were implemented more decisively. In February

1993 the UN Security Council moved to establish the International Criminal Tribunal for the former Yugoslavia (ICTY), located in The Hague, Netherlands. I looked at how the ICTY articulated its mission, which was "to bring to justice persons allegedly responsible for violations of international humanitarian law; to render justice to the victims; to deter further crimes; to contribute to the restitution of the peace by promoting reconciliation in the former Yugoslavia."[21]

The ICTY would operate according to international legal notions of the "fair trial." Testimonies must be true, according to Rule 90 on the "Testimony of Witnesses," which states: "Every witness, shall, before giving evidence, make the following solemn declaration: 'I solemnly declare that I will speak the truth, the whole truth, and nothing but the truth.'" Cross-examination would be allowed (which is not the case in a truth commission). However, Rule 96 on "Evidence in Cases of Sexual Assault" states that for these special cases, "no corroboration of the victim's testimony shall be required" and that "consent shall not be allowed as a defense." Another special concern was support for victims and witnesses. Court documents state: "The Victims and Witnesses Unit . . . is aware that testifying before the Tribunal may, for some victims and witnesses (including women and men testifying about rape), be a traumatic experience." The court said it was its obligation to provide "support and assistance, in the period before, during, and after giving testimony."

The ICTY would eventually set multiple legal precedents and adjudicate important issues of human rights involving genocide, rape, and crimes against humanity. During the first years of its operation, the focus was upon building the institution's infrastructure and issuing indictments. (Radovan Karadzic and Ratko Mladic were indicted in November 1995, although at the time of writing they have not been arrested, even though their whereabouts are known to many.)

The ICTY had its first defendant in April 1995. With the signing of the Dayton Peace Accords in December 1995, the ICTY entered a "new and critical phase," anticipating the cooperation of the Bosnian Serb authorities to "permit the arrest and transfer of those persons indicted to date." The ICTY, which has primacy over state institutions in prosecuting war crimes, cooperates with the state of Bosnia-Herzegovina in gathering evidence on war crimes. The government of Bosnia-Herzegovina has a war crimes commission that is engaged in gathering testimonies for possible use in the ICTY or in other possible future legal proceedings. In 2003 the ICTY was busier than ever. By 2004 all investigations had been completed. As of 2005, most of the cases before the court had been decided and the court had committed itself to a "completion strategy"; several trials were ongoing, including that of Slobodan Milosevic (which was to end with his death in March 2006), and several key fugitives were still at large, notably Radovan Karadzic and Ratko Mladic.

The most obvious difference between the ICTY and journalistic and human rights organizations is that the ICTY has the authority to indict, detain, prosecute, and punish. This means that survivors' testimonies are held accountable to a higher degree of proof and are subject to the legal procedures of fair trials. Thus, testimony in the ICTY is legal testimony, with some accommodations made regarding testimony on sexual assault. Nonetheless, all three types of organizations that I have discussed (journalistic, human rights, and tribunal) claim that there is a preventive logic to their testimony work. They believe that putting testimonies in the public arena will inhibit potential war criminals because they will know that they will face consequences. Although this logic does make sense, retrospectively, it is difficult for Bosnians and Herzegovians to give any of these institutions much if any credit for succeeding in prevention in Bosnia-Herzegovina. They recognized that when disconnected from governmental responses, the journalistic use of testimonies reporting atrocities becomes mere ghoulish entertainment. They knew that journalism and human rights were still beholden to governments, and as Samantha Powers argued, the United States government was never seriously committed to stopping genocide.[22]

In Bosnia-Herzegovina, as the genocide and aggression rolled on, Bosnians grew very tired of participating in journalistic reporting and human rights documentation, but they continued to believe in and support the International Criminal Tribunal. In their eyes, the war crimes tribunal had an institutional legitimacy and an ultimate power that the journalists and human rights organizations never had.

## From Chile to the Former Yugoslavia: Testimonies and Reconciliation

During the years from 1992 to 1995, Bosnia-Herzegovina became the site of an immense humanitarian relief operation. Testimony became part of the efforts to provide psychosocial services to persons in Bosnia-Herzegovina, as well as to those displaced in the new Bosnian diaspora. Millions of survivors in Bosnia-Herzegovina had trauma stories in the sense that they had directly experienced political violence; many persons were telling or would want to tell under the right circumstances. Humanitarian workers and mental health professionals asked: Should survivors be encouraged to tell their stories? Would it help them to heal? During wartime, conditions on the ground were often far too desperate to allow truthtelling to be a prominent part of what governmental and nongovernmental agencies were willing or able to do. Testimony was regarded as too individualistic and too labor intensive to fit in a public health framework of humanitarian interventions in a complex emergency (although many of those same organizations were eager to use testimonies in their public relations and fund-raising campaigns). Nor did it fit in the diaspora, where suffering was also great, and testimony competed against many priorities of life in exile, such as finding employment, housing, health care, and education. But there were some modest attempts to implement testimony work in these contexts. One attempt to use testimony in a time of aggression involved Inger Agger and Soren Jensen, who brought to Yugoslavia what they had learned about testimony in Chile and Copenhagen.

In the chapter at the end of their book *Trauma and Healing Under State Terrorism*, Agger and Jensen have left Chile and ventured into the former Yugoslavia. They describe scenes from inside the wars then raging in the Balkans. Once again, they found themselves speaking with survivors and mental health professionals in the midst of a political and military conflict, although this time it was in Europe.

They came to the former Yugoslavia as employees of major international organizations. Inger Agger worked for the Humanitarian Office of the European Commission, and Soren Jensen worked for the World Health Organization. They were based in Zagreb in Croatia, but their work also took them to Sarajevo and Belgrade. They reflected on what the difference in their official status meant when they made their rounds talking and listening: "We are no longer 'the Danes,' the researchers arriving and asking question 'in the name of science.' We are representing two large international organizations and are expected to represent power structures, and we are therefore potential sources of funding" (*TH* 226).

They brought their Chilean model, rooted in testimony, and wanted to know if this model would fit the situation in the Balkans. Given that they represented international organizations and traveled to all the countries that were party to the conflict, they came to listen to many perspectives: "We can cross front lines and listen to narratives about violence from all sides" (*TH* 227).

Some things reminded them of what they saw in Chile, such as the suffering brought upon individuals and families by political violence; but they were really impressed by what was so different: overwhelming psychosocial needs, wounded professionals, propaganda, nationalism and hatreds, brutality, blindness, and lies. "In our attempts to understand what was going on in this reality, we started from scratch again" (*TH* 214).

However, they did not relinquish testimony. But in order to give their Chilean model greater explanatory capacity in the Balkans, they employed a new concept called "social memory":

> Silent and invisible people are easier to manipulate and dominate. Testimony is one way to ensure that the silent victims are given voice. Testimony documents social memory. However, testimony can also become an important part of a reconciliation process . . . We argue for combining the processes of reconciliation with the construction of social memory. (*TH* 228)

In the Balkans, Agger and Jensen used testimony to say something about the causes of war. They claimed that the war came about in part because people were used—their memories were manipulated—by political leaders. It is possible, they stated, that testimonies could prevent this manipulation of memories. If people knew their stories and the stories of others (including their supposed enemies), then they would not be as susceptible to political leaders telling them who their enemies were and what they should fear. In this sense, Agger and Jensen believed that testimonies could work as grassroots prevention of political and military conflicts. Through testimony, citizens would not be a tabula rasa for demagogic politicians. However, Agger and Jensen were making the assumption that the Bosnian catastrophe was in essence a civil war, not a genocide, and they were not going to take the side of the Bosnian Muslims or any other ethno-national group.

Agger and Jensen also claimed that testimonies could serve the processes of reconciliation. When they talked about testimonies in the Balkans, they imagined testimonies that were not overly colored by ethno-nationalism and were not interpreted through a political lens other than their own. In the Balkans during the time of war and genocide, this was improbable. It was even more improbable that testimonies would fit within the framework of reconciliation. After all, reconciliation would be about putting national stories of suffering and victimhood aside. This would seem to be the opposite of the testimony during wartime, which often brought forward expressions of ethno-national affiliation and condemnation of one's enemy. How could they have it both ways?

Perhaps Agger and Jensen thought that testimonies could be sufficiently free from national identity because they were biased by their own perspective as outsiders moving freely across borders. They did not view testimony and reconciliation from the Bosnian, Croatian, or Serbian side, but from all sides; for example, they did testimony work with people from mixed marriages to help them adjust to living in changed conditions and to help them share their narratives of multiethnic living together in domestic spaces. Agger and Jensen also envisioned reconciliation occurring across national boundaries:

> Reconciliation is thus a process which follows two paths: changing the demonic image of "the others," getting acquainted with their suffering, their feelings and thoughts; and remembering the truth about what some of those others have done." (*TH* 229)

Testimony could be used to get to know the other. People on one side could give testimonies to the other, or each side could read testimonies from the other side. These were the kind of testimonies that Agger and Jensen wanted to produce. So they asked: How was it possible to create such a space in the Balkans? "In the individual and collective healing of the trauma, how do we create ritual spaces where testimony can be given, and where the truth can become an established part of social memory?" (*TH* 230).

This brought Agger and Jensen face to face with the major problem that the Chileans had noted about using testimony in Chile: How did testimony fit within the present social, historical, and political context? As mentioned previously, in Denmark Agger had been able to sidestep this problem by taking testimonies in her apartment's Blue Room, where she in effect created a new space. But in the Balkans, Agger and Jensen were making far more ambitious demands upon testimony, as was each ethnic nation. What would protect testimony from ethno-nationalist policies or programs? How was it possible to oversee the mass public production of testimonies that conformed to such a specific outsider set of notions about reconciliation? Did the institutions exist that could sponsor or shelter this kind of work? I believe that if there were such institutions and systems of understandings, then there probably would have been no genocide or war. Testimony was not going to be able to build those structures overnight. Upon what ground could Agger and Jensen's vision of testimony stand? How could they both oversee the production of testimonies and see that those testimonies changed social memory? They did not consider the distinction between the private spaces where testimony was produced by the survivor with a listener—which Agger had some success in controlling in the space of exile (in her Blue Room)—and the public spaces where testimony entered into culture. These were two distinct spaces, operating under very different rules. Certainly, the latter spaces in Bosnia-Herzegovina, or any other imaginable society during wartime, were not anywhere near as controllable as was the Blue Room in Inger Agger's apartment in Copenhagen.

In their writings on Chile, Agger and Jensen recognized several different levels of social experience where testimony could operate: the individual, the family, the community, and the political. Testimonies may have been produced in a "private" space, such as psychotherapy. In the context of a societal transition toward democracy in Chile, however, those testimonies became involved with public institutions and public conversations, including new leaders in a new government, the National Committee on Truth and Reconciliation, survivor groups, religious groups, and human rights groups. In the Balkans, Agger and Jensen believed that major political and cultural changes in the public realm, brought about by the testimonies, were the fundamental prerequisites that would allow for a subsequent change in social memory. I could not find evidence of such political and cultural changes in wartime Bosnia-Herzegovina or its diaspora.

In the Balkans, Agger and Jensen started from a position of advocating reconciliation across all of the former Yugoslavia. The space of interest to them was not only Bosnia-Herzegovina. They wrote at a time when the idea of reconciliation between those former republics still had some currency in the international community. Reconciliation was beyond belief to most people of those states. However, reconciliation did have a historical precedent, although not necessarily one that Agger and Jensen would want to associate with testimony. To aim for reconciliation across the borders of the new states that had once been the republics of Yugoslavia was to commit to a project not dissimilar from that of Marshal Tito. Tito's project of nation-building in Yugoslavia after World War II insisted that people put away their memories of the war and instead follow the state-scripted narrative of "Brotherhood and Unity" ("Bratstvo i Jedinstvo"). Tito's project involved the suppression of memories through the totalitarian control of the state.[23]

Agger and Jensen did not want a totalitarian solution. Instead, they believed that under the guiding light of the mental health and human rights movement, they could draw on testimonies to reconstruct social memory. Following upon such a reconstruction of social memory, they hoped that reconciliation could take place. In comparison with the ethnic, religious, and nationalistic antagonisms of the Balkans, the assumptions of universal human rights and trauma mental health seemed awfully thin; the institutions of liberal democracies did not offer as forceful mechanisms for controlling private and public spaces as did totalitarianism. Testimony could be produced in an internationally validated human rights movement; but to have an effect locally, they would have to interact with local conditions, without the backing of a totalitarian regime. But because the Yugoslav state had never given people access to social memory, it was far more difficult for its citizens to actively engage in a collective process of testimony work. What is more, beyond the strong impulse to produce testimony, there were also many questions about how to interpret these memories in the building of a larger collective historical memory. For example, pluralists and ethnic nationalists interpreted the testimonies in very different ways.

Agger and Jensen's approach to testimony in the former Yugoslavia was idealistic. They believed that testimony and social memory naturally lead to reconciliation and peace. However, this idealistic belief in the restorative powers of testimony lacked any explicit grounding either in political theories, which draw upon an understanding of ethnic nationalism, or in legal theories, which focus on the prevention of crimes. Instead, they found support for their belief primarily in psychological theories of trauma and recovery. They believed that the testimony narratives produced by the survivors would lead to desired psychological changes (e.g., less toxic traumatic memories) that would diminish the momentum toward vengeance and animosity among the victims and the larger society. And yet Bosnian testimonies could, at one moment, be about forgiveness and living together; and then, at the next moment, be about ethnic hatred and vengeance. Political, social, and cultural theorists alike recognize that often a thin line separates memories that express vengeance from ones that promote forgiveness.[24] In testimony, it does not seem possible to get one without the other.

Mental health professionals who engage with the social, historical, cultural, and political may have something to contribute to this dilemma, but because of their tendency to generalize from individual-level experiences to the levels of community, society, and nation, they are at some risk of idealistic approaches. Agger and Jensen's writings on testimony as a psychosocial intervention demonstrate this risk. Testimony began with mental health professionals, largely because they were there to emotionally heal the survivors. The genres of torture testimony and Holocaust testimony were created as a result of the project of psychological healing (largely of individuals) having merged with the project of remembering (and the related issues of collective trauma, collective memory, and trans-generational transmission of memory). Testimony, as a psychosocial intervention in Bosnia-Herzegovina, extended that same merger—this time under the rubric of prevention and reconciliation. However, testimony was performed in ways that were surprisingly unaware of history and the marked cultural transition that was occurring in Bosnia-Herzegovina as two historical eras collided: living together in the former Yugoslavia and ethnic cleansing from extreme nationalists. If testimony aimed to address peace and reconciliation, then it would need to be based upon a better grasp of historical, social, political, and cultural transitions than the construct of social memory allowed.

## Individual and Collective Traumas

When Agger and Jensen wrote parts of *Trauma and Healing Under State Terrorism* in 1993, it may still have been possible for them to think of reconciliation in Yugoslavia, but as the genocide and aggression continued, belief in reconciliation was no longer a serious possibility. When I began doing testimony work in 1992, my colleagues and I thought of them as "Bosnian" testimonies, not Yugoslav testimonies. Our primary concern was over the national space of Bosnia-Herzegovina and the global Bosnian diaspora. Having chosen Bosnia-Herzegovina rather than Yugoslavia as the context had important implications for the political, historical, and cultural processes that would shape our testimony work.

That national space (and to some extent the diasporic space) was divided between Bosnian, Croatian, and Serbian entities. We positioned ourselves in the Bosnian space, and in the diaspora with those who identified with the multiethnic political vision of the independent state of Bosnia-Herzegovina. During that time, still prior to the 1995 Dayton Peace Accords, however, there was no military or political solution. (Unlike in Chile, where Pinochet eventually stepped down, a democratically elected government held power, and a truth commission was established.) Even during those years of ethnic cleansing and siege, we saw testimony in relation to the wounds that genocide and war were inflicting upon individuals and upon their collective identities as Bosnians and Herzegovians.

I first started doing testimony work with Bosnian refugees in 1992 with Dori Laub, Dolores Vojdvoda, and others at Yale University. We were a group of mental health professionals, interdisciplinary scholars, and community advocates. We tried to help newly arrived Bosnian refugees in Connecticut and New York through clinical and advocacy work, and we did writing and research on testimony.

Beginning in 1994, the Croatian American psychiatrist Ivan Pavkovic and I founded the Project on Genocide, Psychiatry, and Witnessing at the University of Illinois at Chicago, and for the next five years we did testimony work with Bosnians in Chicago and Bosnia-Herzegovina. Testimony was one part of our work, which also included community mental health services and multifamily support and education groups for refugees, and mental health reform in Bosnia-Herzegovina. In all these areas we believed it was important to provide a helpful service, but also to conduct research and intellectual inquiry. In Chicago and Bosnia-Herzegovina, through our Project on Genocide, Psychiatry, and Witnessing, the testimony work grew through a collaboration with two persons who came to work with Ivan and me in Chicago: Alma Dzubur, a Bosnian psychiatrist from Croatia; and Tvrtko Kulenovic, a writer and literary scholar from Bosnia-Herzegovina. Our approach emphasized testimony as a means of addressing both individual and collective trauma, but without assuming that testimony could guarantee desired changes for collectives.

We began this work believing that testimony could function like a brief individual psychotherapy, and that it would help some survivors to suffer less from trauma-related symptoms. The Chileans had reported some clinical improvements in persons who gave testimony, but there had been no systematic study of the possible benefits of testimony upon trauma. The first testimonies that we did in the United States and Bosnia-Herzegovina appeared to help the survivors to feel less distress. So we decided to conduct an investigation in Chicago of testimony as a psychotherapeutic intervention in traumatized refugees from Bosnia-Herzegovina. We thought it was important to get some more "objective" information in testimony, given that most people's opinions on testimony, favorable or unfavorable, were based upon intuition.

Through a scientific investigation and statistical methodologies, we found that giving testimony significantly reduced the symptoms of post-traumatic stress disorder (PTSD) and depression in a group of Bosnian refugees. Telling their stories helped them to feel better. One survivor said:

> When I speak to someone who listens to me, and who respects me, and when I can tell my story to such a person, then I feel good. I don't feel like a zero, and I have felt that way in concentration camp, or even coming to this country. You know, all the time you feel as if you were nobody, nothing, because they can step on you, kill you, humiliate you, at any moment of the day or night.[25]

It was not our claim that testimony was for all persons at all times. Our experiences taught us that testimony should be undertaken only under certain conditions. The relationship between the teller and the receiver must be safe, trusting, and caring. The survivor must be fully told about the aims and procedures of testimony, including the issues of who has access to their testimony. Any concerns that the survivor has about confidentiality or safety must be thoroughly addressed before proceeding. Some individuals with severe clinical forms of traumatic stress or depression may benefit from psychopharmacological treatment before embarking on testimony. Most of all, it is essential that the person wants to tell their story and is not coerced.

We also learned that most of the people who agreed to do testimony had not and would not seek psychiatric services. They agreed to tell their trauma stories, not to receive psychotherapy from mental health professionals. This demonstrated how testimony could help to relieve suffering in those people who were unlikely to seek psychiatric services, but who wanted to tell their story. We found that testimony was a useful tool for addressing the suffering of persons who were reluctant to seek more mainstream mental health services. Most survivors do not seek mental health services, in part because they do not seem themselves as mental patients. However, we found that they often do regard themselves as bearers of a story of injustice. Although many of our testimonies were taken by psychiatrists or other mental health professionals, we strongly believed that they did not need to be. Testimony work is not only for clinical psychiatrists or psychologists in office-based practices. That testimonies could be done by persons who are not mental health professionals opens up more opportunities for doing testimonies in different types of community settings, such as homes, schools, mosques, or cultural centers.

Yet the type of scientific study that we conducted could not answer an important question: How and why did testimony help to relieve the refugees' suffering? To answer that, it was necessary to know what they talked about in testimonies. So testimonies were gathered, collected, read, discussed, reread, and talked over. Some of them were more than a hundred pages long. They brought the experiences of the genocide and war to us in a way that seemed both human and real. These testimonies were comprised of many little utterances that so impressed as to make us feel that these must be a highly significant part of what makes testimony captivating to readers. Words were spoken that could only come from that one person, and yet which seemed to speak for a much larger experience. Nevertheless, the individual trauma frameworks of understanding that we had utilized were not able to account for this power.

We believed that understanding how these testimonies worked could come only from more fully knowing them as individual stories that also connected with history and culture. We recognized that the importance of the story had registered with our professional predecessors in testimony work, but in different ways. Dori Laub claimed that these stories could contain truths not admitted into the actual historical record. For instance, he cited the example of the woman who made the claim in her testimony that in Auschwitz "we saw four chimneys going up in flames, exploding." Laub emphasized that although what she saw was historically inaccurate, there was a great resilient power in her visualizing of the detonation and her imagining that the Nazi death machine could be opposed. Inger Agger's *The Blue Room* emphasized that the restorative power of the narratives of women refugees who survived torture lay in how they were challenging the cultural norms of women in their societies. Although Laub and Agger were clearly reaching toward history and culture, they still anchored their understanding in individualistic, psychoanalytic, and psychiatric frameworks of clinical testimony. For Laub, testimonies were psychoanalytic stories of psychological trauma. Agger told stories in a highly creative metaphoric form and introduced cross-cultural notions of healing, but in justifying her approach, she depended upon the Western mental health concepts of "victimization," "trauma," and "dissociation." For example, she stated: "I thus attempt to write about trauma in a less 'dissociated' language" (BR 7).[26]

The writings of Agger, Jensen, and Laub encouraged us to go further in the direction of stories of life and history. We found textual kin for these testimonies in the literatures of extremity.[27] We learned to say to one another that testimony would have a greater healing power if it was a "good story." It then followed that the role of the person receiving the testimony was to guide and support the survivor in telling such a story, a story that was uniquely theirs. We also came to identify that an explicit aim of testimony was to move the trauma story outside the narrowing prisms of individual psychopathology and the psychotherapeutic dyad, and to reframe the survivor's story in the social and historical context where the etiologic factor of state-sponsored violence originally took place. We thought that for the survivor, this explicit focus on a social and historical context, and not solely on a psychotherapeutic intervention, was a necessary factor that permitted the "entry into meaning" (BR 31).

We did not have scientific evidence to support the claim that testimony as a good story has a greater healing power. That could only come through further investigations. We did find support for it, however, in our testimony work. For example, there was some uniformity to the narratives: they were told chronologically, and they invariably included the personal experience of key historical events, such as Tito's death and the Sarajevo Olympics. Furthermore, there was also specificity of detail and uniqueness of voice. These testimonies also conveyed survivors' beliefs that through telling their story they could fulfill an obligation to transmit their experiences to others. But we did not have a convincing way of explaining how this could work.

As important as the issues of individual suffering and healing were, we also came to see testimonies in relation to collective experience. We regarded the testimony in relation to the collective realm of culture and historical memory. Torture testimony had put torture in first place; ethno-cultural particulars were way down the line. The locale of the Blue Room was taken to supersede the particular places where the women came from. Those other places were named in the introduction, but then more or less dropped. Laub's Holocaust testimony text also paid little attention either to the ethno-cultural origins of the Holocaust survivors, who for all we know may have come from any European nation. In testimony work, the tendency has been to view the teller as a torture survivor or a Holocaust survivor, more than as a Chilean, a Pole, or a Romanian.

Bosnia-Herzegovina, where all hairs stood on end over ethno-nationalist culture and historical memory, required a greater emphasis upon culture in relation to testimony. Even if it were not Bosnia-Herzegovina, this shift of mental health and human rights testimony toward issues of culture could be expected; it was consistent with contemporary intellectual and cultural trends that placed a greater emphasis upon ethnic and national cultures than had been typical in the Cold War era.

We endeavored to know what differences were uniquely associated with being Bosnian and Muslim, or Catholic, or Orthodox, as the case may be. In our testimony work, this meant reconsidering the secular political culture that had predominated in Tito's Yugoslavia and which had allowed Bosnian Muslims to flourish, though at a cost. Thus, testimony work became an opportunity to promote Bosnians exploring their culture and historical memory as Bosnians, especially in relation to war and peace. Stephen Dedalus in James Joyce's *Ulysses* uttered the extraordinary words: "History is a nightmare from which I am trying to awake."[28] We found that nearly all Bosnians who gave testimony shared this dread when they said that their experience as a society was like a nightmare. Those who gave testimony expressed the desire to find a path out of the collective nightmare. This led us to face two central questions: (1) How could testimony work assist in describing the landscape of historical memories in Bosnia-Herzegovina in which survivors were immersed? and (2) How might testimony work contribute to the collective struggles toward more peaceable collective identities?

Listening across many testimonies from Bosnia-Herzegovina, one overall pattern seemed of central importance. What these survivors were saying was: *"In Bosnia, we had a fantastic life, we lived together, and then to our utter surprise, from these others came hatred, massacres, and genocide."* Meanwhile, the standard outsider responses had conveyed two distinct propositions, either: *This is a land of ancient ethnic hatreds* (the "exotic species" focus) or: *The Bosnians were innocent victims* (the "tragic victims" focus).

Most outsiders stopped here, leaving these two propositions separate and unresolved. If you came to prove an externally derived idea, or to extract information, then there was no need to go any further. However, because of what the testimonies were telling us, we could not possibly have accepted this as the whole truth. By engaging survivors in actual conversations and listening more closely, we heard them say both: *"We lived together,"* and *"We knew all along that they were killers."*

These were contradictions crashing together in a narrative that came out of a profound cultural and historical conflict. The Bosnian testimonies presented us with the historical narratives of two eras coming one upon the other: living together peacefully in Tito's Yugoslavia, and ethnic slaughter from World War II as well as the more recent ethnic cleansing. The testimonies showed these two narratives to be proximate to one another, if not talking or colliding with one another.

This collision of narratives then compelled us to advance our inquiry into the truth by asking the question we posed to survivors: *"How can you have it both ways?"* They then offered stories and reflections that detailed their complex, multivoiced relationship with the historical memories of collective traumatization. What the stories said is that nearly every Bosnian family lost a loved one in World War II, yet for the next forty-five years they learned to live together. Listen to B., quoted in my book *When History Is a Nightmare*, who was not only telling his family story, but was actually speaking for a whole way of life: "In my family we always knew who killed my grandfather in World War Two, but we tried not to put it in the first place in our minds, but to put it back and regard it like something that is history, and that will never happen again. We thought of that like the dark side of Yugoslavia and World War Two."[29]

Thus, we came to understand that the testimonies gave an insider's view of the political culture of Tito's "brotherhood and unity," and specifically the culture of *merhamet*. Another young man from Sarajevo first told me about Bosnian *merhamet*. *Merhamet* is a Bosnian cultural value, meaning forgiveness and charity, and was a critical value behind the experience of living together. What we learned about were Bosnians' concerns that *merhamet* left them unable to recognize ethnic nationalism, and unprepared to defend themselves against their enemies.

> We called that "merhamet"—that you feel sorry for someone who has bad luck. Philanthropy. You like all people. You want to support everyone. If you can help, you help. You can even forgive bad things. You can find good in all religions. You will be good and decent to everyone . . . Because of merhamet I think the Bosnian Muslims forgot a very important thing—that it is not the first genocide against them. But people always forget. Bosnian Muslims learned the hard way.[30]

In our quest for understanding the place of historical memories in people's lives and in public life, we looked to other disciplines. The controversial political theorist Carl Schmitt wrote that all human societies have a political dimension that can be reduced to the distinctions made between public friend and enemy. Schmitt wrote: "For as long as a people exists in the political sphere, this people must, even if only in the most extreme case, determine by itself the distinction of friend and enemy."[31]

Schmitt assists us in seeing that there were major problems concerning the place of memories in the political culture of "Brotherhood and Unity." Listening to these testimony accounts of the mentality of multiethnic living suggested that *merhamet* was entirely apolitical in the sense discussed by Schmitt. Precisely because

Yugoslavia was no liberal society, the ideology of "brotherhood and unity" created the false illusion of liberalism amid the totalitarian control of a political state and its culture. Testimonies revealed that Bosnians really believed in that ideology and its sense of *merhamet*, which promised to deliver their historical dreams unto them. It was a shroud that kept them from seeing or attending to the ethnic tensions in Yugoslavian society. It also prevented them from attending to the haunting memories of ethnic nationalist violence, which eventually returned with a vengeance.

Ethnic cleansing in Bosnia can be seen as a collision between those who put those memories behind them and those extreme Serbian nationalists who put them in first place. Those who forgot did so in the name of pluralism and peace. Those who remembered did so in the name of their ethnic nation, thereby putting themselves on a path toward aggression and atrocity. In ethnic cleansing, the rememberers became aggressors against the forgetters, who then became survivors, burdened by new memories. Thus, testimonies helped us to conclude that the Bosnian experience of living together had been real. What proved to be illusory about the Bosnian experience, however, was its political culture which embraced the policy of denial of memories of ethnic slaughter while supporting the ideals of "brotherhood and unity" characterized by multiethnic living together. The suppression of historical memories made ethnic cleansing possible and left Bosnians struggling to reconcile the irreconcilable narratives of ethnic slaughter and living together. In this manner, their struggles over historical memory were at the center of their historical nightmare and were an obstacle in their collective struggle to redefine Bosnian identity in the new Bosnia-Herzegovina and the Bosnian diaspora.

Testimony work turned our attention to the myriad ways that memories of genocide and war entered into the life of the people. We believed that the work with historical memory in Bosnia-Herzegovina and its diaspora must extend beyond a war crimes tribunal. Legal institutions were but one of the voices of historical memory in public life. We wanted to attend to other voices and to reflect on other ways that memories participated in private and public life. We found that testimonies could be used as a means for promoting dialogue and inquiry on historical memory and collective identity in relation to the consequences of political violence. Both during and after ethnic cleansing and sieges, the testimonies helped to examine Bosnians' efforts to reconcile their remembrances of living together in multiethnic Bosnia with the memories of ethnic atrocities—a struggle over memory and culture for the Bosnian future.

For example, the head Muslim cleric of Bosnia-Herzegovina, Mustafa Efendija Ceric, said:

We learned something from this genocide. We can't think first about others and then about ourselves. We must take care of ourselves, think of ourselves. We have learned who we were and who we are. It was they who gave us the name Muslim with a capital M. But then we lost our country. We have been forced to be a part of the worldwide Muslim community, but it was not our prior national identity. So what we learned is that we are Bosniaks. Think of it this way: your first name is Muslim and your last name is Bosniak.[32]

Through testimonies, we listened not to leaders, but to "ordinary" people who were taking part in this enormous conversation. For example, in the testimonies we heard the arguments they were having over *merhamet*, and what we heard were two ways of life struggling with one another. Testimony provided evidence of how *merhamet*, like so many issues of historical memory, was still being contested.

In the period after the Dayton Peace Accords, we used testimony to try to add to that broader collective conversation, both in Bosnia-Herzegovina and in the diaspora. Alma, Tvrtko, and I spent lots of time in Bosnia-Herzegovina, where we engaged in community dialogues, scholarly publications, teaching, and public intellectual work. Our goals were modest. We wanted to promote multidisciplinary scholarship on testimony, especially in order to interest young scholars and professionals. We wanted to promote public discourse on the struggles over memory in the Bosnian landscape and the role of testimony. Although this testimony work was being done amid tremendously hard times for Bosnians and Herzegovians, we found encouraging signs: persons who gave testimonies saw that their testimonies were contributing to a larger process of understanding; more scholars and professionals were focusing upon testimony and memory; and new ideas about the testimony and memory were circulating in the academy and public life. Alma and Tvrtko returned to Sarajevo in 1999, and the testimony continues to be an important part of their respective work in psychiatry and literature.

Nowadays it is hard to find encouraging signs in the political culture of Bosnia-Herzegovina. Although free elections have been held, the people and politics are still divided along ethno-nationalist lines. There is still no justice for the vast majority of crimes of human rights committed in Bosnia-Herzegovina, and there is no sense of lasting security. One way of analyzing this failure is to say that the processes of state-building outpaced the processes of peacemaking, and this has included far too little attention paid to the collective nightmares of Bosnians and Herzegovians and their struggle over culture and historical memories. We believe that testimony work may have helped to address this historical nightmare, but we fully recognize that any broader processes of cultural or social change that testimony might participate in would take far greater investment and far more time. It would also take further clarification of the theory, aims, context, collaborations, methodology, and limitations of testimony.

# 4

# *Kosovar Testimonies*

In 1999 the Milosevic regime's ethnic cleansing of Kosovo, followed by NATO's defeat of the Serbian forces in Kosovo and the subsequent occupation of the region by NATO's Kosovo Force (KFOR) and by the United Nations Mission in Kosovo (UNMIK), brought about a huge expansion of humanitarian activities in Kosovo. Some of the humanitarian intervenors used testimony to treat survivors' traumas and to promote democratization and reconciliation in Kosovar society. In the immediate postwar environment of Kosovo it was difficult, if not impossible, for testimonies to serve the goals of democratization and peacemaking because of how the testimonies embodied the traumas and resilience associated with oppression and war. This chapter rethinks the uses of testimony in post-conflict societies through reporting on the testimony work conducted by one such project, the Archives of Memory, and through reporting on testimony work conducted by our own university-based project with Kosovar Albanians in Frankfurt, Chicago, and Kosovo. Testimony that is done in post-conflict societies confronts high insecurity, overwhelming suffering, tremendous uncertainty, and immediate survival needs; these issues interfere with testimony work and limit how effectively testimony may function as a story of living history.

## Testimony in a Historical Moment

My involvement with Kosovar Albanians commenced in the spring of 1999, just after the regime of the Serbian leader Slobodan Milosevic accelerated its ethnic cleansing of Kosovo and NATO responded with an air war over Serbia and Kosovo. As the situation was worsening in Kosovo, I got to know some longtime Kosovar immigrants in Chicago and some more recent refugees. In May 1999 I traveled to Frankfurt, Germany, to meet with newly arrived Kosovar refugees. Just after the liberation of Kosovo in July 1999, I was able to go there at the same time most of the recently displaced Kosovars were returning. I have continued to be engaged in Kosovo ever since, through a period of major historical, social, cultural, economic, and political transitions. The KFOR and UNMIK occupations continued as a provisional self-government was being constructed and Kosovo's national status was deferred.[1]

Even before I first met Kosovars who had directly experienced the 1999 political violence, I knew that I wanted to try to do testimony work with them. I also believed that any testimony work that I would do had to be carried out as part of an American-to-Kosovar, university-to-university collaboration. But I was also unsure: Would those who survived want to give testimony? Would there be people who wanted to receive the testimonies? What would be the aims of our efforts? I needed to have some experiences that would help me and any potential collaborators to answer these questions.

To intervene using testimony with Kosovars at such a crucial historical moment, in the spring and summer of 1999, was to think of using testimony in radically changing political and social conditions that had not yet finished unfolding. The war had just ended; the peace was tenuous, the wounds raw, and the future highly insecure. Did testimony belong here? If so, what was its role? What were its limitations and risks?

This chapter explores my own and others' experiences of testimony with Kosovar Albanians during those phases of conflict and early post-conflict. It addresses some of the practical and ethical struggles that come with using testimony during and immediately following an armed conflict. Although testimony work is always full of dilemmas and choices, in these conditions some by-now familiar dilemmas are put into bold relief and some new dilemmas are introduced. Testimony work may at times reveal more difficulties and limitations than achievements. When testimony is highly proximate to a situation of catastrophe, it may still function as an energetic story of living history. But I will describe how being proximate to political violence, both in place and especially in time, can both change testimony and create serious problems for testimony work.

All in all, my colleagues and I did about two dozen testimonies with Kosovars in that early phase. It gave us a sense of the conditions and special challenges of doing testimony work in conflict and post-conflict contexts. We were encouraged to see that testimony appeared helpful to the Kosovars who gave it. No one refused or offered any objections to giving testimony. After the telling, the persons always thanked us profusely for our interest, support, time, and commitment. When we asked one man what he thought of testimony, he said: *"I will always remember these things . . . How can I ever forget? . . . We should never forget . . . We should always speak of them in our families and to our children . . . There is no other way."*[2] Overall, Kosovars expressed far less ambivalence than people from Bosnia-Herzegovina had done about giving testimonies concerning memories of oppression and violence. After all, Bosnian identity was more rooted in recent memories of living together with Serbs, whereas Kosovar identity was based more upon a continual history of oppression and violence.

Ironically, I believe that this expression of diminished ambivalence in their testimonies is partly what discouraged us from trying to use testimony to accomplish something at broader social, cultural, or political levels. Lack of ambivalence might have been good for surviving decades of oppression and violence, but it was not good for democratization and reconciliation. In their testimonies, Kosovars were relatively straightforward about the crimes that had been done to them, and also about their identity as Kosovar Albanians. They were not at all ambivalent about who they were, what had been done to them, and what they had done. We set up no official testimony project in Kosovo and made no testimony publications; it did not seem like the best way for us to engage with Kosovars. In this chapter I will explain why, because I believe it reflects something important about testimony.

Given that other organizations had chosen to go with testimony and had organized ambitious projects, I tried to learn from them. While gathering testimonies and peeking through windows and around doors of the organizations trying to help the Kosovars, I kept field notes. I wanted to know if the intervenors were finding that testimony was helpful to individuals. For those organizations that were engaged in testimony initiatives that had an explicit macro-focus (peacemaking, civil society building), I wanted to know what they were finding out about whether testimony seemed helpful at social, cultural, and political levels. This chapter, then, combines reflections on my early struggles with Kosovar testimonies, excerpts from Kosovar testimonies, and reflections on the other organizations' testimony work in Kosovo.

For this chapter, I needed a way to write that communicated the exploration of experiences that were presenting themselves in little pieces, not in one unified whole. I found suggestions of such a form in some writings of the poet Czeslaw Milosz[3] and the anthropological scholar James Clifford,[4] both of whom combined poetry and prose in witness to twentieth-century history. I am no poet, but I do believe that in smaller pieces, rather than in bulk, there may be a better chance of finding meanings concerning testimony that are true to the realities of postwar environments. The writing in this chapter also reflects the fact that I chose to work largely from fragments (of field notes, testimonies, and readings) made as I engaged, listened, observed, and read. I have tried to write an honest representation of the challenges of testimony work in a post-conflict context.

## Documenting Human Rights Violations

Before the 1999 war, during the ten years' occupation by Serbian forces in Kosovo, Kosovars had become more sophisticated at using testimony to document and communicate their experience of human rights violations. The Kosovar sociologist Anton Berishaj wrote of a time when the long-violent Kosovar Albanians shamelessly sought and attained revenge by means of cameras, journalists, photo reporters, foreign human rights workers, etc. Kosovar Albanians no longer hesitated to go naked, bearing raw marks of violence in front of a witness, neighbors and family members, ready to show that they had been wronged.[5]

Visual, written, and spoken testimonies were important tools of human rights documentation. The story that Kosovars were telling the outside world was that they were victims of a cruel and illegal Serbian aggression and that Europe and the United States must intervene on their behalf. Unlike testimony in the postwar context, these testimonies were not done for purposes of healing. They were not intended to document Kosovar life, history, or culture. Nor did they aim to change Kosovar culture or society. The aims of testimony in the oppressed, colonized, and often violently victimized society of Kosovar Albanians were to wake up the sleepy or blind European and American outsiders and to get them engaged in a political and military intervention. This particular use of testimony, done consistently over ten years, and organized primarily by the Kosovar Albanians' political resistance, provides an important backdrop to the subsequent uses of testimony in postwar Kosovo. Their testimonies, in which they told their stories to a few journalists, had for a long time been aimed at changing the outside world's behavior toward them. They were not aimed at changing the Kosovars' interior worlds through either individual or collective healing, as the testimonies solicited by internationals following liberation would be. The Kosovars' testimonies were committed to documenting the historical truths of what was being done to them by the Serbs.

## Taking Testimony in a Complex Emergency

When Kosovar Albanians were ethnically cleansed from Kosovo in April 1999 and ended up in massive refugee camps in Macedonia and Albania, the scenes and stories were covered live across the globe by CNN, BBC, and other networks. The humanitarian organizations mobilized in response to the largest refugee crisis in Europe since World War II. I spoke with several humanitarian agencies about going to the camps to do testimony work. Soon I discovered that it required assertiveness to bring testimony into the fold of humanitarian organizations. I told their program officers that I wanted to "take" testimonies. The word "take" had the feel of using or even exploiting victims, which obviously made them uneasy. One told me, "We are committed to giving, so why should we make space for you who take? If you were a journalist looking for a story, then we could more readily understand." I told them about how testimony work had been done with Bosnians, Holocaust survivors, Chileans, and other torture survivors and refugee groups, but I failed to convince anyone.

Instead, some organizations asked me to do trauma training of local providers from Kosovo in the refugee camps, which is what they tended to expect of international trauma experts. But I did not want to preach trauma psychiatry; I did not want to tell the refugees that they all had PTSD. I know that was the right choice for me, but in retrospect, I believe my attitudes around testimony were naive. The humanitarian intervenors were thinking about trauma relief on a massive scale in refugee camps containing tens of thousands of persons. Doing the laborious, slow, painful work of testimony in a refugee camp must have seemed ridiculous to them. I could not adequately explain testimony; if it is not purely treatment, nor journalism, nor ethnography, then what is it? I also could not counter the humanitarian organizations' need to control the public circulation of survivors' stories through press releases and advertisements, which were useful for their own public relations and fund-raising.

The humanitarian workers also believed that survivors would not want to tell their stories and that doing so was likely to make matters worse. Some intervenors justified their position by equating testimony with debriefing. There is a contentious ongoing debate in the psychological literature about whether debriefing after a trauma works, with many professionals being highly skeptical. I argued that testimony is not debriefing, but these arguments were far too nuanced to be appreciated in a "complex emergency."

So I did not go to the refugee camps in Macedonia or in Albania. I gave up on the idea of doing testimony there, although not on the idea that testimony could have a role in a complex emergency. Having been in refugee camps, I knew that many (but not all) refugees did tell their stories, did want to be listened to, and did find that giving testimony was helpful on a number of levels.

Instead I decided to join Sabina Lluben, a German psychologist at the FATRA organization in Frankfurt, to talk with Kosovars newly arrived in Germany. In Frankfurt, as in Chicago, the field was a lot smaller than it was in the Balkans. This helped, in the sense that the game became simpler and actually playable; we could try to do testimony work. We arranged with German authorities to go to some former barracks for German soldiers, beside the U.S. military base, that then housed the Kosovar refugees who had arrived just a week before from those same refugee camps in Macedonia.

Sabina and I believed that testimonies could help some of the Kosovar refugees. We imagined that they would talk while we listened and recorded their stories, and that we would later give the stories back to them. But beyond that, we did not yet know the shape of testimony. We knew that testimony with Kosovars would have to be different than it was with Bosnians, but not what those differences would be.

We did not assume a priori that these people would do testimony with us, or that testimony would proceed in a prescribed way. With some trepidation, we introduced ourselves to them. We asked each one: What were you told? "That some people wanted to talk with us, including a doctor from America." It was up to us to introduce the idea of testimony, and to invite them to participate. For Sabina and me, this beginning raised some serious questions:

> What choices did we have about how to introduce the testimony? This
> of course depended upon our initial aims. Were we trying to treat their
> traumas, document historical truth, or change their culture?
> What choices did they have over how they testified? Certainly their testi-
> monies would be structured by language, culture, and history, but we
> did not know how.
> How might the Kosovars and we negotiate a way of doing testimony work
> that addressed both their concerns and ours?

Sabina asked Afrim, a young Kosovar man, to work with us. He was a Kosovar from Prizren living in Germany who had done some interpreting for FATRA. We arranged to meet Afrim in Offenbach. We first glimpsed him on the platform of the S-bahn. Two transit police officers were escorting Afrim to their security post from the train that had just arrived. Afrim shrugged his shoulders and motioned us to wait; he came back from the police shortly. "I forgot my pass at home."

Afrim had been up all night, watching the TV, waiting for any news from his family. They had just been forced to leave Prizren; their whereabouts were unknown. Were they alive or dead? Then at 4:00 A.M. he received a phone call from his sister in Tirana. "They arrived. They are OK."

Sabina worried about Afrim. He was half in Frankfurt, and half in Kosovo. He planned to travel to Tirana any day now to reunite with his family. How would Afrim cope with hearing the other refugees' stories? Would it be too much for him? Perhaps all the reasons that Sabina was concerned about whether Afrim would be able to withstand the testimony work were the same ones that made him the right person for the task. He was inside the experience, and was thus well positioned to be a bridge between the Kosovars and us. Afrim volunteered to work for no money. We insisted that he be paid for his time, but clearly he was not doing it for the money. "I am interested in this. It's a lot better than staying home and worrying about these matters." We did not disagree with Afrim that it was better to listen to the stories, but still we had our concerns. As mental health professionals, Sabina and I were able to help Afrim manage the risks of retraumatization. We could talk with him before, during, and after about its effect upon him; we could look for signs that it was too much.

We sat in an outdoor café at the S-bahn station and described to Afrim what we proposed to do. I spoke of our previous testimony work with Bosnians and our initial conversations with Kosovar refugees in Chicago. I said: "We want them to tell stories of their lives, of history, of their lives in history, and history in their lives. We think it can be valuable as a documentation of their experience as Kosovars, and for some, as a way of helping to lessen their suffering." He replied: "Yes, this makes great sense to me. It is a very interesting framework, very appropriate. But we do not know if these people will want to tell." "That is up to you, Afrim, to introduce it to them, to make them feel comfortable, to answer all their questions, to reassure them that it's OK." Afrim took to the idea readily, and his comfort was a great reassurance to the Kosovars. Without Afrim's enthusiastic support, the testimonies would not have proceeded. We caught a taxi to the place where the Kosovar refugees were staying. We wondered what would it be like to people who had only been in refuge for a few days or weeks; would they want to give testimony? Would being in refuge make it easier or harder for them to tell their stories?

## Transit

*"Where are you sending us?"*

After the knock on the door, the flight from the burning houses, nights spent sleeping in gardens and on mountaintops, rifle butts in the chest, Kosovar Albanians were put on trains, carried across Kosovo on the way to Macedonia, stopped several kilometers short, and then made to cross the border on foot, arriving at Blace, from where they were bused to Stenkovec, met by German officials seated at tables who took their names and then put them on planes to Frankfurt, where they were processed, then bused to industrial zones on the city's outskirts and put in former military barracks, then visited by an American Jewish doctor from Chicago who wanted to hear their stories. All this in less than a month. Yet it was not only these experiences, but also the decades of suffering under oppression that had prepared them for the testimonies that they gave.

*"Yes, of course I want to return. We did not run away. We were forced."*

In what kind of space did ethnic cleansing occur? It was a space not of one room, like torture. Nor of a concentration camp, as in the Holocaust. It began in the family home, with the fist or the rifle butt on the door, or the megaphone telling the block to vacate immediately. But the true space was that of transit—trains, walking, buses, and airplanes. As in Bosnia-Herzegovina, ethnic cleansing was a campaign of depopulation, consisting of scores of particular acts of forced removal, extending into oblivion. The trauma of ethnic cleansing was being forced to leave your home and your homeland. For these families in Frankfurt, this trauma would only end with their return to Kosovo. They were waiting for liberation to return. Meanwhile, they waited as families in their flats. Although they were still far from home, they made the former military barracks into a Kosovar family space.

## A Family Event

Kosovars' giving of their testimonies in Frankfurt was a family event. The available physical settings reinforced this. Testimonies were performed in their temporary living quarters: a large room with four, five, or more beds, a large table, a kitchenette, perhaps a television set. Although the walls were barren and there were no family belongings to mark the space, it nonetheless had the feel of being theirs. They invited us in with such hospitality as if it was a home they had been in for years.

A child sat next to his father, and when the father spoke of the moment when the child was threatened at gunpoint, the child had a heavy expression, shaking hands, and tears. A woman sat between her husband, who said, "Go ahead, it's OK, tell them more details," and her sister-in-law, who said, "Do not fear, you can trust them." The children, who listened to every single word, chuckled when their mother spoke of being courted by their father. It was not only that the family listened and helped to support the teller, but that the story each told belonged to everyone in the family. These testimonies could hardly be more different from those of the Blue Room, where a refugee woman sat with a therapist woman, and the story told was often about reclaiming the self outside of the family space. Here each individual spoke from within, and in support of, their family.

## The Historical and the Clinical

In these testimonies, survivors searched for a means to make what happened knowable. They had to speak of all the atrocities committed over the past ten years, but they needed to avoid presenting a pornography of violence. They did so by not only revealing the horror but also the dignity of their families' and nation's struggle throughout history. Their testimonies demonstrated that this is where they had found their resilience.

Sabina and I felt a tension between an anguished but proud history that wanted to tell itself and the helping hand of trauma psychiatry that we brought, which wanted to focus mostly on the memories of trauma. There were traumatic memories in these stories, but also so much more. To allow the testimonies to be open and energetic stories, we had to let testimony stay clear of our narrowing professional agendas. For example, if Kosovar testimony was really a family event, as these testimonies suggested, then this called for many important modifications to the individual basis of testimony work so that the family story could be told.

We wanted the experience to be "healing" for them, but we were not sure exactly what that meant here. We had to let go of the focus on individual and traumatic memory, and let the family members tell the story of their journey through history as Kosovars. We just tried to help them to say as much as they could about what happened to them, their families, communities, and nation; we also wanted to know their ideas about the future and what all of this meant for them.

## Archives of Memory

When waves of international humanitarian intervenors came to Kosovo in 1999, some were prepared to integrate testimony into their interventions in ways that were more ambitious than what was ever attempted by internationals in Bosnia-Herzegovina. The International Organization of Migration (IOM) was the most explicitly focused upon testimony of any of the international psychosocial organizations. The IOM secured funds from the government of Italy and the U.S. Department of State and organized a multimillion-dollar, multiyear initiative called "Psychosocial and Trauma Response in Kosovar"; this included the Archives of Memory project, which involved collecting testimonies, engaging international trauma experts, publishing scholarly texts, and training local psychosocial workers. I will describe this project and its testimony work.

In his article "Beyond the Archives of Memory," Natali Losi, the IOM project director based in Switzerland, conceived of the Archives of Memory initiative as an intervention challenging Kosovars' "mythical formation."[6] Losi believed that the Kosovars had a rigid and false way of understanding their own history that "had effectively fossilized the environment, interpreting it through the plot: aggressor/victim/rescuer" ("BAM" 7). Losi was concerned that Kosovars always saw themselves as the victim of Serbian aggression and would look toward internationals as the rescuer. The project's aim was "to help them break away from this rigid and limiting constriction" ("BAM" 7). The IOM project imagined that testimony would change these culturally embedded understandings of Kosovars through engaging them in "re-narrativizing, re-storying" ("BAM" 13). Testimony was to be a crucial step in helping the Kosovars to find "less restrictive and more vital alternatives to the fossilized story frozen around the dominant constellation" ("BAM" 13).

From the perspective of these outside intervenors, the war was over and it was time for making peace. Kosovars had to relinquish what the internationals perceived as nationalistic attitudes associated with war and their struggle for independence; testimony offered a way to help them get there. This view of testimony as a vehicle for democratization in a postwar context was remarkably different from the view of testimony as a vehicle for human rights documentation performed by Kosovars during the years of active struggle. It was also different from the accounts that Kosovars gave to Sabina and me. The primary obligation the Kosovars presented in those testimonies was to the truth of the injustices experienced by the

Kosovar Albanians. They wanted the world to know and accept this truth. It was not clear how to reconcile these contrasting perspectives on testimony, or whether reconciling them was even possible.

The Kosovars' testimonies that Sabina and I received all began with the Serbian offensive that drove them from their homes and ended with the refugees in Frankfurt, thinking about their uncertain futures. When the giver of testimony found that beginning point, he or she performed like the turntable needle that has found its groove; the story seemed to tell itself, whether we said a little or a lot, gave instructions or said nothing at all—the giver of testimony always found that groove. Some found it right away, whereas others took more than an hour. There was greater variability concerning what was said outside of that groove, but there was still a remarkable similarity in these stories of their families' recent nightmare. The testimonies described in the IOM report sound similar to those that we received in Frankfurt and even later in Kosovo. However, it was as if the Archives of Memory project had expected something very different.

The humanitarian intervenors operated under a different set of pressures than Sabina and I. They had to justify an intervention and claim that it was successful. In effect, they claimed that the testimony worked, but that the Kosovar Albanians were nationalists. I would argue that in the situation of conflict or post-conflict, both the testimony itself and the IOM's use of testimonies were problematic. Yes, it is true that in the Kosovar testimonies there was chauvinism, sometimes nationalism, and sometimes even extreme nationalism. But there was also moderation, patience, and tolerance. One problem with giving testimonies in proximity to political violence, and not just for Kosovar Albanians, is that the testimony itself may concentrate expressions of nationalism; these may appear more nationalistic than they really are. It was difficult for internationals to see this in context because of the ways that many of them engaged in Kosovo. There was too little collaboration and dialogue. In testimony work, the internationals were selective in what they quoted from testimonies. This made it more likely that they would find what they had come looking for (including a rationale for their program of intervention) and that it would express preexisting biases about Kosovar Albanians. This was not the Kosovars' bias, but the internationals'. However, there was little that Kosovars could do about it as long as they did not control the structures, ideas, or methods of testimony.

## A Proper Team

When I first entered Kosovo thinking about testimony, in July 1999, I came with the view that testimony must primarily be done by and for Kosovars. This meant that I would have to find partners in local professionals, scholars, and institutions who also wanted to engage in testimony work and who shared a similar vision. I soon found out that this introduced a dilemma familiar to Kosovo and its leaders. Ibrahim Rugova, who became the first president of Kosovo, said in a radio interview in 1990: "The only aim of us Albanian intellectuals is to make it possible for new politicians to emerge in the future. Because, you know, now we still lack a proper team who could lead the people and society."[7] This posed several immediate problems for testimony. If testimony was to go beyond the act of producing a few testimonies, then who were the teams? If there were yet no teams, then could the use of testimony somehow help in the making of teams? How would Kosovars and Americans (or other internationals) reconcile discrepant views of testimony, such as those mentioned before: testimony as democratization versus testimony as documentation; testimony as individual versus family story?

I talked with the local mental health professionals and psychiatric leadership. They were open to hearing about testimony and read the professional and scholarly texts on testimony that I provided, but then clearly let me know that testimony was not their priority. They were more concerned about improving basic clinical mental health services and building a public system that could address the basic mental health needs of Kosovars. Testimony may have been helpful in healing some traumatized persons, but in a society overwhelmed by multiple public mental health problems, this was clearly not where they wanted the work to go. They too expressed the concern that for many people who were still vulnerable and insecure, giving testimony might not be a good idea. In making their arguments, they were not focusing on the political dimensions of testimony. Unlike the IOM, they were not at all concerned that testimonies would express nationalism or that the problem of nationalism needed to be addressed through testimony.

These Kosovar mental health professionals did not want to make a major institutional investment in the testimony and did not see it as the path to the future in mental health work in Kosovo. There is little doubt that if I had come with some decent money to support it, then they would have enthusiastically endorsed the project and entered into a collaboration. However, that was not how we chose to proceed together. Through months of dialogue with the Kosovar mental health professionals, my colleagues and I decided to leave testimony aside, and to enter into a project that focused on the Kosovar family as a basis for organizing mental health professionals and services in Kosovo. But I did not cease looking to see what others might do with testimony in Kosovo.

The members of the IOM project, along with their funders, followed a different path. They designed and funded the Archives of Memory project. They did not seek the involvement of local psychiatrists in this project until everything important had been worked out. Nor did they focus on the middle and senior generation of professionals, but instead engaged directly with university students. One goal of the IOM project was to build a cohort of young people who could engage in psychosocial work. But they did not want to be limited by either the clinical framework of institutional psychiatry or by what they perceived as the nationalistic framework of the Kosovars' political culture. Their project tried to achieve this goal by making the training of Kosovar psychosocial workers one of its focal points. These psychosocial workers were 18- to 22-year-old youths recruited from the University of Prishtina. They were accepted into the program and were expected to participate in its training. Participation in the testimony project was one of the key training experiences for these workers. Each testimony interview was done by a psychosocial worker paired with an international staff member. The idea was that the psychosocial workers would learn how to conduct testimony interviews.

At this point, it is hard to say exactly what resulted from the psychosocial workers' involvement in the Archives of Memory project. None of the psychosocial workers appear as authors or coauthors in the Archives of Memory book (although multiple students from Italy do appear as authors and coauthors). As of spring 2006, twelve of the seventy persons trained as psychosocial workers were employed by the Ministry of Health in Kosovar community mental health centers. Some others were enrolled as students at the new Psychology Faculty of the University of Prishtina.[8]

These mental health workers became the most concrete legacy of the IOM project. They had become a part of the new generation in the Kosovar mental health system, and that in itself is an achievement. It is too early to determine what more might come of that. But it is fair to say that their current level of involvement does not appear to have made substantial changes in the practices or attitudes within the mental health system, and the psychosocial workers en masse do not appear to have changed the larger social, cultural, and political field of Kosovo. Investing in youth had its advantages. But there were disadvantages too, apparent in the lack of ability of the IOM project to have a more immediate impact on Kosovar professionals, managers, and leaders. The emerging public mental health system in Kosovo has not yet engaged with the issues of clinical trauma treatment or reconciliation.

## Testimony in Kosovo

I first went to Kosovo in July 1999 with Merita Zhubi, a Kosovar immigrant from Chicago. We thought that Kosovo would be an appropriate context for gathering testimonies. Actually, we did far fewer formal testimonies there than we had imagined doing. Doing testimony in Kosovo felt more awkward than doing testimony in Frankfurt. The families were not sitting around waiting, but were busy with their daily lives. Many families also appeared to be sad and fearful. Oftentimes we did not ask people to do testimony because we felt that it might add to the suffering and discomfort of the family members. Meeting families in villages and towns was closer to the experience of meeting with whole families in Frankfurt, whereas in the large cities, it was more often the case that we would talk with one or two family members.

We were constantly talking with Kosovars about the war. They would so often spontaneously tell their trauma stories that it seemed like our time in Kosovo was one nonstop testimony with myriad Kosovars. And yet it still seemed awkward for us to impose the formal structure of testimony upon these conversations. Had we done so, I do not believe that many of them would have agreed to tell their stories. This left us feeling unsure: where does conversation become testimony, or testimony become conversation? At times I questioned what is gained by bracketing off testimony from conversation. It could be that doing testimony in the usual way was just not compatible with the conditions in Kosovo immediately following liberation. They had their own ways of talking about those experiences, and they did not appear to need our way of doing testimony.

*"This is my story, but also the story of many people. This is not something so unique."*

Merita reassured them in Kosovo, like Afrim did in Frankfurt. Still, they wanted to know about me. They noticed the Slavic spelling of my first name and wanted to know where I was from. "Are you a Serb?" they asked. I told them, I am a Jew, and my grandparents were Russian Jews. Funny, I already knew far more about their past than I did about my own. In contrast, they knew far more about their past and that of their families than they did about other people. They especially knew about the traumas they suffered.

*"We are all sick here from what we saw. Killing and destroying. All killing and destroying."*

They spoke to us because we asked. Because of Merita, the insider, and me, the outsider and professional. Never did we ask anyone to tell us their trauma stories. Nonetheless they all did. In homes, cafés, streets, schools, barbershops. Often what we heard was not spoken of outside of families, nor even inside them. But these stories could be told to us because of who we were to them: an American doctor and a Kosovar family friend.

*"Snipers killed a fourteen-year-old girl. Her father took his coat and put it over the girl and ran away."*

Although it is believed that family is the most appropriate basis for organizing mental health services in Kosovo, it was clear that the majority of the testimonies we gathered in Kosovo could never have been done in the presence of whole families. Unlike the special circumstances in exile, where they were all more or less forced to be together, in Kosovo they could take leave of one another. A son told of his father's murder. His mother could not stand to be around when he spoke, so she left for the afternoon. A woman's husband was still being held in a prison in Serbia. Her mother stayed with the children as she told her story. On the one hand, I felt that it was probably better that other family members were not there to listen. But if doing testimony was not going to involve families, then what good could it be in a Kosovo where life revolved around the family? I noticed that even when all the family members were not present, the story was still highly focused on the family and all its members. The story that they were telling was still the family story, and other family members were later very interested in hearing what was said.

## Losing a World

Entering Kosovo I thought: we who came, gained a world. They who are here, lost part of theirs long ago. Those propositions of ours, including testimony, that depend upon a sense of individual ownership over experience meant little there. The Kosovars have two core reference points: one is family, and the other is their ongoing national struggle for freedom and independence. To be useful, testimony would have to fit with their sense of family and national struggle.

I also noticed that in Bosnia-Herzegovina, everyone had spoken of the Holocaust. In Kosovo at that time nobody spoke of the Holocaust, or of ethnic cleansing in Bosnia-Herzegovina; although they were aware of these histories, they tended to minimize their expressions of other peoples' suffering. What so impressed me was their total preoccupation with the suffering of their families and their nation. They did not experience this as an expression of selfishness or unhealthiness, but as a strength and a necessity. Nonetheless, it challenged many of us coming from outside. We believe that our humanity resides in our ability to recognize crimes done to others and to lend them a helping hand. When we encounter persons who do not share that same directedness of self toward others, then it strikes us as wrong. But with the Kosovars' help, I came to recognize how this was not our space. Given Kosovo's culture, history, and what these families had experienced, it was not surprising that they would have these attitudes, nor was it surprising that their testimonies would reflect them. *"I need two days to explain what happened."* In a time of war, family and national history were speaking so strongly and abundantly in each testimony that there was little room for much else.

## A Flaw of Testimony

I consider it a flaw of testimony that I worried about inserting a meaning into the person's story. The vulgar debate on false memory in the United States has made this unavoidable, but in Kosovo it took an entirely different twist. My initial bias in Kosovar testimony was to do as little as possible to shape the testimony narrative. It was better to leave it up to the testifiers. I waited for the ambivalence, something like the Bosnians' conflicts over *merhamet*, but that ambivalence never emerged. I waited for the Kosovars to speak about possible conflicts about living with Serbs.

I waited for them to speak about concerns over the retaliatory violence against Serbs that was then commonplace. I wondered if I should keep waiting or if I should ask them about these issues that seemed important to me. Most difficult for me were those infrequent occasions when they did speak of violence against Serbs, but did not condemn it. I felt uncomfortable, as if I had to say something. Still, I hesitated because I thought it important to respect their freedom to tell their stories as they wanted. Then I realized that each question, each statement, each glance was an insertion. There were already lots of these. This could not be avoided. I said something back to them that expressed my own discomfort. I had to be careful what I said or I might lose their support.

Never did I believe that I should try to change the politics in their testimonies through insertions, or that I could. In the immediate postwar setting, their testimonies reflected the traumas and resiliencies associated with oppression and war. Kosovo would have to be a completely different place for the testimonies to be other than they were. This may sound pessimistic, but I did not believe that testimony could change their views, or make them think differently, let alone think like I did. The Archives of Memory project, on the other hand, wanted to change people through testimonies. The IOM intervenors also sounded like pessimists, but instead of placing that burden upon testimony or upon themselves, they laid it upon the Kosovars. Instead of concluding that testimonies could not fully function in the midst of conflict and post-conflict, or that their project was not able to change the Kosovars, they used testimonies to try and show that there was a flaw in the Kosovars.

## A Monolithic National Identity

The Archives of Memory project's international and local staff (psychosocial workers being trained by the IOM) conducted forty interviews in Prishtina, Mitrovica, and Peja (with twenty-one Kosovar Albanians and nineteen Kosovar Serbs).[9] Scholarly papers were presented in Fiesole, Italy, in May 2000, and a compilation of those texts was published in 2001. Silvia Salvatici, in her contribution entitled "Memory Telling," wrote that "narratives of suffering seem directed at the construction of a monolithic national identity" ("MT" 15–16). This Kosovar Albanian identity, characterized as nationalistic and exclusionist, is described as both the consequence and the creator of ethno-political conflict. She also found some narratives that were "not unified, but fragmented along socio-cultural, gender and generational dimensions" ("MT" 16). She regarded the latter as a "resource" for "plurality" and a challenge to "homogeneity" ("MT" 49).

Luisa Passerini endorsed the "trilateral engagement" of psychology, anthropo-history, and narratology in testimony work and wished for it to be undertaken on a larger scale.[10] She hoped that this would lead to narrativizing multiple subjectivities based on "transversal communications . . . that could interfere with the persistence of a 'public, nationalist discourse.'"[11] For example, she found hope for breaking up the Kosovars' monolithic identity through evoking gender, generational, and rural/urban distinctions.

In its analyses, the Archives of Memory project juxtaposed monolithic vignettes with multiplistic vignettes. Would both the monolithic and the multiplistic ever have been present in the same testimony? Or perhaps in the same family? Did these testimony narratives vary with some factors of the interview—who were the interviewers? What did they elicit? What were the survivors' worries that day? I question whether these testimony narratives were actually so totally one or the other. I also question whether it makes sense to draw a linear correlation between a nationalistic attitude and a national political agenda. Might an attitude like Kosovar national pride be more appropriately viewed as a rhetorical figure, something that floats in the culture and society, rather than as the worst kind of nationalism?

The Archives of Memory project was conceived as an intervention that aimed to change how Kosovars narrated their traumas. The way in which the IOM came to target a monolithic national identity as being the primary problem seemed unlikely to engage Kosovars' interest or support. It reflects more a judgment than an understanding of Kosovar culture and history. I suspect that the IOM project members believed too much in testimony and in themselves to notice that the immediate postwar context may not have been the right time or place for testimony work that could be as productive for Kosovars as it apparently was for the internationals.

The contributor who came closest to questioning the faith in testimony was Enrica Capussoti, an Italian cultural historian. She worried that through conducting testimony she might return "a gaze" which could confirm and reinforce rigid stereotypes. She articulated the challenge for oral history as being to "criticize the [Kosovars'] mechanism of inclusion and exclusion, and the process of identity construction based on territories and national values."[12] I would only add that critical reflection should also include outside intervenors critically reflecting on their theory, methods, and behaviors. In the IOM's case, an insufficient amount of such critical reflection significantly contributed to the representations of those same nationalistic mechanisms and processes that they condemned in the Kosovars.

## Testimony and Obligation

*"I will tell you my story and my vision."*

Testimony can cause vertigo. You may already know the major contours of the history, the most obvious events and the biggest players. But before you is one person, chosen for their ordinariness, who you ask to tell their story. It starts out as an ordinary story, about their village, their upbringing, and making a family of their own. But as you detect that history is leaning into their life, their story, it becomes less ordinary. Then there is that moment in the story, and there is always that moment, when the person takes you (but remember it is because you asked) to the edge of a precipice and you look over and what you see is a life that has been occupied by a nightmarish history, and a nightmarish history that is populated by actual lives, and then the lines start to blur between history and lives, and then you fall right into that history with the person.

Because you are the one who encouraged it, who may even have pushed it, it is then part of your obligation to help them out. Yet you recognize that often this is not actually possible in one encounter. It is a process that requires attention over time. What also requires attention are the stories themselves, and the other obligations that they create. How will you respond to them? What you do with those stories after the telling is done is part of your obligation to them. These are stories that want to be heard. They may want to teach, to inspire, to frighten, to console, or to question. They do not want to be put in a box.

There were many testimonies from Bosnia-Herzegovina, and then new ones from Kosovo appeared. At first I allowed myself to respond to a technological viewpoint that "sophisticated computer software could show us" the shape of testimony. I believed that there were certain rules governing the world of testimony. My hope was to do an analysis and generate a spreadsheet on the survivors' stories that would prove that no matter where testimony was taken, the structure of the story remained the same. But when we started tinkering with the program, we found that it could not be done. One could demonstrate a Kosovar story and a Bosnian story, but the two would not line up on the page. This was not a defeat but actually a triumph; Kosovar testimonies do not have to look like Bosnian testimonies.

*"Thank you very much for your interest in people who were very close to massacre and had weapons in their chests. The next generation will never forget about that. They will hear about that forever."*

We gave the testimonies back to the families for them to read, to keep, to use as they pleased. The testimonies did help us to better understand Kosovars; we put this understanding to use in developing and implementing other efforts to help larger numbers of Kosovar survivors and their families (those in Chicago through TAFES—Tea and Family Education and Support, and those in Kosovo through the Kosovar Family Professional Education Collaborative).[13] But because we did not believe that we could truly fulfill the obligations that testimony created in the postwar context, we decided not to make a testimony project in Kosovo.

Five years later, in March 2004, ethnic violence exploded in Kosovo, with Kosovar Albanians burning over a hundred Orthodox churches and displacing several thousand Kosovar Serbs. Three days of violence revealed that Kosovar Albanian hardliners could mobilize large segments of the public to violent acts; equally problematically, it demonstrated that moderate Kosovar leaders or institutions had difficulty speaking out against nationalist violence. It was a pessimistic sign of both how far the Kosovars still had to go and how deficient had been the humanitarian interventions in discouraging political violence. When I saw what happened those three days in March, I regretted that my Kosovar colleagues and I had not done more to build tolerance in survivors, communities, and institutions. But I did not believe in using testimony to make them "break away" from who they were, and nothing since has made me think otherwise. Unfortunately, it appears that as long as Kosovars remain vulnerable to ethnic nationalist violence, both Kosovar Albanians and Kosovar Serbs will continue to pay an enormous price.

## Incompleteness

*"I can talk enough to fill one big book."*
How many times have I seen the amazement when witnesses held the typed pages in their hands and asked, "How did I say all this?" What was it that surprised them? A person was impressed by his or her capacity (albeit facilitated) through the testimony to produce from misery, formlessness, and devastation something that is whole, beautiful, concrete—a personal and historical speech gift. Yet there will always be testimonies that for one reason or another do not achieve this level of wholeness. Perhaps this is more likely in the testimony done in the crisis or postcrisis context, where there are so many difficulties that may interfere with it.

Rereading those testimonies, I become aware of thinness; it seems like more was actually said when we sat together. The stories seem incomplete. There is no reason to be disappointed; there is certainly no good reason for transferring that frustration onto the givers of testimonies. All testimonies are filled with gaps; some more than others. Incompleteness is tolerable. Incompleteness in testimonies may even be necessary, because it indicates that the story and the understandings are unfinished. In Kosovo, I believed that there was hope in the testimony narratives' incompleteness, but neither I nor the other humanitarian intervenors really knew how to work with either the incompleteness or the hope in the testimonies.

# PART II

## Testimony as Dialogic Work

*We shall live again, we shall live.*
—Patti Smith, "Ghost Dance"

# 5

# Introducing Bakhtin's Dialogic Work

The overall aim of part 2 of this book is to articulate a narrative approach for understanding and engaging with testimony as a story of living history. I will rethink testimony in relation to the three aforementioned human developmental concerns regarding the consequences of political violence. Once again, these are: How to relieve suffering? How to create cultures of peace and reconciliation? How to document histories?

In part 1 of this book, I discussed several examples of testimony as a story that were drawn from the testimony literature, but without considering theorists or theories about the narrative. This second part of the book introduces some narrative concepts from outside of testimony work that will aid in this exploration. There are many scholars who could have been consulted. However, my intention was not to plunge this discussion into a deep sea of theory and lose contact with the survivors' worlds. I have chosen to employ a narrative theory that I believe will sharpen and strengthen the perspective of testimony as a story of living history. To me, the best choice was Mikhail Bakhtin's dialogic work and several related narrative concepts described by him and his disciples.

Mikhail Bakhtin (1895–1975) was a man who wrote extraordinary books in incredibly difficult times. He had a passionate commitment to literature and philosophy. This passion carried him through a life of extreme hardship from chronic pain and political persecution, although not political violence, like those Chileans, Jews, Bosnians, and Kosovars that were discussed in part 1. It was not only Bakhtin's writings but also his life of inquiry and struggle—which yielded to no system (neither his own nor any other)—that was so compelling to me, and so relevant to testimony. Bakhtin never gave his testimony nor described how his approach would apply to testimony, but in this book I extend some of his ideas as a basis for rethinking testimony in relation to political violence.

One problem that I immediately faced was that there are actually so many Bakhtins. It was clearly beyond my capacity to offer a comprehensive reading of all of them; nevertheless, it is necessary for me to say which Bakhtin it was that I have responded to. The Bakhtin that is a primary focus for this inquiry was the author of

*Problems of Dostoevsky's Poetics* (1929). I also focus on some later Bakhtin, especially his "Toward a Reworking of the Dostoevsky Book" (1963) and his essays "On Speech Genres" and "Toward a Methodology for the Human Sciences" (both published in Moscow in 1979). My picture of Bakhtin has also been shaped by direct interactions with several leading Bakhtin scholars. I had the privilege of conversations on Bakhtin and testimony with two leading Bakhtin scholars: Caryl Emerson, author of *The First Hundred Years of Mikhail Bakhtin,* and Gary Saul Morson, author of *Narrative and Freedom.* I also learned from reading the works of other Bakhtin scholars, especially Michael André Bernstein, author of *Foregone Conclusions: Against Apocalyptic History.*

Another potential problem in my use of Bakhtin to rethink narratives of political violence concerns the appropriateness of applying literary interpretations to social realities. Morson has said that Bakhtin "took seriously the analogy between a literary work and the real world" (*NF* 82).[1] However, I do not claim that what Bakhtin wrote regarding a literary text (e.g., *The Brothers Karamazov*) should be directly applied to the lives of survivors of political violence (e.g., families of the missing from Srebrenica). Overall, my position is that what Bakhtin wrote regarding a literary text may be used to further our understanding of real-life situations, but we should never simply equate literature with life.

Another challenge for me in reading Bakhtin was to decide whether his visionary ideas were to be regarded as the "hope" or the "steps."[2] If they are the hope, then they represent the ideal conditions that we eventually want to reach. If they are the steps, then they represent the means by which we may be able to get there. Bakhtin's visionary ideas may be taken as both the hope and the steps or as either one alone. In this book, I use them both ways because I believe that testimony needs help with both. Bakhtin's ideas are not offered as definitive proof that testimony works, but rather as helping to develop a new conceptualization of testimony that might be further analyzed, implemented, or scientifically investigated in future works.

Bakhtin's writings present an array of concepts that are relevant to testimony, but the primary focus of this text is on three concepts: *polyphony, dialogism,* and *unfinalizability.* To say that there is only one definition of each of these terms would be fundamentally anti-dialogic. Let each person say what they mean to them and let the conversation begin. As a starting point, consider these simple claims about what polyphony, dialogism, and unfinalizability mean to me:

> Polyphony: A multitude of voices interact with no predetermined result.
> Dialogism: The voices speak and listen to one another openly and responsively.
> Unfinalizability: Events are multi-potent.

My aim is not to freeze one understanding of Bakhtin's concepts in a few words, but to start a discussion that considers and reconsiders their multiple possible meanings as I reflect further on testimonies and on narrating the traumas of political violence. Let me now introduce "dialogic work," a core concept that Bakhtin used to explore literary texts and the human experience. Bakhtin wrote: "Life by its very self is dialogic" (*PDP* 293).[3] In his book on Dostoevsky, Bakhtin described what he called "dialogic work," which Caryl Emerson explained as follows:

> By dialogue, Bakhtin meant more than talk. What interested him was not so much the social fact of several people exchanging words with one another in a room as it was the idea that each word contains within itself diverse, discriminating, often contradictory "talking" components. The more often a word is used in speech acts, the more contexts it accumulates and the more its meanings proliferate. (*FHY* 36)

Emerson explained that words carry meanings and that repeatedly used words accumulate more and more meanings. This creates ever more complex webs of voices, memories, emotions, and experiences. Dialogic work holds that truth is sought through a vigorous discourse involving the dynamic interactivity of multiple voices and points of view. One voice/point of view/word is shaped by its connections to the others and is held together with them in an ongoing dialogic relation.

Dialogic work is never easy. That is certainly true when applied to testimony. However, dialogic work can assist in getting a handle on the ongoing conversation to which the testimony belongs. First, let's consider the circumstances of the production of testimonies. The naive assumption, too often made, is that what the survivor wants is pure telling. Survivors want to get the story out, and the receiver wants to support that. But the receiver, who asked that the story be told to them, also wants to insure that there is some uniformity to the telling. Dialogic work assists in clarifying how the testimony cannot be said to be only a product of the survivor, who of course speaks it, but also of the receiver with whom words, memories, and stories are exchanged. A receiver stimulates and structures what is said (or not) and then documented (or not) and then transmitted (or not). Receivers inevitably want the testimony to adhere to some kind of structure, informed by their own sense of what a testimony ought to be. Therefore the receiver often supplies much of the structure, even if unwittingly. For example, sometimes the receiver insists on a before, during, and after, even though the survivor may not be bound to a linear chronology. In chapter 8 I will discuss how Gary Saul Morson and Michael André Bernstein extended Bakhtin's ideas concerning more open models of time sense, exploring literary works and theory in ways that have valuable implications for testimony work. Another important issue is to what extent the survivors are telling their stories dialogically in the testimony, and how the receiver has helped or hindered dialogic exchanges.

Of course, testimony is more than production. It is also reception, gathering, interpretation, rearticulation, and communication. Bakhtin should be useful here because these too are potentially dialogic relations. In considering the relationship between testimony narratives and readers, it is important to ask: What allows readers or listeners to enter into a dialogic relationship with testimony narratives? How might they respond with a dialogic narrative of their own and so on down the line? Could dialogism be a productive path for the social communication of testimonies and their entrée into a culture?

In the clinical testimony literature discussed in part 1, these interactions and transformations were often not considered. Sometimes it was claimed that it is all the survivor, and sometimes that it is all the listener. Insufficient attention was also paid to the contexts of testimony, including the roles of institutions watching over the telling and listening. It was also forgotten that the broader contexts are history, culture, and life itself, which is intuitively known, but which I find becomes more addressable when the concept of dialogic work is employed.

This exploration claims that if testimony were approached as dialogic work, then it would be more likely, but not guaranteed, that testimony would realize its potential for doing good in serving survivors and their communities. I believe that the power of testimony as an agent for change comes from its dialogic properties. When dialogism is forgotten, then testimonies' potential for helpfulness diminishes. I am not saying that dialogic testimony is without risks, failures, or limitations. I believe that testimony can sometimes do no good or even do harm; however, that too, may be understood from a perspective of dialogism and narrative.

The chapters of part 2 that follow are "Relieving Suffering" (chapter 6), "Creating Cultures of Peace and Reconciliation" (chapter 7), and "Documenting Histories" (chapter 8). Thus, part 2 envisions testimony as a dialogic work that takes shape around the three imperatives that emerge from survivor communities. The mental health worker wants to free the survivor from the suffering of traumas; the peace worker wants to build cultures of peace and reconciliation today, despite what happened before; the documentarian wants the survivors' stories to be remembered throughout time. As important as each of these are, we must also recognize that at times they may conflict or be incompatible with one another.

Dialogism has been mentioned by others in the testimony literature, but not in a way that adequately capitalizes on the gravity of Bakhtin's contribution.[4] Dialogism is truly a philosophy in Bakhtin's writings, and it has been productively extended into many different questions and experiences. This dialogicity is what I will bring to this exploration of testimony, but not monologically so, I hope. To introduce Bakhtin as a grid to which everything else is fixed would be a betrayal of the values of dialogic work. To offer up dialogism as a panacea for testimony would be a betrayal of all the difficulties and struggles characteristic of Bakhtin and the discourse on his ideas. It would also be a betrayal of the difficulties and complexities of testimony discussed in part 1. Rather, my approach is to have Bakhtin's ideas respond to what we have already learned about the testimony. If this brings us closer to testimony as a story of living history, then it might better help us get to a place where those badlands start treating us good.

# 6

# *Relieving Suffering*

According to the traumatic stress theory that is widely accepted by mental health professionals, relieving survivors' suffering depends upon reducing the adverse influence of traumatic memories on the survivors' cognitions. Clinical testimony is thought to be one way to achieve these cognitive changes in traumatic memories. However, in focusing largely on the cognitive mechanisms of traumatic memories, the traumatic stress approach to testimony forgoes an understanding of survivors' suffering in relation to broader human developmental struggles, including the potentially helpful roles of testimony as a story.

Bakhtin's "dialogic work" suggests an alternative theoretical understanding of testimony's role in relieving suffering among survivors of political violence. The perspective of dialogic work does not depend on the claim that traumatic memory is the source and memory disorder is the form of survivors' suffering. Rather, Bakhtin's dialogic work suggests approaching suffering following catastrophe as a metalinguistic condition. In testimony, the survivor works with a receiver to create a story that, as a polyphonic and dialogic narrative, offers the survivor potential for growth in consciousness and ethics in regard to his or her experience of political violence. Whether testimony helps to make such changes, and whether this relieves suffering, is always difficult, by no means certain, and sometimes not even achievable. But under the right conditions, this approach claims, producing a polyphonic and dialogic testimony narrative can be a helpful act for the survivor who is suffering.

## Survival, Consciousness, and Ethics

Survival, not death, was Bakhtin's preferred subject. For example, he wrote about a Dostoevsky tremendously preoccupied with the "crises and turning points" of survival; its presentness, struggles, contestations, and meanings (*PDP* 73). Bakhtin drew a sharp contrast between the deaths presented in Tolstoy's novels and what he imagined Dostoevsky would have done with similar material. Tolstoy presented deaths "from within" as the extinguishing of the dying person's consciousness; whereas Dostoevsky described deaths "observed by others" with a radically different sensibility whereby "death finalizes nothing" (*PDP* 290).

To Bakhtin, survival was closely linked with the phenomenon of "consciousness." For the purposes of this book, I assume that consciousness has the following characteristics: it is a mental process that encompasses such essential human qualities as information-processing, subjectivity, self-awareness, and individual diversity. As the Nobel Prize–winning neuroscientist Gerald Edelman explained, consciousness is one of the most powerful human forces in existence: it makes new associations and connections; it creates new thoughts and feelings; it seeks to know the self and the world.[1] Trauma psychiatry and clinical testimony have considered the disturbances of consciousness during and after trauma far more so than the potential of consciousness as a source of growth and renewal for survivors. The consciousness that interested Bakhtin, and that he found in Dostoevsky, was not psychopathology but a transformative life force. To Bakhtin, Dostoevsky explored and reported not "the depths of the unconscious" but rather the "depths of the heights of consciousness" (*PDP* 289).

A key passage on Dostoevsky from Bakhtin's 1963 "Toward a Reworking of the Dostoevsky Book" linked consciousness with catastrophe: "Catastrophe is not finalization. It is the culmination, in collision and struggle, of points of view (of equally privileged consciousnesses, each with its own world). Catastrophe does not give these points of view resolution, but on the contrary reveals their incapability of resolution under earthly conditions" (*PDP* 298).

Here I will apply Bakhtin's approach to catastrophe and consciousness in the novel in order to achieve a new understanding of catastrophe and consciousness in life. Bakhtin is not saying that after catastrophe, you are just supposed to get over it. I do not read him as unempathic or callous toward survivors. After all, if you were tortured and raped, or if your loved ones were killed and you were forced to leave your home and your country, then it is impossible to claim that these were not finalizing events. Bakhtin's stubborn, optimistic challenge is: what if catastrophe was not a terminating event? What if catastrophe was open-ended in how it could influence life, history, and spirit?

Even when people die or communities are destroyed, consciousness of the lost ones and of the event lives on in those who survive: their loved ones, their neighbors, their community, and other witnesses. The consciousness of survivors could potentially overgrow even the most crushing traumas with new connections, new meanings, and new purposes. For Bakhtin, consciousness was not only an essential element of human existence; it was also one of the most tenacious forces in the world.[2] The collisions and struggles of consciousness are what underlies suffering as a metalinguistic condition. In some respects, Bakhtin was more concerned about consciousness being diminished by objectifying and closed human responses than he was about consciousness being diminished through catastrophe. Thus, Bakhtin encourages us to rethink whether the responses to catastrophe from psychiatry and clinical testimony serve to diminish or to enhance the transformative potential of consciousness.

Let us continue by inferring something new about catastrophe: it may be as much of an energetic, as it is a destructive, experience. Catastrophe is energetic in that it disrupts the strictures that have controlled consciousness, restricted meanings, and limited human freedom. It may be argued that this interpretation of Bakhtin fails to acknowledge catastrophe's destructive effects on people's lives. Yet what Bakhtin says to me is that catastrophe neither erases nor invalidates life's other struggles. For those struggling to rebuild a life after political violence, catastrophe becomes a point on the lifeline. That point may be as dark as its crimes are evil, but it is also as shimmering as the potential energy it contains. Catastrophe is not an end point on a lifeline of many other events and meanings. Even after catastrophe, there is still room to hope for better days, for love, and for a life that is more free. Nor is catastrophe a solitary point. A given catastrophe is marked by many shades of many colors because the experience inevitably contains many views, many voices, and all kinds of crucial choices.

These ideas push against today's clinical psychiatric approach to testimony as often expressed in torture testimony, Holocaust testimony, mental health and human rights, and refugee mental health. As discussed in part 1, these genres have tended to emphasize the exclusivity of traumatic events, the corrosiveness of traumatic memories, and the extreme suffering that besets the victims of political violence. Bakhtin helped me to recognize the limitations of the psychiatric emphasis upon psychopathologic symptoms as a result of catastrophe, which has been psychiatry's primary framework for understanding survivors' suffering and for justifying psychological interventions, including clinical testimony. This, of course, does not mean discounting the crimes or the human costs of political violence or the important role of psychiatric treatment, but it does require supplanting the vantage point of clinical testimony that has at times overstated trauma mental health consequences.

Speaking from within the framework of clinical testimony, Dori Laub wrote of one survivor that "after the Holocaust, life lost its seasons," and Laub characterized trauma as a "black hole."[3] Many other mental health professionals, including myself, have stated that the traumas associated with political violence occupied first place in the lives of its survivors. As mental health professionals, many of us believed in diagnosing political violence victims with mental conditions because we thought this was in itself a meaningful way of documenting the crimes and the victims' suffering. In some respects our professional interventions did help; some got treatment, some got disability assistance, some found understanding. But I fear we went too far in emphasizing trauma as psychopathology. At worst, we fetishized traumatic memories and let them eclipse history, politics, art, love, and life itself, including the power that lies in consciousness.

I regard Bakhtin as saying that once having occurred, these catastrophic events are answerable at multiple levels: individually, familially, communally, aesthetically, spiritually, morally, politically, and socially. Bakhtin stated: "As long as a person is alive he lives by the fact that he is not yet finalized, that he has not yet uttered his ultimate word" (PDP 59). People are open and free, although this may not be realizable on any given day, or perhaps not for many years, and maybe not ever for any one survivor in all the ways desired or deserved; but the possibility is always there, if only in waiting. Bakhtin was an irrefutable optimist. For every catastrophe, there was always a response.

According to Bakhtin, because responses depend upon consciousness, the specific problem of the denial of the supreme role of consciousness is far bigger than any crime and all suffering, whether ordinary or extraordinary. After catastrophe, look not only to diminish the manifestations of suffering, but look also to draw upon all the collisions of consciousness. By "collisions" Bakhtin did not mean more death and losses, but instead other life changes that are coincident with or follow from extreme events. The more collisions the better, because collisions produce energy, and energy can be used to produce changes in consciousness. Later in this chapter, I will consider some key ideas of Bakhtin that suggest dialogic ways of working for growth in consciousness after catastrophe.

Bakhtin also saw the possibilities for ethical change in catastrophe's aftermath. By "ethical change," I mean the person being faced with new or different combinations of obligations. Catastrophes and collisions of consciousness produce new obligations because survivors are faced with all sorts of new boundaries and positions, which offer new perspectives with which one has to interact and new choices that have to be made. To Bakhtin, this was good; the self needs interactions with new people in new and different positions in order to achieve a greater sense of responsibility with respect to their dilemmas and choices, and to grow ethically. Gary Saul Morson wrote: "Might not catastrophe—or for that matter, extraordinary good luck—also generate ethical accomplishment?" (CP 26).

Ethical change following catastrophe has been a matter of concern to important scholars who worked in the psychohistorical vein, including Erik Erikson and Robert Jay Lifton. In the 1960s, Lifton, the prolific scholar of Cold War-era political violence, made a crucial turn away from clinical psychoanalytic preoccupations with survivors' "anxiety" into a broader consideration of meaning and "moral anxiety."[4] By moral anxiety, I mean that Lifton was focused on the survivor's enhanced, painful knowing of right and wrong and the citizen's concern about what states and societies do to promote a more peaceful and just world. This was the basis for Lifton's landmark inquiries into "mass psychohistorical dislocations," which he conducted over several decades in multiple historical contexts including communism, nuclearism, genocide, war, and Nazism. For example, Lifton investigated the psychological processes involved in the political transformation of anti-nuclear activists, as well as the psychology of the Nazi doctors who led the genocide against European Jews. Although not all survivors will become activists or leaders, this enhanced moral knowing and potential for ethical change is often inherent to the experience of surviving political violence.

With the hyperbolic growth of the traumatic stress field in the 1990s, for many trauma mental health professionals, concerns over meaning and ethics became supplanted by a focus upon the clinical psychiatric facets of traumatic stress symptoms. Although the trauma mental health movement regarded Lifton as an early pioneer, it spawned a trauma industry that largely followed the path toward PTSD; prioritized relieving traumatic stress symptoms; and squeezed out concerns over ethical change amid historical change. My inquiry into testimony seeks to retrieve and revive both the ethical line of inquiry carried by Lifton (and his mentor Erik Erikson, and another prominent disciple of Erikson, Robert Coles) as well as Bakhtin's focus on consciousness. I will do so by next turning to Bakhtin's concerns over the authoritative position of psychology.

## Psychological Laws

Bakhtin emphasized Dostoevsky's staunch rejection of the claim that he (Dostoevsky) occupied a psychologist's position for understanding human experience. Here is Dostoevsky's view as it appeared to Bakhtin: "He saw in it a degrading *reification* of a person's soul, a discounting of its freedom and its unfinalizability, and of that peculiar indeterminacy and indefiniteness which in Dostoevsky constitute the main object of representation" (*PDP* 61).

Bakhtin condemned psychologists for imposing a "ready-made definitiveness" that was "naturally" and "normally" predetermined in all its words and acts by "psychological laws" (*PDP* 62). Bakhtin's confrontation with clinical testimony and trauma mental health boils down to a question that is as simple as it is radical: are trauma-related cognitions (e.g., traumatic memories) so real that they should supplant consciousness and ethics? Bakhtin never actually addressed this specific question, but I believe his answer would have been no, trauma should not supplant consciousness and ethics. I will explain this position by connecting Bakhtin's concerns with the writings of Ian Hacking, the philosopher critic of trauma psychiatry. Two of Hacking's books, *Mad Travelers* and *Rewriting the Soul*, are inquiries into the validity of historic and contemporary trauma psychiatric diagnostic constructs and treatment approaches, including post-traumatic stress disorder and multiple personality disorder.[5]

Hacking argued that psychiatry took elements of the human responses to suffering that were originally found in religious and cultural activities and then tried to render them accessible only to itself by employing highly privileged technical understandings. That is to say, psychiatrists made the claim that the phenomenon of trauma could not be grasped without understanding traumatic memory as only they understood traumatic memory. Psychiatry prioritized trauma-related cognitions and in comparison deprioritized other dimensions of human experience, including consciousness and ethics. Hacking did not doubt that these cognitions existed, but he critically examined the processes that led to their prioritization by a profession trying to establish a legitimate niche in its society.

These concerns about psychiatry laboring to establish its legitimacy also extend to the issue of treatment. Hacking questioned trauma mental health professionals' claim that they alone could perform treatment and interpret the meaning of its content and of trauma in general.[6] Although he did not specifically address the situation of clinical testimony for survivors of political violence, Hacking's analysis enables us to rethink this key question: is relieving survivors' suffering through testimony best approached as a clinical activity to be performed by psychiatric professionals upon PTSD patients? In my opinion, it is not. However, further clarification is warranted. I certainly do believe that some persons suffering with symptoms that are above a particular threshold may benefit from psychiatric treatment for trauma-related disorders, including the use of psychotherapy and medications. These persons may in fact be suffering too much to benefit from testimony. However, I do not believe that this justifies subjugating all testimonies or testimony as an intervention to a cognitive psychiatric framework. My analysis in part 1 found that through clinical testimony, trauma psychiatry has used technological understandings of traumatic memory to assert control over the testimonies so as to try to help survivors. I am concerned about the limitations of this approach. Often it seemed more assured that psychiatric professionals would gain legitimacy from clinical testimony than it did that either individual survivors or the public at large would derive benefit from it. After Bakhtin, I am proposing that testimony might be more helpful in relieving suffering if it were not subjugated to trauma psychiatry. I do believe that there is a need for psychiatric leadership in the realm of testimony, but this role would be vastly improved if psychiatry sought to create legitimacy in testimony work less through monologic ways and more through dialogic approaches.

Bakhtin did not know of early twenty-first century trauma psychiatry, but he did reject the psychology of his day because he regarded it as opposed to his philosophy of dialogic work. For the same reasons that Bakhtin condemned psychology in his Dostoevsky book, I am critical of contemporary psychiatric thinking and our overemphasis on universalized psychopathological conditions and traumatic memories at the expense of consciousness and ethics. Also suspect to me is the trauma mental health profession's view of trauma's "forgotten history," an attitude that drives the contemporary trauma mental health movement and its tendency toward monologism.[7] This view, which is often espoused by trauma mental health professionals, centers on the belief that because knowledge of trauma has been "forgotten," professionals must spread the word, missionary-like, about the professional views of trauma. Far less emphasis is put upon hearing survivors' stories because, in essence, we as mental health professionals believe too completely that survivors' stories are bounded by our universal theories of psychological laws. As professionals we already know what the survivor's story is: a story that emphasizes traumatic stress and its variants, which can be healed by our standardized interventions. But we in trauma psychiatry too often do not hear other people's voices, and this is precisely what would be needed to correct our teleological views. Thus I find here the contemporary equivalents of the "ready-made truth" and "official monologism" that Bakhtin in his day came to deplore (*PDP* 110).

Yet isn't the testimony literature a departure from standard mental health practice? As discussed in part 1, the psychiatric authors who wrote of testimony went out of their way to confirm that departure by virtue of the different approaches they employed—telling and listening to stories, human rights, and cross-cultural sensitivity. They believed that testimony was better able to reach the authentic survivor than were the mainstream psychiatric approaches. In some senses these proponents of clinical testimony were right: testimony is always based upon a narrative, whereas so much of psychiatry is not. Where there is a narrative, there is going to be some degree of dialogic give-and-take between survivor and listener. Furthermore, the testimony writers may have been more aware of what differentiated them from more traditional psychiatry and psychoanalysis than what actually did not. However, in other hands, the narrative-induced tendency toward dialogism can easily be squashed by other disciplinary forces, such as the cognitive paradigm that is central to traumatic stress theory and trauma mental health. For example, when we put the focus on faulty processing of traumatic memories as an underlying theory that drives the testimony, and claim that narrative is needed to integrate memory fragmentation or to extinguish "fear networks," then we are using narrative, but we do so in a cognitive way that is counter-dialogic.

Bakhtin was inalterably reluctant to grant one element, individual traumatic memory, such a high place in psychic life, relegating all else to the distant background. He was against this ordering of psychic life because it would interfere with the possibility of dialogic work. The problem with overemphasizing either the pathological or therapeutic processes concerning traumatic memory is that it turns survivors into passive objects of a mechanistic process. If there is not openness and responsivity in the story and in the life, then there is no room for consciousness and ethics, for growth in consciousness, or for ethical growth.

Bakhtin cited the famous example from *The Brothers Karamazov* where Dmitry was subjected to an investigation and trial, which Bakhtin harshly condemned:

> All who judge Dmitry are devoid of a genuinely dialogic approach to him, a
> dialogic penetration into the unfinalized core of his personality. They seek

and see in him only the factual, palpable definitiveness of experiences and actions, and subordinate them to already defined concepts and schemes. The
authentic Dmitry remains outside their judgment. (*PDP* 62)

How much better off is the survivor's authenticity today in the hands of clinical testimony? From Hacking's vantage point, not much better, especially if the diagnoses
of dissociative disorder or PTSD are being prioritized. To Hacking, these diagnoses were signs of illegitimacy and were of questionable benefit to victims and suf-
ferers. But Hacking's inquiry did not extend to the traumas and testimonies of political violence. To search further for more legitimate paths for testimony as an
intervention for relieving suffering, I will return to Bakhtin. For Bakhtin, the path
toward legitimacy could only be realized if survivors' suffering and testimony were
regarded not as treating a psychiatric condition, but as addressing a metalinguistic
condition and a human developmental struggle. To illustrate this, I will use Bakhtin
to go beyond the cognitive approach to traumatic memory.

## Beyond Traumatic Memory

A key premise of clinical testimony and its putative role in healing is that suffering
is in large part due to the burdensome presence of traumatic memories. You suffer
because these memories occupy the mind and the brain and interfere with their
healthy, normal processing. You are healed, then, if that occupation can be diminished. In a thoughtful critique of trauma psychiatry, Patrick Bracken wrote: "The
trauma, or the traumatic memory, is understood to be 'stuck,' or 'repressed' some-
where in the individual's mind. It has to be brought forward, center-stage, examined
and processed."[8] Because trauma mental health work typically regards traumatic
memory as residing in individuals, it looks to individual interventions and focuses
on changing individuals' cognitions in order to diminish trauma-related symptoms.
Even those trauma theories that attend fairly well to social and cultural contexts,
such as Judith Herman's popular "trauma and recovery" model, which also integrates feminist theory and women's lives, have at their core these basic assumptions
about the centrality of the individual's traumatic memory cognition in suffering and
healing.[9]

Bakhtin would have raised objections to all such privileging of traumatic
memory in the trauma mental health field. After all, he did not accept the Freudian
view of an unconscious. Why privilege one part of consciousness over another?
There was simply too much happening with consciousness to justify the preoccupation with an unconscious. To selectively emphasize traumatic memories was a
similar reification of one part of the self to the exclusion of other parts and their
myriad interactions. Most important, it was also a denial of the many other dimen-

sions of consciousness. Therefore, Bakhtin could not accept our contemporary focus on traumatic memories. Bakhtin's perspective would fit with contemporary critiques of trauma mental health coming from cultural and medical anthropology, including those made by Ian Hacking, but also by Allen Young, Maurice Eisenbruch, and Michael Humphrey. These scholars have argued that contemporary Western societies are overly preoccupied by traumatic memory, and that psychiatry has established its claim over certain human experiences through prioritizing and technologizing traumatic memory.[10] From Bakhtin's perspective, interventions to relieve survivors' suffering would have to be aimed at something other than traumatic memories.

Bakhtin's position on consciousness also makes it difficult to accept the rudimentary distinctions between individual and collective memories that are commonly made in the trauma and testimony literatures. Testimony has to be more than just two types of memories, two narrative structures, interacting. Remembering is a highly fluid process, an interaction of direct memories from an event, your subsequent remembering, your retelling, your receiving the remembrances of another, and so on and so forth. When speaking of memories of an event of political violence that was not strictly personal, but also belonged to the collective realm of experience, consider how many facets there are to that memory of an event in history. For example, there is the state's current version of that event; the repudiated state's version of that event; other political views of that event; ethno-religious views of that event; spiritual views of that event; secular views of that event; family views of that event; a view you long believed was true; a view that you came to accept; what you could talk about in your family; what you could talk about with people in the café, with people at work, and so forth. The survivor lives with and within a distributed network of points of view (and memories and voices) regarding the experience of political violence.

In recognizing the influence of so many points of view upon experiencing and remembering political violence, even within one person, we have identified the core Bakhtinian concept of "polyphony." In Dostoevsky's polyphonic novels, Bakhtin found "a plurality of independent and unmerged voices and consciousnesses, a genuine polyphony of fully valid voices" (*PDP* 6). Within one point of historical experience, even within one person's narration of surviving political violence, there are many different ways of seeing many different things, and each connects interpersonally, culturally, historically, and spiritually with many other views. Moreover, speech itself is comprised of "utterances" and sometimes "double-voiced words" which are shaped through "dialogic interaction," and which bear not only the speaker's words and meanings but also those of the listeners (*SG* 60–102). Thus the survivors' storytelling contains words that carry points of view that belong to a larger distributed network of experiences and meanings.

From this vantage point, the critique of clinical testimony can be sharpened, and the roles of testimony as a polyphonic and dialogic narrative come into view. If the survivor's narrative is truly polyphonic, then it is difficult to accept the proposition that testimony works via cathartic recall or some other mechanistic cognitive restructuring. If you simply go ahead and say it, then can you really get these things off your chest? Are they really out of you, and are you better for it? Bakhtin would have rejected these ideas because he believed that neither catastrophe nor narration involved the self letting go of memories and experiences. He wrote: "Catastrophe is the opposite of triumph and apotheosis. By its very essence it is denied even elements of catharsis" (*PDP* 298).

Life, including catastrophes, and its narration, is full of many, many views and voices. They are never out of you, nor are you ever out of them. If so, then how might testimony work? In testimony, the survivor who is speaking asks the receiver who is listening to help the survivor in telling a story that respects (not denies) the polyphonic nature of experience. Instead of the cathartic model whereby the memories flow out, in the polyphonic and dialogic approach, the survivor and the receiver work together in such a way that the many different, perhaps even disparate, aspects of their experience are put together into a whole. Importantly, this is a whole that does not sacrifice either the singular or the multi-voiced meanings of the person's experience of political violence. It is a whole in which the different positions and voices are given the chance to interact with or even speak to one another, which creates the possibility of new positions and meanings, and thus growth.

In polyphonic and dialogic testimony it is the elaboration, not the erasure, of the picture that is the important element. It is also essential that this elaboration not stop at some boundary just outside of the self, and fail to consider broader social, cultural, political, spiritual, developmental, and ethical concerns and struggles. A more elaborated story may help the survivor to grow in terms of his or her consciousness and ethics. The Chileans, Agger and Jensen, and Laub were each aware of the importance of contextual understanding in testimony. But without the principles of polyphony and dialogism as anchors, their model of testimonies could easily be pushed in a monologic direction (e.g., the narrative elaboration of one memory chosen by the clinician), especially when relying upon traumatic stress explanations that kept testimony within the realm of the clinical. Bakhtin challenges us to rethink the potential for promoting development and relieving suffering by sticking with a polyphonic and dialogic approach to testimony.

But Bakhtin's views leave little if any place for PTSD, the contemporary psychiatric diagnostic approach to traumatization, or clinical testimony. His staunch opposition to diagnosis is obvious and understandable. But then what would he say about the psychiatric profession's obligation to relieve suffering? Did he really desire to address suffering in his intellectual project? I believe that he did not, at least not in the way of contemporary psychiatry's focus on disorders and cognition. This is important, because the professional obligation to relieve suffering is central to what legitimizes clinical psychiatry and gives it a claim over testimony. To understand what kind of claims can be made regarding relieving suffering from the perspectives of dialogic work, I will now say more about the psychology advocated by Bakhtin.

## Bakhtin's Psychology

For most of his adult life Bakhtin suffered from a chronic bone disease. There was no treatment and no painkillers; his leg eventually required amputation. In 1928, just after completing the Dostoevsky book, Bakhtin was arrested in Moscow because of his participation in outlawed religious activities; his sentence was commuted from a prison camp (which would have likely meant death) to internal exile in Kustani, Kazakhstan.[11] Despite these personal sufferings, Bakhtin never gave his testimony. Caryl Emerson wrote: "He was, I repeat, a person who profoundly did not like outpourings of a personal nature" (*FHY* 50). This would make Bakhtin an unlikely proponent of testimony. But there is more to it. If Bakhtin was struck by catastrophe, his primary concern, according to Emerson, would not have been about what was lost or broken or how to get healed, but, "How much time do I have to become something else?" (*FHY* 158). Bakhtin envisioned the healthy, lively self in constant motion, intensely involved with other persons and continuously desiring change. To stay healthy and lively, the self needed contact with others of a special and rather specific nature. The self that Bakhtin pictured did not seek completion by the merger with another who supplied everything it needed. Rather, the self wanted to "expose itself to a multiplicity of inputs and perspectives from the outside" and to "maximize its choices and thus reduce its impotence in the world" (*FHY* 214).

Emerson asked an important question about development and answered it as Bakhtin would, from the perspective of creativity: "How do I get outside of my life—with its pain, indignity, missed opportunity, crimped perspective—so as to shape it into something I can live with, that is, shape it as I might shape an artistic creation?" (*FHY* 217). Catastrophe, and the metalinguistic condition that it caused, were potentially positive forces because they created fragments and boundaries in their survivors. In response to these adversities, you were not supposed to dwell too much on your self and your miseries. You were supposed to use the momentum supplied by catastrophe to get out of your own orbit; this leap forward could potentially be achieved through the dialogic work of testimony.

"If I wish myself to be healthy, I must seek to be finalized by as many different people as possible" (*FHY* 223). Not with one person but with many. Not through one-way but two-way interactions. You tell your story to others, who add to it, and make it something new. You take that in, and tell it again. You also listen to other people's stories or testimonies. This may help them, but it also helps you to step out of your own story into something new. Thus, giving and receiving testimonies should help to move the survivor further into that distributed network of experiences and meanings. As your involvement with stories, both others' and your own, grows, so might you. This is the psychology that Bakhtin wrote about, and according to those who knew him, it is also how he lived. "They sat around the table all night and smoked and talked, smoked and talked." For this reason, Bakhtin was nicknamed a *mezhdusoboinik,* a "just-between-you-and-me-nik" (*FHY* 5).

It is no surprise, then, that Bakhtin was highly critical of academic and professional psychology. For example, he wrote:

> A sort of peculiar periodic alternation seems to take place between an elemental psychologism, which subjects all the ideological sciences to inundation, and a sharply reacting antipsychologism, which deprives the psyche of all its content, relegating it to some empty, formal status . . . or to sheer physiologism. (*FHY* 31)

Here Bakhtin's insights on psychology anticipated contemporary disagreements over trauma mental health involving recent developments in psychiatric memory science. He implied that attempts to reduce psychology to mechanisms and structures would be inadequate, also anticipating some of today's critics of trauma psychiatry.[12] For example, in his writings about multiple personality disorder and PTSD, Ian Hacking described the ascendancy of the "memory sciences" and discredited the impact of "memoro-politics" upon clinical practice with trauma survivors.[13] Another professional voice critical of trauma psychiatry, Patrick Bracken, wrote that the focus upon memory is so highly biased toward individual cognition as to remove persons and their stories from cultural, social, and historical contexts.[14]

In the present era, innovators in philosophy and neuroscience, such as Christopher Koch and Semir Zeki, who are trying to understand human consciousness, are attempting to link brain structure and processes with perception and the highest reaches of consciousness, including cultural experiences. In his era, Bakhtin believed that the brain could be linked to culture through attention to speech and language. There were different levels to dialogue, and these coincided with different levels of "signs," ranging from more inner to more outer channels. At one extreme were the body's own physiologic channels for communicating only to itself. From there communication extended outwards, becoming progressively more dependent upon translations into signs, with language and with culture, to the self, to other individuals, to family, to community, and so forth. Bakhtin was hopeful that scientific work would eventually connect the neurological or biological processes with the communicative ones.[15] But the view of science that Bakhtin suggests—a science able to discern the multiple levels of communication underlying dialogue—

is different from the view of science dominating trauma mental health that investigates pathological cognitive mechanisms and largely ignores dialogue and consciousness. Unfortunately, in the contemporary trauma field, when the technology to do brain science actually exists, Bakhtin's vision of science supporting dialogic work is just as radical a proposition as it was when there were no such technological advances. Nonetheless, I believe that a science of dialogue concerning trauma is still necessary and possible.

I am aware of several contemporary examples of "engaged scholarship" from outside the field of trauma mental health that satisfy many of Bakhtin's concerns and manifest the polyphonic and dialogic view of testimony. They focus upon survivors' stories, but without being too individualistic, or too cognitive, or too positivistic. Rather than focusing upon trauma per se, they frame the problem in more social terms as "social suffering" (Kleinman), "positional suffering" (Bourdieu), and "social trauma" (Das). I will briefly discuss each of these.

The psychiatrist and anthropologist Arthur Kleinman has expressed hope about the use of ethnography as a means of addressing social suffering, which he defined as "an assemblage of human problems that have their origins and consequences in the devastating injuries that social force can inflict on human experience."[16] Ethnography is a narrative-focused method of inquiry centered on stories of and from people's lives that aims to be answerable to a people's experience of social suffering in the wake of catastrophe. Kleinman described several ethnographies that he claimed succeeded because they promoted "a convergence of the local moral processes and ethical discourse—resulting in practical means that measure up to ambitions."[17] Kleinman's emphasis upon the moral and the ethical is refreshing in comparison to the narrower trauma mental health discourse, and it is reasonably close to Bakhtin's ethical concerns (although Bakhtin did not have the same practical ambitions of social change as these ethnographers). Kleinman's description of the impractical methodology of ethnography has much in common with Bakhtin the "just-between-you-and-me-nik":

> Ethnography is a backwards methodology. More nineteenth than twenty-first century, it starts with face-to-face engagements enabling both indirect participant observation and direct questioning with a small number of informants. And it takes time, a great deal of time: months and years, not hours, days, or even weeks. It requires rapport, trust, and intimacy . . . Ethnography requires the capaciousness of the book-length monograph to work out what its findings signify. ("ME" 87)

According to Kleinman, "the ethnographer is 'called' into the stories and lives of others by the moral process of engaged listening and by the commitment to witnessing" ("ME" 89). In his fieldwork, the ethnographer functions like a receiver of testimony. But in the writing of his ethnographic book, the ethnographer becomes the authoritative author. The stories may come from individual inhabitants of a local world who have survived catastrophe, but in Kleinman's conception of ethnographic writing, a lot is left up to the ethnographic author and his "instrument of interpretation and comparison" ("ME" 91). In the quest for a "new bioethics," Kleinman has praised a type of ethnographic authorship that integrates "the ethical and the moral aspects of serious human problems strong[ly] enough to permit a move from description to action" ("ME" 81). Burdening the ethnographic author with a mandate for action would appear to give the author an authority that runs counter to the ideal of Bakhtin's polyphonic novel, where the author does not impose upon the independent voices of his heroes or close down the openness of their stories. However, overall Kleinman and Bakhtin share much common ground. Kleinman sees ethnography as at best producing "mixed knowledge" that does not guarantee "good outcomes" ("ME" 92), and Bakhtin would likely agree that some kind of "essential surplus" organizing vision of the ethnographer is needed for all the stories to be organized into a larger narrative (NF 44; CP 241–43).

The French sociologist Pierre Bourdieu produced another type of contemporary scholarly narrative that focused on listening within catastrophic social and historical contexts. Bourdieu worked in what he called "difficult spots . . . difficult to describe and to think about."[18] He described intentionally departing from the dominant professional discourses because they failed to adequately address the problem of a person's social and cultural marginalization. Bourdieu's writings, such as the majestic Weight of the World, were explicitly based on the Bakhtinian polyphonic novel; they brought together multiple voices in an unwieldy but exciting text. Bourdieu provided multiple perspectives via multiple interviewers and interviewees who practiced what he called "non-violent communication" (WW 608–9). He was equally concerned with avoiding representations that failed because they were "objectifications" of the subject, and with those that failed by inadequately taking into account "the objective conditions common to an entire social category" (WW 609). Bourdieu also invested less than Kleinman in the moral authority of the solitary author, and in that sense I consider Bourdieu closer to Bakhtin.

Yet another approach can be found in the work of Veena Das, whose focus upon "social traumas" has involved depictions and analyses of the "remaking of everyday life" in survivor communities.[19] She showed survivors trying to reassert the normal in their lives, after experiencing the extremities of atrocity and loss, and how this necessarily involved them struggling with language. Das contrasted the efforts of individual survivors and communities to remake everyday life with professionals' heavy-handed efforts to claim those experiences as a part of the clinical enterprise. Das expressed a faith in survivors' ways of working things out in their lives that is close in spirit to Bakhtin's polyphony and dialogism. To Das, survivors were conversing, sharing, and exchanging in many ways that facilitated healing, and what her text did was document, rather than engineer, those processes.

It is reassuring to recognize that there are humanities and social science scholars who share some of the same concerns as Bakhtin and apply them to understanding the consequences of political violence. However, more work is needed to use the approach of polyphonic and dialogic narrative to conceptualize interventions for survivors of political violence that are alternatives to the clinical testimony and the cognitive- and memory-focused trauma approach. This requires a better understanding of Bakhtin's view of the narrative forms that characterize testimony and that explain how testimony may cause psychological change.

## Testimony as Personal Confession, Biography, or Autobiography

To Bakhtin, the problem introduced by catastrophe and suffering would never have been conceived as a psychiatric condition requiring treatment. Instead, this problem was a metalinguistic condition that required human communication. Regarding catastrophe and suffering from Bakhtin's perspective of metalinguistics commits me to a response that is necessarily different from today's trauma psychiatry. If the testimony narrative is not a trauma psychotherapy narrative, then how may we characterize testimony as a narrative form? I find some help answering this question in some early Bakhtin writings, such as *Author and Hero*, where Bakhtin compared several literary genres. Like Bakhtin, we can ask if testimony is confession, biography, or autobiography.

In the personal confession, the "I as subject" and the "I as narrator" are one. No other presence is there to finalize the self and its narrative. In contrast, the examples of testimony that I discussed in part 1 were each indelibly bounded by the presence of a receiver; this person was most often physically present in the room, listening and interacting, but was sometimes an imaginary figure for the speaker (which Bakhtin elsewhere referred to as the "superaddressee"; *FHY* 231). These examples demonstrated that the receiver's active or even imagined presence has a huge influence on the survivor and on the testimony narrative. Because the personal confession, as depicted by Bakhtin, did not account for this receiver and his or her influence, testimony cannot be considered simply a personal confession.

The biography, in contrast, is defined by the aesthetic property of being fully possessed by the narrating other. It is this characteristic of possession, more than the giving of information about the life story, that is unique to the biography. Regarding testimony, earlier I claimed that the survivor is not speaking alone. There is another, a listener, who sets the frame, invites the survivor in, and guides the journey of truth-telling. The question is: Can this be characterized as possession in a biographical sense? In most instances it cannot because the survivor, not the biographer, is the one who is supplying the narrative through his or her telling. For this reason, testimony is not a biography either.

In his Dostoevsky book, Bakhtin described another important finding from

Dostoevsky's novels that also discounted the biographical in testimony. Bakhtin admired Dostoevsky's refusal to inhabit just one kind of space, the space of biographical life, where the author has completed the subject and finished the dialogue on the subject. Instead, Dostoevsky insisted upon inhabiting different types of historical and existential spaces in his novels where dialogue was paramount.

> In comfortably habitable interior space, far from the threshold, people live a biographical life in biographical time: they are born, they pass through childhood and youth, they marry, give birth to children, die. This biographical time Dostoevsky "leaps over." On the threshold and on the square the only time possible is crisis time, in which a moment is equal to years, decades, even to a "billion years." (PDP 169–70)

This passage and Bakhtin's key term of "threshold" assist us in thinking about the kind of spaces in which testimony may reside. To have endured political violence means to be exposed to a shattering of the biographical life. Thus, although testimony is personal and must engage the story of the survivor's life, it is a story that must be told in far broader contexts. It is a paradox of testimony that we ask individual survivors to tell *their* story when fully realizing that this story is not solely *their* individual story, but also a story that belongs to collective groups and to their histories. One liability of clinical testimony is that it tends to focus too much upon the individual's trauma story, and not enough on testimony in relation to historical, social, and cultural changes affecting many. Clinical testimony gives us one voice, whereas the crisis of political violence on the threshold "takes place on the boundary between one's own and someone else's consciousness" (PDP 286).[20]

Although testimony is not biographical, there may be possession, not in a biographical frame, but in a more limited sense. This can happen when the receiver attempts to squelch or stifle the narrative into some systematized given. This can be personally motivated, as when the receiver is retreating defensively from something that is threatening because it is too painful. This is what psychoanalysts call countertransference, which is certainly elicited by survivors who may confront the listener with much too much to bear. Or it can happen when a system of values, derived external to the testimony itself, becomes imposed upon the testimony being spoken. This can happen rather insidiously, as when survivors censor themselves, or more overtly when the listener is imposing censorship. It is something that you can see happening when the receiver is prioritizing, selecting, or preferentially seeing or not seeing certain aspects that do or do not fit with the externally derived given.

Is testimony like autobiography? Is it an "I for myself" kept in balance with an "I for another"? Here, one part of the self is selecting, editing, changing because it anticipates the other's experiencing of their life story. In testimony, however, there are two parties directly present who are occupying the role of the "I for another."

There is the actual giver of testimony who is a listener to himself or herself. And there is also an actual "another" present in the room, the listener and recorder of testimony. And they bring with them an actual recording device (an audio recorder), which is another kind of presence, an impending promise of possibly a great "many others" who may eventually listen to the testimony. They also bring with them some guidelines or understandings that are to varying extents institutionally or conceptually derived. And all these parts of another are pressing upon the survivor. Does the receiver's behavior give rise to an enlivened "I for another" in the survivor, or is so little choice given to the latter by forceful external conditions that no survivor's "I for another" need be there? It is an important distinction, which would become sharpened later in his intellectual development when Bakhtin shifted his attention to the form of the novel and moved into the frameworks of dialogism, polyphony, and unfinalizabilty. But the idea of testimony as autobiography seems fairly promising as a way to explain how testimony works in that it locates the testimony in an interactive relational context. Together, teller and receiver may explore the polyphonic and dialogic potential of the story. The individual story is allowed to interact with other cultural, social, and historical stories and processes. It is a hint of the radical concepts that would come later for Bakhtin, especially in the Dostoevsky book.

## Novelistic Selfhood and Testimony

Nowadays it is not uncommon for humanities scholars to answer the "call of stories" and to go to novels in search of truths about the helping professions. The legal scholar Martha Nussbaum, for example, wrote books that showed what the literary imagination adds to the work of courts and the law.[21] What she has been teaching to future lawyers and judges, the psychiatrist and author Robert Coles has been teaching to future doctors, in a lifetime of literary reflection upon William Carlos Williams, Walker Percy, Flannery O'Connor, George Eliot, Raymond Carver, and Bruce Springsteen.[22]

Like these contemporary helping professional humanists, Bakhtin looked to the novel to find the most profound truths about humanity. But what made Bakhtin's use of the novel strikingly different, if not "revolutionary," was that the ideas he found in novels were so original and powerful. A novel did not just reinforce an existing idea by putting it in context. A novel was the source of a new idea. A novel did not communicate emotionally what a theory communicated abstractly. A novel was the seat of a new philosophy.[23] A novel did not just illustrate the complexities of a theory of selfhood. A novel revealed a new concept of selfhood. Thus, Bakhtin's reading of a novel was not going to deepen the understanding of testimony and suffering. Rather, it was going to suggest an entirely new potential role for testimony as a story in relieving suffering.

When Bakhtin made these claims for novels, he spoke not of all novels, and especially of one: *The Brothers Karamazov*. The radical truth at the center of his Dostoevsky book was a new conceptualization of the self as "novelistic" (*PDP* 220). I will use Bakhtin's idea of the "novelistic self " to further explore testimony as a polyphonic and dialogic narrative and its role in relieving suffering as a metalinguistic condition.

The self is novelistic in that it contains "many voices within." These voices partake in "an independent, responsible, and active discourse" (*CP* 216–18; *DI* 349–50). For Bakhtin, these characteristics were fundamental indicators of a "healthy self" (*DI* 31). Or as Gary Saul Morson wrote, "The truly novelistic, mature, and responsible self knows a minimum of authoritative discourse" (*CP* 220). Bakhtin was contrasting this openness of discourse essential to an "ethical, legal, and political human being" with the "authoritative discourses" that Bakhtin staunchly opposed, which came from the state, the professions, and the monologizing author (*DI* 349–50).

Bakhtin's notion of discourse is based upon his identifying Dostoevsky as the inventor of the polyphonic novel, of which *The Brothers Karamazov* is the epitome. The polyphonic novel is inhabited not just by "characters" that are mere marionettes in the author's all-controlling hands, but by actual "personalities" invigorated by their own "voice ideas," their own "consciousness" (*CP* 237).[24] The author participates in this dialogue as another voice that can speak in response and that tries to shape the exchanges.

Morson and Emerson describe polyphony as a theory of the creative process. In their interpretation, polyphony consists of two essential components: "a dialogic sense of the truth and a special position of the author necessary for visualizing and conveying that sense of truth" (*CP* 234). Bakhtin was arguing against the romantic notion of creativity in which the writing of a poem is described as a sudden burst of inspiration (*CP* 243–46).

Bakhtin's argument also holds against the romantic notion of cathartic healing in the sudden draining away of suffering. The problem with romantic inspiration and catharsis is that they are both monologic propositions. They regard the self as suddenly possessed by, or dispossessed of, an occupying force. For trauma psychiatry the self is possessed by traumatic memories, and giving testimony is supposed to rid the self of the memories and yield the desired cognitive changes. Just as polyphony enabled Bakhtin to offer an alternative model of creative works, polyphony (and associated concepts of the novelized self and dialogism) enables me to present an alternative view of testimony and relieving suffering.

Reconceiving testimony begins by assuming that the survivor is not simply an isolated vessel who passively carries the residue of traumatic memories or the documentation of criminal events. Survivors can actively tell stories that embody personal, truthful, and ethical narrative representations of the experiences of political violence. As active participants in living historical, social, and cultural domains of experiences, they carry within them many different voices; these voices speak of themselves, of their journey, of those around them (friends and enemies, living and dead), of the eras in which they lived, and of their unique consciousnesses struggling over the odysseys of survival and witnessing. In the face of the centrifugal pull of these voices and experiences, survivors struggle for clarity, structure, purpose, and meaning. Work is required, especially work involving dialogic interaction, in order for survivors to tell a complete story that contains all these parts of the narrative and that retains a sense of openness. Giving testimony always presents the risk of succumbing to a monologizing proposition, coming from either survivors or receivers, that would squelch the heterogeneity of voices and experiences.

The survivor has primary responsibility for producing a polyphonic and dialogic narrative. But the receiver who is listening and interacting has a special obligation to help the survivor to resist the tendencies toward monologism. The receiver must not regard the survivors as objects, but as "subjects of their own directly signifying discourse" (*PDP* 7). The receiver should not overwhelm the survivors' voices with his or her own "surplus" of information or understanding, for example, coming from academic theory or political ideology (*PDP* 73). The receiver is not to approach the giving of testimony as a "system," but as an encounter which adheres to what Bakhtin found in the polyphonic novel: "a concrete event made up of organized human orientations and voices" (*CP* 117, 23).

For both the survivor and the receiver, polyphonic and dialogic testimony requires keeping the communication open-ended, multileveled, and multivoiced. Plot is secondary in the testimony, just as in the novel. Neither the author nor the characters are made simply to serve a plot. To the contrary, Bakhtin wrote: "Dostoevsky seeks words and plot situations that provoke, tease, extort, dialogize" (*PDP* 39). He "placed the idea on the borderline of dialogically intersecting consciousnesses . . . and forced them to quarrel" (*PDP* 91). The receiver of testimony should help the survivor in such a way that the multiple voices and positions speak and listen to one another openly and responsively. One way to bring these voices into contact with one another involves transforming the sense of time, with less sequentiality and more simultaneity.

Gary Saul Morson and Michael André Bernstein described the deficiencies in some narrative strategies for representing the Holocaust and other historical catastrophes. Attempts to narrate the "unimaginable" have too often fallen back upon the most limited of rhetorical strategies. This diminishes both the horrific dimensions of the catastrophe as well as the range of human possibilities and responses in its wake. Drawing upon Bakhtin and Dostoevsky, Morson proposed a more open modeling of time called "heterochrony" that will be discussed further in the chapter on documenting histories (*CP* 48). At this point, it is necessary to say that Bakhtin encourages us to favor more open conceptions of time in testimony because such conceptions would make it far more possible for the narrative to address the uncertainties, ambiguities, tensions, and contradictions in survivors' experiences. Polyphony and dialogism urge the survivor to loosen up the clamps that plot has on the testimony. Survivors' testimonies have a tendency toward a chronological form of three periods: before, during, and after. Instead, the aim of polyphonic and dialogic testimony is to create satisfying narratives that are not necessarily symmetrical in how they structure time. Testimony also should be open to embodying what Bakhtin called the "unfinalizability" of events and experiences.[25] For example, the survivor is likely to communicate the sense that he or she did not know what would happen next, and even now may still not. It is important to resist the allure of closure and certainty that would trade in the unfinalizability of living histories for some kind of certainty.

The survivor and receiver would be well advised to learn from what Bakhtin found in Dostoevsky's novels regarding multiple voices:

> Where others saw a single thought, he was able to find and feel out two thoughts, a bifurcation; where others saw a single quality, he discovered in it the presence of a second and contradictory quality. Everything that seemed simple became, in his world, complex and multi-structured. In every voice, he could hear two contending voices, in every expression a crack, and the readiness to go over immediately to another contradictory expression; in every gesture he detected confidence and lack of confidence simultaneously; he perceived the profound ambiguity, even multiple ambiguity, of every phenomenon. (*PDP* 261)

Testimony as a polyphonic and dialogic narrative places a value on the elaboration, articulation, and relatedness of experiences toward an unpredictable end. As such, it does not work toward extinguishing one memory or its "fear network," but instead sets its sights on the interactions of multiple memory networks within the broadest possible constellation of meaning and experience. Memories do not simply disappear, but they may become thicker, longer, more interconnected, more flexible, and more vibrant. Memories become more, not less, a part of life itself and all its processes and complexities.

Testimonies need not be symmetrically organized around the claim that one crime deserves another, because that too goes against polyphony. In other words, they need not settle for what might be called affective symmetry, often observed among survivors, where loss and mourning are substituted for by hatred and the desire for vengeance. An affectively asymmetrical narrative would not disallow the expressions of hatred and vengeance. As a matter of fact, these expressions would be expected. Instead, an asymmetrical narrative would also expect different affects, such as compassion and love; the testimony would aim to somehow keep these contradictory feelings in relation to one another as part of a multidimensional experiencing of the traumas of political violence.

In aiming for asymmetry, testimony is trying to remain open to the varieties of possible human responses to political violence. The role of the receiver of testimony is not to impose a particular symmetry that would betray the openness of testimony. More than that, the receiver's role is also to question when the testimony narrative is leaning too far toward symmetry, and to help the survivor to express different, even contradictory affects, thoughts, and choices. Testimony should not be expected to heal survivors by resolving these asymmetries, discrepancies, or the dilemmas and conflicts that they prompt.

Polyphonic and dialogic testimony also does not culminate in a straightforward resolution of ambivalent, contradictory, or uncertain meanings; nor does it seek closure, either by the survivor or by the listener. For example, testimony may help survivors, who find themselves caught between the contradictory historical narratives of two eras, to articulate their struggles dialogically; they learn to see how these two narratives are in proximity to one another, if not talking or colliding with one another. Survivors may come to have a greater capacity for experiencing that struggle dialogically, rather than rejecting the dialogic and being forced into a monologic response. The principle of dialogic work holds that if survivors are able to achieve this in their testimony, then this may help them to grow in the areas of consciousness and ethics, which may help them with their suffering.

## Uses and Limitations of the Polyphonic and Dialogic Narrative

In this chapter I have used Bakhtin's ideas to specify strategies for testimony as a polyphonic and dialogic narrative for relieving suffering in survivors of political violence. I am not simply saying that giving testimony reduces suffering and that everyone should do it. Nor am I saying that testimony as a polyphonic and dialogic narrative is unconditionally beneficial. But I am saying that approaching testimony as a polyphonic and dialogic narrative may help survivors who are suffering in ways that the cognitive approach to testimony does not. I will briefly summarize my conclusions.

Bakhtin's ideas encouraged me to choose different foci than the disorder of PTSD and the symptoms of traumatic stress that are prioritized by trauma psychiatry. After political violence, survivors may also experience suffering in relation to broader human developmental struggles. This suffering is viewed not as a constellation of symptoms that needs treatment, but instead as a metalinguistic condition involving collisions and struggles of consciousness that may benefit from dialogue.

Rather than focusing on cognitive changes in traumatic memories as a way of relieving suffering, Bakhtin's ideas encouraged me to consider other narrative processes through which testimony as a story may play a helpful role. Testimony entails producing polyphonic and dialogic narratives and identifying and exploring key struggles over consciousness and ethics related to surviving political violence.

Consciousness is important in that it is a potentially powerful and underutilized transformative force in the lives of survivors. Ethics is important in that survivors are often faced with situations of competing or conflicting obligations. Producing testimonies may offer the survivor potential for growth in these areas.

Bakhtin's ideas suggest two major ways that testimony may work in the realms of consciousness and ethics to possibly produce these changes. These are: (1) to produce testmonies that respect the polyphonic nature of survivors' experiences of political violence (e.g., trauma stories in broader contexts; open sense of time); and (2) to produce testimonies in which multiple voices and positions are given a chance to speak and listen to one another openly and responsively (e.g., asymmetrical narratives; novelistic selfhood).

I have not offered scientific proof that polyphonic and dialogic testimony relieves suffering. I have no such proof. Rather, I have made these claims on an intellectual and pragmatic basis: intellectual in the sense that these claims are derived from Bakhtin's theory of dialogic work; and pragmatic in that compared with the cognitive approach to trauma, these claims bring us closer to the real worlds of survivors as described in part 1. I hope that the approach of polyphonic and dialogic testimony can help to open up new worlds for testimonies' role in relieving suffering. I emphasize again that ultimately it is important to see evidence of whether using polyphonic and dialogic testimony makes a positive difference with respect to a range of outcomes, including, but not necessarily limited to, suffering as measured by traumatic stress symptoms. That requires investigation. But it is important that the methods of investigation not be overly biased against dialogue by leaning too far in the direction of traumatic stress and cognition.

Because there is often something about the experience of trauma that stimulates the desire for magical healing responses, it is necessary to be wary of the dangers of recognizing only the promise and not the pitfalls of testimony (or for that matter, any intervention). Furthermore, there is no doubt that using polyphony and dialogism for testimony to relieve suffering has its limitations. This was implicit in Morson's and Emerson's comments on Bakhtin's Dostoevsky: "In his novels, however, Dostoevsky's form-shaping ideology—his way of visualizing the world—led him to portray people as completely beyond genetic approaches and as ultimately capable of remaking everything about themselves (or so Bakhtin contends)" (CP 262).

No one could reasonably argue that survivors are completely free to remake themselves. Not given the many severe social problems that survivors of political violence face: immense losses, unemployment, displacements, poverty, lack of freedom of movement, unpunished crimes. Polyphonic and dialogic testimony does not have answers for these problems, which are really very common to the experiences of political violence.

Nor does testimony necessarily have answers for severe mental health problems: major depression, post-traumatic stress disorder, psychotic disorders, alcohol or substance abuse, and stress-related medical illnesses. More than that, it is entirely possible that testimony could make any of these conditions worse.

Another limitation that is inherent to polyphonic and dialogic testimony pertains to the tension between the authority of the receiver of testimony compared with that of the giver of testimony. Paradoxically, testimonies may need the authority of the receiver, guiding and supporting the making of a polyphonic and dialogic narrative, in order to be more open and free to reduce the survivor's sufferings. This is the opposite of what I argued in chapter 4: testimony may not work as well when it is not allowed to be free and open. Testimony is in a bind between openness and closure, and the receiver has to make important choices about how to use his or her authority in the testimony. I would argue that testimony should be as polyphonic and as dialogic as can be tolerated in a given specific context.

If we want to think about polyphonic and dialogic testimony as a psychosocial intervention for trauma survivors, then it is helpful to think of indicators and contraindicators for testimony's usage. Testimony probably works best when people are prepared to tell their stories. People are more prepared to do so when their degree of suffering is less than severe. Stated in clinical terms, persons with severe depression or PTSD should probably not do testimony before getting appropriate clinical psychiatric treatment.[26] Those professional or lay persons who receive testimony should be attentive to the psychiatric needs of the survivors giving testimony.

Testimony probably works best for suffering when a survivor already has some footholds outside his or her experience of political violence. Being without threat may help. Being free to choose and to move may help. Being in exile may help. Being young may help. Being disposed to reminiscence may help. Having time to become someone else may help. Having others to tell may help. Each of these factors may contribute to the loosening of the hold of the traumas, and may make the survivor more able to benefit from testimony. Therefore, the effectiveness of testimony in relieving suffering is likely to depend upon these types of conditions. In the first half of the book, I spoke of testimony being conducted in several locations where these conditions were not met (for example, immediate postwar Kosovo). There, testimony was bound to fail. This should serve as a reminder that it is just as important to know when testimony is not going to work as it is to know when it is likely to work.

It is important to recognize the value of testimony framed not as a clinical mental health intervention but as a form of human communication to address a metalinguistic condition. Polyphonic and dialogic testimony provides the basis for innovations in trauma interventions that are consistent with the current questioning and revision of clinical psychiatric approaches to trauma intervention. Community-focused perspectives point out that there are many survivors who are highly disinclined to seek or accept clinical psychiatric treatment from mental health clinicians. In comparison, giving testimony may offer a higher degree of fit with populations of community-based survivors. In fact, the group that may best be able to benefit from testimony is precisely a group of survivors who would not be found in a mental health clinic. The fact that testimony deals explicitly with the social, historical, and political dimensions becomes important as a motivator to recruit survivors and give testimony, especially in the absence of help-seeking behavior that would otherwise lead to mental health services.

Another implication is that the persons who receive testimonies need not be mental health professionals. But they need to know how to engage in dialogic interaction with survivors and to help them to produce a polyphonic and dialogic narrative. This may come naturally to some people, but most likely, it would still require training and supervision. I have not forgotten that this then poses a challenge very familiar to Bakhtin: how to introduce a system that does not kill freedom. There is no way to escape Bakhtin's vigilance regarding freedom, but as far as I am concerned, there is no need to either, because there is significantly more hope with it than without it.

# 7

# Creating Cultures of Peace and Reconciliation

How can people who have been wronged live in peace? What is to be done with the memories, thoughts, and emotions related to the traumas of political violence? Many fear that these traumatic sequelae could exacerbate hatreds and vengeance and thereby lead to further conflicts and violence. Contemporary theory and practice in mental health and human rights often makes the assumption that after political violence, trauma-related disturbed cognitions in many individuals pose obstacles to peace and reconciliation. Psychosocial interventions, according to this view, are needed to transform these disturbed cognitive mechanisms, including through survivors' telling their trauma stories. Giving testimony, then, will help people to transform the memories, thoughts, and emotions of trauma and to move on.

This cognitive view of the role of testimony in peace and reconciliation, however, is at risk of paying insufficient attention to historical, legal, social, and cultural contexts. It also risks misunderstanding, neglecting, or even disrespecting particular cultural meanings that may potentially facilitate peace and reconciliation. Such an approach may fail to adequately acknowledge the dialogic processes that actively shape private and public meanings related to the traumatic consequences of political violence. The testimony is thus at risk of becoming reduced to something one-dimensional and fixed—either a dreaded cauldron of extremism or an idealized reservoir of understanding—that may further complicate the problems that intervenors seek to address.

Mikhail Bakhtin's dialogic work suggests a different approach to testimony in peace and reconciliation work. Bakhtin did not focus upon decontextualized memories, thoughts, and emotions. Instead he focused upon the narrative processes that are the bases of culture in everyday life. Bakhtin's definition of the "human sciences" may serve as an alternative framework to cognitive approaches to peace and reconciliation work. From a human sciences vantage point, I propose the concept of "cultural trauma" as a focus for testimony work regarding peace and reconciliation. Other Bakhtinian concepts may also help in understanding and addressing cultural trauma through testimony. "Creative understanding" provides a vision of how testimonies may build knowledge that is linked to efforts for peace and reconciliation in the broader field of culture. The power of "outsideness" resides in testimony, and the cultural work of peace and reconciliation could better utilize it. Testimonies of political violence possess an "eventness" which could be the source of an ethical obligation toward peace and reconciliation. Lastly, the idea of "speech genre" suggests how testimonies may make contact with prevailing social discourses on peace and reconciliation.

## Peacemaking as a Cognitive Science

One goal of peace and reconciliation work is to build cultures that are conducive to peace and reconciliation. Some of the most common activities to achieve this goal are truth commissions, peace education for youth, building a free press, oral history projects, interfaith dialogues, multiethnic cooperation, and artistic creation. Although all these activities are very different from one another, testimony is a concern whenever there is the matter of survivors telling their stories of their experience of political violence. To think of testimony in relation to culture requires expanding the level of interest far beyond testimony production itself, and thus including testimonies in religion, media, education, and the creative arts; importantly, it also requires acknowledging listeners' or readers' responses to testimonies. Admittedly, this paints a very broad canvas. However, this breadth is necessary given the focus on culture and cultural change.

Because many persons from different sectors work (either directly or indirectly) with testimonies, many persons may be involved (to varying degrees) in the cultural work of peace and reconciliation. These include journalists, historians, religious clerics, educators, psychologists and psychiatrists, academics, humanitarian workers, lawyers, curators, writers, and artists. They may include people from the country of interest, but are also especially likely to involve outside intervenors. Very often these are professional or cultural elites coming from Western countries to poor or undeveloped countries. The presence of the internationals can be both helpful and problematic, especially in relation to testimony work.

These international helpers often introduce scientific and professional approaches that are biased in favor of Western values of individualism, confession, empiricism, and positivism. When these approaches are applied in such ways that local cultural values and practices are not respected, the potential for misunderstandings and unhelpful or even harmful psychosocial interventions is substantial. Multiple scholars critical of trauma mental health, including Derrick Summerfield and Maurice Eisenbruch, have described this problem in trauma mental health.[1] Another scholar, Lawrence Kirmayer, wrote of the negative impact of PTSD and traumatic stress theory:

Morally, it simplifies the issue of responsibility, guilt and blame that plagues survivors, and authorizes their righteous anger or forgiveness; scientifically, it suggests a linear causal model amenable to animal models and simple experiments; therapeutically, it allows clinicians to attribute a wide range of problems to a single wound, and so to organize treatment along clear lines that may include both the moral and scientific models.[2]

In his thoughtful book critiquing the current discourse on trauma, Patrick Bracken described the cognitive bias in trauma psychiatry and human rights intervenors as a reflection of Western Cartesianism.

A basic assumption in the cognitivist framework is that the meaningful nature of reality is something "conferred" on it by the schemas, or the programs running in individual minds. Trauma disrupts the meaning of the world through its impact on these schemas. Trauma is thus conceived of as acting on individuals, and therapy is oriented towards restoring or renewing the schemas in discrete individuals.[3]

Bracken strongly questioned the appropriateness of applying these Western assumptions in cross-cultural settings, especially in postwar countries. Although Bracken's focus was primarily on suffering and healing, he found a similar pattern of assumptions operating in peace and reconciliation work, as in the example of truth commissions. Bracken noted that "they are also about 'processing' the experiences of war and violence. I believe that both types of endeavors work within certain assumptions (most often unacknowledged) about memory and truth."[4]

I agree with Bracken that many of the same cognitive assumptions are often used in peace and reconciliation work. There is a tendency to overemphasize that trauma-disturbed cognitive mechanisms in individuals pose obstacles to peace and reconciliation, to extrapolate these individual phenomena to the larger group level, and to believe that these must be transformed through clinical or psychosocial interventions. Michael Humphrey pointed out that even when these psychosocial interventions are orchestrated on a societal level, as in the truth commissions, there is still a tendency to focus on individual victims.[5] One example of this tendency may be found in the writings of the political psychologist Ervin Staub, whose theorizing called for trauma mental health work directed at the "healing of wounds" so as to prevent political violence.[6] Although he cited a broad range of possible activities for "healing and reconciliation" (e.g., diplomacy), Staub's conceptual framework foregrounded the terms and concepts of Western trauma mental health (i.e., trauma, healing, and wounds) and did not go far in terms of contextual understanding (for which he used the term "difficult life conditions"). Applying Western trauma mental health frameworks to peace and reconciliation work in different cultures may have liabilities. Veena Das and Arthur Kleinman, in *Remaking a World*, warned that by imposing theory-driven "social scripts" explaining collective violence, "global institutions and agencies of the state have often inhibited the mechanisms of restraint and notions of limit that have been crafted in local moral worlds."[7]

Human rights theory and practice may have partially contributed to this cognitive focus, which may be inattentive to local and everyday contexts. First, the human rights movement's focus on legal rights, such as the individual rights of the victim and the legal responsibility of individual perpetrators, concentrates on the individual as the locus of both sufferings and crimes. Das and Kleinman noted that "those writing on behalf of human rights groups are constrained by the immediate needs of victims and by a mode of storytelling that is anchored in judicial ideas of what testimony can stand up in court."[8] When the everyday contexts of family, community, religion, and society are backgrounded, it becomes easier to settle upon narrower individual-based explanatory theories regarding cognition.

Second, there is often a troubling gap between the human rights abuses that the movement documents and the will or ability of states to either end the conflict or to bring perpetrators to justice. As a consequence, instead of doing peace and reconciliation work with the perpetrators and aggressors, humanitarian intervenors often end up working with survivors and victims. What follows is that when survivors and victims express frustration, impatience, hatred, or even the desire for vengeance, these thoughts and feelings, rather than the actual crimes committed against them, then become the central problem and the focus of intervention. This leads the intervenors to identify cognitive changes in the survivors as the primary targets for psychosocial interventions as part of institutional peacemaking operations.

Through its reliance upon clinical theories, such as traumatic stress theory and the diagnosis of PTSD, the trauma mental health movement has been the most avid promoter of cognitive approaches among the respondents to political violence. Western trauma professionals have come to the consensus understanding that exposure to the political violence of torture, genocide, or war changes the brain and the mind. They have also come to believe that these traumas leave individuals with specific traumatic memories, thoughts, and emotions which could potentially lead to further aggression, and thus limit the potential for peace and reconciliation. Western professional and scientific descriptions of these cognitive changes are introduced increasingly as explanations or rationales into the discourses on peace and reconciliation, even by those who are not mental health professionals.

I am not disputing the existing scientific knowledge about how trauma changes the brain and mind. Nevertheless, I am concerned about the limitations of the cognitive perspective when it is extended from trauma in individuals to peace and reconciliation in large groups such as communities, societies, states, and civilizations. For instance, there is a tendency to regard nationalist attitudes as a post-traumatic reaction that needs to be rooted out. This view tends to assume that all kinds of national allegiance are equally bad and essentially pathological. In exhibiting such strong nationalist foregrounding, the cognitive view seeks first to identify and then to eradicate local nationalistic attitudes by replacing them with internationally derived pluralistic attitudes. This approach fails to grasp the complete picture by choosing to overlook the ways in which longstanding attitudes of national allegiance may have functioned within the local sociocultural and political system of meanings. It can overlook local structures and processes that may have worked to keep nationalist attitudes in check.[9] The sociologist Eduard Tiryakian has written that nationalist attitudes per se are not dangerous, but of graver concern is nationalism combined with race, ethnicity, and religion, in what he called a "cultural bundle."[10]

The opposite is also possible, as some survivors may express memories and emotions that they or others may try to associate with the desire for peace, love, and understanding. My concern is that the cognitive view of testimony forgoes the necessary tools for understanding or shaping testimony as anything other than an expression of what is dreaded (hatred and violence) or what is desired (peace and reconciliation). Lacking more sophisticated methods of cultural understanding, the individual cognitive framework fails to appropriately interpret and shape testimony work in its proper social, historical, and cultural contexts.

The cognitive perspective further breaks down when one considers the lack of interventions that could possibly act to change attitudes toward peace and reconciliation. Culture simply cannot be reduced to cognition. Thus, it is interesting to note that the work of peace and reconciliation has shifted away from across-the-board cultural change and toward piecemeal attempts to make changes in individual cognition, such as the ones facilitated through truth commissions or trauma mental health treatment. The cognitive approach to peace and reconciliation, so it seems, provides a cover for the lack of ability or the lack of will of states to address political violence through more comprehensive political, military, or civil solutions. The humanitarian interventions of the late twentieth and early twenty-first century have not attempted the total refashioning of a society and its culture, such as was conducted in postwar Germany and Japan.[11] The inadequacies of contemporary humanitarian interventions' approaches to peacemaking are even more apparent in conditions of "state failure" such as exist in Afghanistan, Iraq, the Congo, Sudan, and many other places.[12] Most often, too little is done; but actual accomplishments may be trumped up by cognitive theories that exaggerate small examples of peace work into forms of perfection.

Earlier, I considered several examples of testimony work that made at least some attempt to address broader contexts. Agger and Jensen envisioned that testimony work could change "social memory" in the former Yugoslavia. In Chile, they were interested in healing at the community and societal levels. The primary emphasis of the testimony work that they discussed, however, was mostly upon the production and analysis of individual testimonies. The IOM's Archives of Memory project in Kosovo aimed to help Kosovar society to rewrite its narratives of political violence. The emphasis, however, was again upon identifying disturbed patterns of cognitions in individual testimonies. Although each of these testimony projects aimed to effect change broadly, they were essentially applying an individual cognitive framework to explain collective cultural experiences. Is it possible to do better? What kind of theory of narrating the traumas of political violence would help?

## The Human Sciences

The last work of Mikhail Bakhtin was a set of notes that he wrote on an unfinished essay from the 1930s. Just before his death in 1975, Bakhtin returned to this text and wrote the piece entitled "Toward a Methodology for the Human Sciences."[13] Anticipating the end of his writing journey with a new sense of urgency and gravity, this text rearticulated some of Bakhtin's longstanding concerns. I believe that this particular Bakhtin text offers an alternative framework to the previously discussed cognitive approach to peace and reconciliation work with testimonies. In the first place, it helps to both clarify and sharpen the objections to the cognitive approach. Second, it helps to pose an alternative approach focusing more closely on narrative and dialogic work.

Bakhtin's proposal for the "human sciences" teaches that using testimonies for creating cultures of peace and reconciliation would only be possible through dialogic listening and response. However, this kind of dialogic work is highly difficult to achieve and the results can never be guaranteed; but Bakhtin postulated no other way to approach the processes of cultural change.

Bakhtin regarded the hard sciences as inherently limited in promoting humanistic values because of their methodological preoccupations and ideological biases. Bakhtin wrote: "The exact sciences constitute a monologic form of knowledge: the intellect contemplates a thing and expounds upon it." The "natural sciences" are committed to an "object system" and are "subjectless" (SG 168). In trying to elucidate the underlying systems that govern many individuals or a society, the sciences center on "voiceless things" (SG 161). Bakhtin, on the other hand, wrote the following about structuralism in literary study: "I am against enclosures in a text. Mechanical categories . . . sequential formalization and depersonalization: all relations are logical" (SG 161).

I have similar objections to the cognitive mechanisms used to approach the traumas of political violence. In sharp contrast to these, Bakhtin claimed, "I hear voices in everything and dialogic relations among them" (SG 169). For Bakhtin, viewing subjects in dialogical relation to one another was an essential prerequisite for addressing "context." This dialogical relation between subjects was the seat of understanding in his proposed "human sciences." It may also be the basis for developing alternative approaches to testimony work for peace and reconciliation. The cognitive approach to testimony and peace and reconciliation does not offer much promise for building cultures of peace and reconciliation. This approach is more committed to elucidating underlying individual cognitive mechanisms related to a presumed universal trauma response than it is to listening and responding to any one person, let alone to the many people of a community, society, or nation. Because the cognitive approach does not listen to enough voices, it cannot begin to know the culture or to recognize trauma to the collectivity. Because it does not respond with other voices, it cannot facilitate cultural change.

The aforementioned critics of Western humanitarian interventions regarded the act of imposing the cognitive approach as a form of disrespect for local cultures of local people. For example, Patrick Bracken wrote:

> "A Western, 'technical' way of thinking about suffering and loss is being introduced to people at a time when they are weak and vulnerable. The effect is often to undermine respect for local healers and traditions and ways of coping that are embedded in local ways of life."[14]

I believe that Bakhtin, like Bracken, would also be uncomfortable with the strictures inherent in the human rights legalistic approach that favors the truth of its universal doctrines above other local and historical truths. Human rights field workers may favor one form of perception, direct eyewitness, far and above all other possible personal and public views of political violence and survival. On the other hand, Bakhtin suggested no answer as to how to determine whether or not a given testimony is true. Those who do testimony work in legal or forensic contexts have struggled the most with this concern. For example, Peter Brooks in *Troubling Confessions* wrote that "we want confessions, yet we are suspicious of them."[15] As for truth commissions, I believe that Bakhtin would be suspicious of state institutions using survivors to propagandize official memories (anticipating some of the critiques of the South African Truth and Reconciliation Commission).[16] Truth commissions might be more acceptable as dialogic work if they led to an expanded dialogue on political violence and if their outcomes were not predetermined. Then again, as a philosopher Bakhtin was not all that interested in social justice and political questions. As a sufferer of a severe chronic bone disease, perhaps he believed that it was pointless to turn to politics to take away one's pain.

Bakhtin, who was thoroughly a "non-modernist," certainly did not anticipate the global successes of the modern human rights movement. This is understandable, given that no international authorities came to his rescue in Stalin's Soviet Union. Perhaps if Bakhtin had known what human rights would achieve, he might have changed his position. Nor did Bakhtin anticipate the human rights movement's struggles and challenges in implementing universal human rights principles, such as the United Nations Declaration of Human Rights, in ways that really do honor and respect different societies and cultures. Regarding mental health, I suspect that Bakhtin would probably be more sympathetic to what Patrick Bracken calls the "new cross-cultural psychology," including Bracken's own definition of "post-psychiatry," based upon the phenomenology of Martin Heidegger. These newer approaches reject the modernist principles that Bakhtin found so troubling. For example, Bracken's post-psychiatry prioritizes "ethical issues," "contextual understanding and practice," and the "recognition of power differentials."[17]

I propose a human sciences approach to testimony that challenges the underlying principles of clinical testimony and trauma mental health, whose rigid focus on psychopathology has removed experience from context. In the latter approach, the truth imposed by the trauma-related cognitive mechanisms in individuals has greatly superseded the truths derived from collective contexts stemming from subjects in interaction with one another. By contrast, in the human sciences approach to testimony, the testimony is from and for ordinary survivors. The appropriate context for understanding testimony is not that of psychiatric disorders, but rather that of personal, social, legal, cultural, historical, and ethical relations. There is simply no way that culture, cultural change, or peace and reconciliation can be explained by PTSD or other notions of individual psychopathological disorders or processes.

A human science of testimony does not fall back upon either the human rights or clinical approaches that risk moving testimony away from culture. Instead, Bakhtin framed the larger purpose as follows:

> "The task consists in forcing the thing like environment, which mechanically influences the personality, to begin to speak, that is, to reveal in it the potential word and tone, to transform it into a semantic context for the thinking, speaking, and acting (as well as creating) personality" (SG 164).

Instead of rendering the testimony into a listing of things, which in modern social science parlance is referred to as "reification," the human sciences challenge is to use the testimony as a means for moving beyond the thing and into culture. The human science of testimony respects testimony's true nature as a narrative by lifting the discourse on testimony out of that of things and into that of dialogue. This should be a science highly attuned to "such absolutely unrepeatable individualities as utterances" (SG 108).

Bakhtin's "prosaics," as Gary Saul Morson and Caryl Emerson named it, offers another element of an appropriate foundation for testimony to address cultural work after political violence (CP 15–36). According to Morson and Emerson, prosaics is a theory of literature that privileges prose and a form of thinking that presumes the importance of the everyday. Prosaics is not concerned with making overarching generalizations about experience and does not look to interpret or create great systems of knowledge or to clean up the "mess" of culture. Rather, prosaics is concerned with the nuances of narratives that come from the ordinary language of everyday life. In stories, prosaics sees complex layers of interacting meanings and the traces of dialogues that have unfolded in cultures over historical time. These elements of prosaics are of central interest in the human science of testimony.

Human sciences work seeks to liberate testimony from the cognitive science strictures that render it into something less than the story that it really is. A human science of testimony has to hear the voices after catastrophe; hear voices responding to other voices and to themselves; hear today's everyday voices and the voices from past histories; and hear voices that try to make order and voices that find only chaos. Only by embracing such a melange of voices can the human science of testimony interpret and impact the communicative potential of the testimony as it enters into a culture. Only as such might testimonies earn private and public responses, and generate dialogue. Only in dialogue does there exist a potentially transformative cultural force that might further the efforts of peace and reconciliation.

Of all the genres of testimony that we have discussed, Holocaust testimony appears to come closest to the work of a human science of testimony. Holocaust testimony is highly engaged with culture. It is firmly rooted in literary narratives, memoirs, films, museums, and in other imaginative means of cultural expression. This is not surprising given that Holocaust testimony has had more than fifty years to evolve, far more than most other contemporary testimony genres, and has been well funded. Although Holocaust testimony can be criticized for institutionalization and excesses, it has by and large not become relegated to a scientific mode of knowing. Holocaust testimonies have been used widely in America, Europe, and Israel to promote peace and reconciliation. (Although some would argue that in the state of Israel, the narratives written about and from Holocaust memories have contributed to a hardening of attitudes toward the Palestinians, and have led away from peace and reconciliation and toward confrontation and violence.) It is sobering to note that outside of the Western context, it is difficult to find examples where Holocaust testimonies have contributed to peace and reconciliation work.

If Bakhtin's idea of the human sciences is to help us, then other examples of testimony are needed that come closer to creating cultures of peace and reconciliation. This requires a closer look at how testimony can link with culture and address trauma at the level of culture.

## Cultural Trauma

Because culture is so much more than individual cognition, building cultures of peace and reconciliation simply cannot be based solely upon identifying, treating, or preventing disturbed cognitive mechanisms in individuals. Therefore, a human sciences approach conceptually frames trauma around the phenomenon of culture rather than cognition. "Cultural trauma" refers to changes in shared meanings and behaviors that come about as a consequence of traumatic events that impact social groups. Among "traumatic events" I include direct acts of violence and aggression against a people, but also social, economic, political, and cultural processes that collectives perceive as threatening to their existence. Thus, my definition of "cultural trauma" is related to several existing concepts that also attempt to conceptualize trauma from the vantage point of social and cultural theory, including Kai Erikson's notion of "collective trauma," Veena Das's notion of "social trauma," Maurice Eisenbruch's "cultural bereavement," Arthur Kleinman's "social suffering," and Pierre Bourdieu's "positional suffering."[18] In this book, I am talking about cultural traumas that come when political violence affects a society.

Cultural trauma is not individual trauma writ large. It does not share the same individualistic values and assumptions embedded in traumatic stress theory, such as those that Bracken critiqued (e.g., meaning is all internal; the brain's information processing is disordered due to trauma; and talking about trauma heals). Nor does it rest on the simple dichotomy between the individual and collective that hampers much of the trauma mental health discourse as it is applied to mental health and human rights. Instead, cultural trauma may induce significant changes in the culture of the surviving groups. Cultures may fragment or coalesce; they may be poisoned, or nourished, and perhaps some of both. Shared meanings and behaviors may change, but there is no predictable pattern to these changes.

This is in part because cultural trauma releases both centrifugal and centripetal forces in a culture.[19] Some existing values may be shattered, or threatened in the face of new circumstances. Some cultural figures or products may be destroyed, discredited, or become just plain irrelevant in new times. Some means of communication may be broken, overwhelmed, or become out of touch with the new experiences. Yet cultural trauma certainly does not mean that all has been lost or destroyed. Some existing values may remain present and strong, and may grow yet stronger. Some core cultural elements, such as tradition, family, rituals, obligation, and patriotism, may be reaffirmed and reasserted.

This concept of cultural trauma suggests that political violence may bring a wide and nonuniform array of cultural changes. These are likely to involve such important issues for peace and reconciliation as otherness, identity, race, religion, nation, historical memory, plurality, and democracy. Areas of cultural change may not actually focus directly on traumatic events, but may address other cultural changes brought directly or indirectly, or by other coincident processes of change, such as globalization or migration.

Given that communication is crucial for a culture to exist, a human science of testimony approach to cultures of peace and reconciliation after cultural trauma uses the perspective of communication in culture.[20] This type of cultural work entails specific concerns over whose testimony is being given to whom, in what ways, and with what responses. One matter of particular importance is the testimony's ability to reach beyond the realm of private confession into broader spheres of communication, through communities, organizations, governments, media, art, nations, and global systems. Testimony may enter into some sectors of culture, but not others. Testimonies may have different impacts when communicated through various cultural media, such as linguistic versus visual, or documentary versus artistic. Susan Sontag wrote about the special power of photographs, paintings, and drawings in documenting war and political violence: "The Western memory museum is now mostly a visual one, " she claimed.[21]

One especially important aspect of a cultural trauma following political violence that involves narratives concerns the ways in which a people explain to themselves and to others their journey through history: what they tell and what they do not tell of their history. This type of cultural discourse typically stems not only from written documents, but especially from oral stories which further allow for previous explanations to be supplemented or modified. Older generations use testimony as one way to transmit their knowledge of their historical experiences to younger generations. The sharing of testimonies might become linked to processes of moral teaching and learning in a society. The leading moral voices of a culture may become involved in or implicated by the testimony work, so as to influence the testimonies' impact upon cultural trauma as well as peace and reconciliation.

The idea of cultural trauma is linked to larger ethical questions concerning people's obligations to their history and culture, questions such as: Who are we? Who are our friends and who are our enemies? What is the purpose of our existence as a society? What are the values that unite us? A human sciences approach to cultural trauma is interested in how these important questions are being asked and answered at multiple levels in a culture.

When a culture engages with these questions through testimonies, the testimonies are supposed to offer explanations that help people to better understand and face the demands of the present and the anticipated demands of the future. After political violence, testimonies should help a culture to address such important concerns as how to redefine itself after suffering losses, and how to redefine the other or the enemy. But a human sciences approach to testimony work does not believe that these questions are to be answered in any particular way, or that doing so promises any predictable resolution of them. It seems just as likely that testimony work may support cultural illusions that would diminish people's capacity for understanding their situations and for building peace and reconciliation. Although a human sciences approach presumes that there is an important link to be made between testimony and the cultural work of peace and reconciliation, it does not imply that all survivors should give testimony, and that testimony is going to magically accomplish peace and reconciliation. In some instances, testimony may have precisely the opposite effect.

One thing for certain is that after cultural trauma, a culture can no longer go back to what it once was. Therefore, responding to cultural trauma requires finding ways to creatively combine some of the old with some things new in ways that may better facilitate peace and reconciliation. These are processes and they take time; but this does not mean that one should only sit back and wait for changes to transpire. A human sciences approach asks: If there is no testimony, no storytelling, no open entrée of survivors' stories into culture, then what kind of cultural change can there be?

## Creative Understanding

In "Toward a Methodology of the Human Sciences," Bakhtin also sketched the concept of "creative understanding," which has useful implications for testimony in relation to the cultural work of peace and reconciliation. Bakhtin was trying to achieve a means of understanding that was both a science and an art. As a science, this means of understanding was a disciplined way of inquiring and learning. Conversely, as an art, it was nonreductive, formal, thoughtful, and expressive. Bakhtin identified four essential tiers in this process of "creative understanding": perception, recognition, contextual significance, and active-dialogic understanding (SG 159). I will discuss each tier and show how it can help to link testimonies to the broader cultural work of peace and reconciliation.

The first two tiers in the process of creative understanding imply that testimony is fundamentally built upon the survivor's uniquely authored *perceptions* ("psychophysiologically perceiving a physical sign [word, color, spatial form]") and *recognitions* ("recognizing it [as familiar or unfamiliar]") of their personal experiences (SG 159). This particular idea also calls to mind the "personal" aspect in my definition of testimony that was mentioned in this book's introduction. There, I defined the "personal" characteristic of testimony as the survivor's account of the events of political violence that they themselves endured or witnessed.

When survivors are given support and freedom to tell their stories, perception and recognition usually emerge. In many instances, however, when testimonies are taken, perception and recognition are either constricted or shut down. This inability to get past these first points of entry into creative understanding was the stumbling block for some of the cognitive science and legal rationalist methodologies critiqued earlier. From Bakhtin's perspective, both perception and recognition are the necessary prerequisites for helping testimony to engage with culture in the work of peace and reconciliation. Thus, when approaching a testimony, one should first ascertain if the chosen methodology of engaging with testimony facilitates genuine perception and recognition.

That being said, Bakhtin placed even greater emphasis upon the latter two aspects of creative understanding. *Context* ("understanding its significance in the given context [immediate and more remote]") is critical in several ways (*SG* 159). This is the true province of the human sciences, given that the natural sciences are often so inattentive to contextual understandings. One specific form of contextual understanding bears special mention. In the human sciences, Bakhtin asked that context be understood from the perspective of "the authored text." He wrote: "The text lives only by coming into contact with another text [i.e., with context]" (*SG* 162). A text (in the case of testimony) is a product not just of one delimitable speaking or writing act, or of one isolated moment in time. Instead, the text is itself the narrative response to many other texts and to many voices over many moments in time. Testimony as text is both personal and public, but not only that. When one person gives testimony to another, together they are making a textual whole from many, many textual parts. Bakhtin asked that the text (testimony) be seen as the narrative embodiment of those many texts, and of the huge swaths of human activity to which they are linked. Thus, for the reader or listener of testimony, a given testimony is not to be regarded in isolation, or as only private or public. On the contrary, it may be perceived in relationship with many other texts, and through them with multiple voices and responses outside of these texts.

Context is highly linked with the last requirement of *active-dialogic understanding*. The phenomenon of multiple voices responding freely to one another supplies the context for testimony. This polyphonic nature of interaction can occur in several different ways. First, in the testimony itself, the survivors may themselves be speaking in multiple voices arising from different cultural perspectives or vantage points upon the experiences of political violence and cultural trauma. The survivors' voices may even reflect different historical eras (i.e., before and after political violence). Second, the receiver of testimony may also facilitate the multiplicity of voices, either by introducing an outside voice or by enabling an alternative voice within the survivor. Third, the testimony as a wider medium of communication opens up the possibilities for responses by the freely expressed voices of persons other than those of the survivor and the direct receiver of testimony. Overall, what is important is the particular nature of communication between the interlocutors of testimonies. By interpreting, reframing, or retransmitting the testimonies, to what extent are all parties encouraged to engage in freely responding to both the testimonies themselves and to each other's respective responses? Inspired by Bakhtin, we may envision a snowballing of freely voiced responses emerging from testimonies as stories of living history.

The very freedom and openness that Bakhtin insisted made creative understanding possible poses problems for the cultural work of peace and reconciliation. If the desired outcome is peace and reconciliation, then only so much freedom and only a certain kind of openness can be tolerated. Given this complication, how then can cultural work for peace and reconciliation legitimately utilize creative understanding? One possible alternative is to consider creative understanding not as an end point in itself, but rather as a means to be paired with other means to achieve other ends. In other words, given the objectives of promoting peace and reconciliation, there needs to be as much active-dialogic understanding as possible. This kind of active-dialogic understanding should serve to enhance the testimonies' impact upon the culture. Nevertheless, it should not be so open and free that one loses control over the meaning and the purpose of the testimony, which is to facilitate peace and reconciliation (e.g., no openness for racists). The balancing of Bakhtin's "non-predetermination, unexpectedness . . . surprisingness, absolute innovation, miracle" with the ethics of peace and reconciliation will never be easy (SG 167). This is one of many ways in which the application of dialogic work to testimony demands a lot of the survivors, the receivers, and the many responders.

## Testimonies' Outsideness

Bakhtin mentioned another requirement for creative understanding that is useful in thinking about testimony in cultural work for peace and reconciliation: "In order to understand, it is immensely important for the person who understands to be located outside the object of his or her creative understanding—in time, in space, in culture" (SG 7).

Creative understanding depends upon the existence of a boundary or boundaries. The traumas of political violence create boundaries, lots of them. Trauma survivors can claim that they stand outside of society and their culture because of their experience of trauma. What they went through is not what someone in their society was supposed to experience; it is, as the *Diagnostic and Statistical Manual of Mental Disorders (DSM-III)* stated, "outside the range of normal experience."[22] Trauma can push survivors into an outside space, in the sense that trauma may radically change what Bourdieu called the "habitus," the manner in which people normally experience and occupy social spaces.[23] What was once presumed to be safe is now experienced as dangerous; people cannot be trusted; what was once predictable can no longer be counted on. When testimony is spoken from within the world of traumatic experiences, it is outside of ordinary life. Because the survivors have crossed the boundary posed by trauma, we naturally assume that they possess knowledge and understanding that those on the ordinary side do not have. We assume that they know what is valuable and meaningful about life, including knowledge of war and peace, vengeance and forgiveness. The survivors often believe this too, and they want to share their knowing with those who are outside of the outsideness of trauma. In addition, if the survivors are refugees in exile, then they are geographically "outside" of their home: living in another place in their country, or maybe even abroad. With these boundaries may come new and valuable perspectives. Because of their trauma, survivors have experienced "an ousting of one's self to some outer, and thus more privileged, position from which to then look in" (*FHY* 211). Because of their experience of outsideness, survivors now have unique perceptions and recognitions. They can, furthermore, pass this outsideness on to the receivers of testimony.

Even among entire communities or societies that have experienced political violence, there are innumerable ways that political violence creates boundaries; and some, but by no means all, may help to facilitate creative understanding. For example, each different type of traumatic experience, such as being in a concentration camp or being sexually assaulted, is bounded. Each boundary can be a locus of a particular kind of special knowledge. Although not all boundaries are equally desirable, from this perspective, the more boundaries the better; it increases the possibilities of outsideness. According to Caryl Emerson, Bakhtin would have wanted "benevolent demarcation, without border disputes" (*FHY* 135). Granted that the boundaries created by political violence are full of "border disputes," these are obviously less than ideal for Bakhtin. Nevertheless, I doubt that this belligerent demarcation would stop Bakhtin from championing boundaries and outsideness. Bakhtin, after all, lived through Stalin's reign of terror in the Soviet Union.

Outsideness is not only a matter of position, but also one of process concerning the production of testimonies. The acts of telling, listening, and retelling continually involve crossing and recrossing boundaries. Outsideness may facilitate the survivors' telling when the person who receives the testimony is someone who was outside of the trauma experience itself. For example, many times I have been told by survivors: *"I can tell you my story because you are outside of it."* Explaining one's traumas to an outside person can be helpful to the survivor because it gets them out of their own life, "with its pain, indignity, missed opportunity, crimped perspective—so as to shape it into something I can live with, that is, shape it as I might shape an artistic creation" (*FHY* 217).

The outsideness of survivors' testimonies is likely to intensify or alter preexisting views about the identity of one's own group and may contribute to the sense that the outside other is to be feared. The fear that comes from traumatic experiences of political violence may act to deplete cultures of tolerance for otherness. When faced with the fear-evoking outsideness of an enemy, a society may also accept fewer internal boundaries; it may seek to minimize perceived outsideness within its own walls.

Survivors' testimonies, on the other hand, may also be a countercultural force to these fears associated with cultural trauma. Testimonies can provide documentation of important exceptions to the dehumanizing categorization of the outside other. They may introduce boundaries where it was assumed that there were none (i.e., they may demonstrate the heterogeneity of the other group). Testimonies' inherent outsideness can serve as a check upon the centripetal force of narrowing institutional or state responses to political violence. In testimony, survivors are encouraged to engage in their own personal struggle of consciousness and ethics, rather than to simply accept the externally defined narrative. Testimonies may prompt dialogues that promote acceptance and understanding of differences rather than minimizing or rejecting them.

Listening to testimonies means joining the survivor and crossing a boundary into the world of trauma. What exactly is to be gained from crossing over there? Dori Laub claimed that there was a healing benefit for the survivor; when the listener crosses over with them, survivors feel less alone. Bakhtin would also emphasize the benefits of crossing over for the receiver of testimony. By crossing over into the world of trauma, the receiver may come to learn something new from survivors that would change his or her views about war and peace, conflict and reconciliation. Yet it may be just as important for the giver of testimony to cross over into the world without trauma. Having to articulate his or her story to one who stands outside is a step in the right direction for the survivor who must return to the everyday and find a code to live by.

Emerson shared with Bakhtin the recognition that being outside changes the self. This process of change entails "an ousting of one's self to some outer, and thus more privileged, position from which to then look in" (FHY 211). Each links outsideness to the healthiness of the self. "A healthy self, in order to maximize its choices and thus reduce its impotence in the world, will always strive to expose itself to a multiplicity of inputs and perspectives from the outside, that is, it will strive toward a novelized state" (FHY 214).

This concept of a healthy self can apply not only to the giver and the receiver of testimony, but in a sense, to any persons who are part of a culture in which testimony has a presence. A culture after political violence can also be made healthier through the outsideness that testimony is able to provide to survivors, and to many possible receivers. Testimony releases many different voices, speaking of and from many different experiences regarding political violence. Having such a multitude of voices to draw upon promotes a culture that is not limited to one master narrative, but is novelistic in the sense of being polyphonic and dialogic. Bakhtin believed that outsideness was something that could be shared. With respect to testimony, outsideness begins with the survivor. Outsideness, however, does not belong solely to the survivor, or to the receiver of testimony. Once the testimony has passed between them as dialogic work, then the survivor, the first receiver, and all subsequent receivers are linked in dialogic relation and may experience the "shared status of outsideness."

Bakhtin believed in outsideness: "In the realm of culture, outsideness is the most powerful lever of understanding" (SG 7). The outsideness that testimony carries is a potential source of power that can be tapped to make testimonies more effective in the cultural work of peace and reconciliation. Like most of Bakhtin's major ideas, outsideness may be regarded as both an attribute and an end point. When outsideness becomes identified as a fixed end point, it can lead to rigidly scripted social roles for victims, which Michael Humphrey has critiqued as an undesirable outcome of truth commissions and trauma mental health treatment. If peace and reconciliation are the desired end point, then outsideness in testimony is more useful as a means that will help to get there.

## Eventness in Testimonies

Bakhtin used the concept of "eventness" to indicate that the meanings of a given event are open, and are created and re-created through dialogue. Bakhtin further declared his commitment to the open concept of eventness when he referred to "the world as an event (and not as existence in ready-made form)" (*SG* 162). Eventness is also important as the link between events and obligations or ethics. Obligation is located "in eventness—still incompletely, of course, but much more fully than in other available forms of representations" (*CP* 27). Bakhtin was interested in how obligations are created, and ethical understanding achieved, but not at all in making a system of ethics.

In contrast to Bakhtin's focus on eventness, the human rights and mental health fields have tended to prioritize the events in a testimony. The human rights movement tends to see testimony as offering a fixed picture of criminal events that the person witnessed, putting the person's subjectivity aside. Clinical testimony considers the individual's psychological response as the primary event, which it often frames in the universal terms of a trauma response, and relegates historical experience and remembrances to the distant background. But in addition to containing criminal or psychological events, testimony may be brimming with eventness. The eventness in testimony often represents the interactions of the historical with the personal, without neglecting either. The quality of eventness seeks to know and represent how the experience of the event was and still is being processed by the person, with an emphasis upon the openness, uncertainty, and ambivalence of all possible responses to events, and upon the vicissitudes of obligations.

Testimony inspired by "eventness" contains not only the knowing of events, but the knowing of "eventness." In learning of events through testimony, the receiver learns of the multiple obligations that were experienced by the persons caught up in those events. The receiver may see how they understood those events, how they articulated them to themselves, what they saw and what they were blind to, and how they made choices, for better or worse.

Through testimony, survivors and receivers engage with some of the most critical political, existential, and moral questions that a society can ask concerning identity, otherness, existence, values, and enemies. After the experience of political violence, these questions are especially important for individuals, families, groups, organizations, and communities. These questions are at the core of how a society and its people redefine themselves and the codes by which they live.

Testimony is able to contribute to this process of questioning and redefining

precisely because it is a carrier of "eventness" and what Bakhtin called "event potential." Eventness means that testimony carries ideas as well as events. Bakhtin
would say that the retelling of only events doesn't go anywhere. But when there are
both ideas and events, as there is in eventness, then something important may be
ignited. Bakhtin said: "Like the word, the idea wants to be heard, understood, and
'answered' by other voices from other positions" (*PDP* 88). Still, there is no guarantee that the processes kindled by testimonies' "eventness" will be good for peace
and reconciliation. Testimonies increase the number of variables and the potency
of the variables, but they do not provide solutions.

But in situations of political violence and cultural trauma, this is desirable because the risks of succumbing to trauma's centripetal culture-degrading processes
are so great. Dialogically engaging with the eventness of the traumas of political
violence through testimony may promote a better awareness of people themselves
and of the world. Fostering this specific kind of awareness may invigorate a culture
and may help that culture to make better choices. Bakhtin's idea of the speech genre
can help us to think of how speaking about these matters may be arranged in a
culture.

## Speech Genres of Testimony

> A thing, as long as it remains a thing, can affect only other things; in order to
> affect a personality it must reveal its semantic potential, become a word, that
> is, assimilate to a potential verbal-semantic context. (*SG* 164)

Bakhtin's idea of the "speech genre" can serve as a further guide for how testimonies
may participate in a culture and address cultural trauma. The speech genre was another relatively late idea of Bakhtin, extrapolated in his essay "On Speech Genres,"
written in 1952–53. Thomas Kent wrote that Bakhtin's concept of the speech genre
refers to a body of language responses "to something within a specific social situation" that "creates effects in the world."[24] According to Michael Holquist, Bakhtin's
speech genre is defined through three kinds of restrictions. The first concerns "what
is perceived as the imminent semantic exhaustiveness of the utterance's theme—
how much elaboration and effort is felt to be adequate" (i.e., what one needs to say
when telling one's story). The second restriction refers to "the speech plan of the
speaker—what he or she intends to accomplish" (i.e., the aim to spread the truth
of what happened). The third concerns "the typic generic forms of finalization"
(i.e., terms like "trauma" and "reconciliation").[25] Holquist makes a further important
distinction between primary and secondary speech genres. Primary speech genres,
which correspond to how trauma survivors talk about trauma, are those that "come
into being before they are specified into institutional forms." Secondary speech

genres are the "norms governing professional language," such as how mental health professionals communicate with one another about trauma.[26]

This idea of the speech genre has several implications for testimony. Testimony, when considered as its own speech genre, may share certain aims and themes that are similar to what Bakhtin identified in Dostoevsky: "a genre of ultimate questions," "confessional self-utterance," and "a moral torture" (*PDP* 56, 54). As a distinct speech genre, the more different that testimonies' aims and themes are from the speech genres of daily life the better. They then pose a better chance of provoking changes. However, I have also implied in this book that the secondary speech genre of testimonies' professionals and managers threatens to limit and contain the unique voices of the primary speech genre of the survivors' testimonies themselves. The more heavily testimonies are managed, the less potent they may be as a source of cultural change.

This very large speech genre of testimony may be subdivided into different genres according to the sociohistorical sites of political violence (e.g., torture testimony, Holocaust testimony, Bosnian and Kosovar testimony). The stories told within each genre typically resemble one another, and differ somewhat from those in other sites. To make the testimony speech genre stronger, we should seek as much diversity as possible within every genre, and all the various subgenres should be as different as possible from one another. But this distinctiveness should not go so far as to close off testimonies from interacting with other speech genres in the culture. Bakhtin wrote: "Each fundamentally and significantly new genre, once it arrives, exerts influences on the entire circle of old genres; the new genre makes the old ones, so to speak, more conscious; it forces them to better perceive their own possibilities and boundaries, that is, to overcome their naïveté" (*PDP* 271).

Testimonies should not stay sequestered in their own genre in just one part of the culture. Cultural change is more likely if there is movement and contact with other speech genres. This could happen, for example, when testimony narratives enter into literature, film, or other forms of popular culture, or when they become a part of children's education or clerical training. These uses of the testimony speech genre in order to foster processes of cultural change are to be distinguished from the isolated appearances of testimony in the mass media, which often do little more than create a spectacle that enrages, entertains, and works to affirm the status quo.[27]

The place of testimonies in the speech genres of a society may be actively managed by political authorities, who control public expressions and public memory. This may be both worrisome and promising. Totalitarian regimes, including the former Yugoslavia and the Soviet state that oppressed Bakhtin, put the clamps on public memory.[28] But so did the United States in its de-Nazification of Germany. Ambitious state approaches to reshaping post-conflict cultures are not at all a part of Western peacemakers' agendas in the late twentieth and the early twenty-first century. Given the piecemeal nature and cognitive biases of today's civilian peacemaking efforts, it is unrealistic to expect anything other than limited state efforts to manage speech genres of testimony on behalf of cultural changes for peace and reconciliation. Still, I claim that should states choose to undertake such efforts, they would likely be more effective if they were designed and implemented as cultural projects that aimed to enrich and strengthen speech genres, rather than as efforts to create spectacles or to reach fixed conclusions (e.g., "never again").

Within the broader culture, there are two key questions for testimony work to address in order to help with cultural trauma and to further peace and reconciliation.

*How can we forgive and trust those who have been against us?*

Offering forgiveness and reestablishing trust are both processes. Along the way are many important dilemmas and choices, and testimony may be helpful in exploring them (i.e., concerning attribution, blame, wrongdoing, evil). No one but survivors can offer forgiveness. Because testimony is a place where this is often contemplated, testimonies can introduce survivors' views on these issues into a culture and prompt dialogue and cultural change.

*How can we identify and protect against our enemies?*

Peace and reconciliation are not possible if a society is not reassured about its own security. Societies are obligated to know who their enemies are and when it is necessary to take action against them. But there can be tremendous ambiguity and ambivalence around knowing who your friends and enemies are, and choosing what to do about that. Testimony often explores these issues with respect to the past, present, and future, and can prompt a broader dialogue on what to believe and do about friends and potential enemies.

Both of these questions in the speech genre of testimony are also linked to multiple other speech genres within different sectors of society. For example, forgiveness and trust may be spoken of in a religious community, a civic meeting, and a youth group. The cultural aim of testimony work is not to convert all conversations to ones that are about testimony; but to use testimony to enter into and change each of those genres in their own contexts, so that these two central questions keep getting talked about and worked on, creating the possibility for cultural change.

## Not Better Than My Time

The Bakhtinian ideas that I have presented in this chapter do not determine the end points of peace and reconciliation work. Those long-term aims are peace and reconciliation themselves. Bakhtin's ideas have suggested several concepts and methods for working with testimonies in approaching these questions and traversing that path. They may be summarized as follows.

Testimony work with survivors of political violence is a human science based
upon creative understanding that centers on attention to perception,
recognition, context, active-dialogic understanding, and voice.

The human sciences approach to testimonies is concerned with responding
to cultural trauma as it impacts the processes of peace and reconciliation.

Boundaries and outsideness are sources of narrative power that can facilitate
the processes of producing testimonies and testimonies' entry into a
culture.

Eventness in testimonies is to be nurtured, since it may be linked to ethics
and obligations concerning peace and reconciliation.

Testimony as a speech genre aims to diversify and to make contact with
other speech genres in a culture with regard to peace and reconciliation.

Given that testimony work regarding peace and reconciliation requires a long-term
perspective, these concepts and methods are best approached as processes that
evolve over time.

In a confession late in life to a friend, Bakhtin made a profoundly leveling comment: "I was not better than my time" (*FHY* 180). This is astounding given that
it came from the writer who claimed that "even a word known to be false is not absolutely false" (*FHY* 124). For Bakhtin, "it always presupposes an instance that will
understand and justify it" (*FHY* 124). The comment "not better than my time" revealed a Bakhtin who not only struggled but recognized the human limits of what
it meant to be living in this place, in this time, in this culture, in this life, with this
language. Events may be unfinalizable, but because life is short, the present and history are also binding. We should stay aware that there are considerable limits for
testimony in relation to peace and reconciliation work.

I have already spoken of some of testimony's limitations with respect to diminishing suffering. Even if we imagine that the peacemaking power that resides in
testimony could be realized, many of these limitations also apply to peace and reconciliation. Governments or other political agents may use the memories of political violence to shape the history that they prefer, and their views of historical
memory may become fixed within a society. Nongovernmental organizations and
the media may use testimonies to create a spectacle centered on atrocity to elicit
what Michael Hardt and Antonio Negri describe as a "universal moral call."[29] Although we may hope that testimonies provide foundations for peace and reconciliation, it is just as possible that testimonies will be used to contribute to hatred and
violence. Any time testimonies are spoken, it is within a society and its culture at a
particular historical moment, and any of these factors are potentially binding. Testimonies cannot readily undo what has become part of a culture. Societies that experience cultural trauma from political violence do not shed violence easily. At
best, culture change is a process and a long-term project.

Simply producing testimonies will not achieve peace and reconciliation any more than simply producing testimonies will lead to healing. Rather, testimonies introduce a potent new centrifugal energy source into a culture that may induce changes that could promote peace and reconciliation. However, Bakhtin does not write that these would be guaranteed. Once again, testimony creates options, not solutions.

As long as there is political violence, there will be the testimonies of survivors and witnesses, and states and societies will be faced with the question of how to respond to them. Bakhtin helps us to be aware that the professionals and institutions that are involved in peace and reconciliation work are often oriented in centripetal directions. I worry that they may put testimony through a cognitive machine that renders it into something that it is not. Bakhtin has also helped to identify alternative principles for approaching testimony in the work of peace and reconciliation: human sciences, creative understanding, outsideness, and eventness. However, the project of getting those institutions and professionals that do peace and reconciliation work to commit to the "dialogic work" that Bakhtin described can be immensely difficult.

Another important limitation regarding the use of Bakhtinian concepts for testimony is that Bakhtin the writer was not interested in politics. Emerson notes: "His temperament was not that of a testifier or witness. He worked largely with attitudes and responses, not with policies or events" (*FHY* 25). Bakhtin's philosophy was far more "moral" than political, and his approach focused upon "communication," not political change (*FHY* 28). Bakhtin would probably be the last person to claim that testimony guarantees any particular political outcome. I for one do not share his rejection of politics, but I can understand it given the circumstances of his arrest and exile in the Soviet Union. I also believe it is impossible to completely sever efforts to create cultures of peace and reconciliation from the political context; the political is one of the most important contexts for testimony work. But perhaps Bakhtin's position can be interpreted to mean that the political realm is not the primary context for testimony. The dialogue that begins in testimony and reverberates throughout a culture will at some points touch the political. For example, political ideas about social change may frame how testimonies are produced, interpreted, represented, or retransmitted. But the point Bakhtin's writings suggest is that testimony does not belong only to the political, but also to the cultural.

Testimony is like the short novel. It is not an efficient institution, but it has to exist. Both are deeply storied but appallingly impractical propositions in the fast-paced, quick-fix, media-driven, technologically oriented culture of the early twenty-first century. That, however, may be precisely why they need to exist, because artistic models can address human needs that otherwise cannot be addressed. While in the short term, testimony demands expenditures of human energy that may be nonproductive; in the long-term, testimony work offers an honest and valid path toward creating cultures of peace and reconciliation.

# 8

# Documenting Histories

From the Holocaust to Chile, South Africa, Cambodia, Rwanda, the Balkans, the Mideast, and September 11 in New York (to name only a few), historical accounts of mass political violence have often included survivors' voices and perspectives. Journalists, artists, educators, politicians, human rights activists, and historians have relied upon the powerful legitimacy, sensibility, and moral strength that survivors' voices add to histories. Survivors' testimonies carry obligations to uphold the historical truth of events of political violence; but in the context of many complicating factors, the role of testimony in documenting histories of political violence may be limited by the lack of appropriate frameworks to tell, represent, and interpret these histories. Testimonies play a more limited role in documenting histories when, for example, they are used only as sources of facts about historical events; when they express that the outcomes and analyses of history were always known and certain; when they are rejected because they are considered too subjective for history; or when they are exclusively focused either on the personal or the historical. These and other shortcomings in using testimony for historical documentation show up in some of the institutional practices for managing survivors' stories and producing knowledge about political violence. This includes institutions associated with mental health and human rights.

Mikhail Bakhtin devised several important ideas about narratives that I find may enhance the historical uses of testimony with regard to political violence. "Unfinalizability" implies that the historical processes and meanings documented through testimony are not to be foreclosed. An open sense of time termed "heterochrony" and Morson's related concept of "sideshadowing" offer alternatives to fixed or distorted frameworks of time that are often used with testimonies. The "novel of historical emergence" is an artistic model for innovations in narrating personal and historic experience that can facilitate survivors' documenting their histories through testimonies. Lastly, Bakhtin's understanding of "heroes" and the "heroic idea" may guide how testimonies may create meanings from survivors' historical journeys. Applying these ideas of Bakhtin may help to document histories of political violence as a living history and to preserve the openness of historical events, processes, and meanings.

## Elusive Histories

In South Africa, the Truth and Reconciliation Commission (TRC) was established by the government of national unity in 1995 to "help deal with what happened under apartheid" and to facilitate the country's transition to democracy.[1] Survivors were invited to tell their stories, and many of those stories were broadcast on national television. Truth commissions had been used before in other countries, including Chile, and in several of the former Communist states of Central and Eastern Europe. In South Africa, as in those other countries, this nationwide telling of its history was claimed to be the right type of intervention to help the nation and those who had suffered injustices to move out from under the great historical crimes of apartheid. A truth commission does this in part because it is believed that it can provide a fair and objective documenting of historical truths. In South Africa, some but by no means all survivors, witnesses, family members, and perpetrators were given an opportunity to participate in the public truth-telling. The issue of who gets to testify is a serious concern. Until its closing in 2001, the TRC had about 2,400 survivors testify. South Africa is a country that has lacked any systematic accounting of the true number of persons subject to human rights violations.[2] However, 27,000 victims submitted statements to the TRC, and at least 8,000 more were submitted after its closing.

The Truth and Reconciliation Commission in South Africa has had its critics. The expatriate South African writer Breyten Breytenbach wrote of "the inquisition called the Truth and Reconciliation Comission." It was comprised of justices he called the "dogs of God" who made arrogant claims upon what was the historical truth, claims that to Breytenbach were terribly out of touch with South Africa's peoples.[3] Breytenbach wrote: "Misery and devastation and iniquity and treachery and pain are staged before a bench of the pure and beamed into the living rooms of the populace. So that memory may be excavated, shaped, initiated and corrected where needed to serve as backbone to the new history of the new nation."[4]

If the TRC was at the politicians' mercy, Breytenbach scornfully asked, then what kind of historical truths could emerge that would be of any possible help for a desperate nation trying to find the path to a better future? War crimes tribunals (for example, in Nuremberg and in The Hague) have been criticized on similar grounds.[5] If testimonies were selected, influenced, or used by leaders to further political aims, then citizens would stop believing in the historical truth of the commission. If citizens did not believe that the history was truthful and fair, then the truth commission would lose credibility and the historical basis for reconciliation would be undermined.

Breytenbach was not the only South African critic of the Truth and Reconciliation Commission. Merle Friedman, a South African psychologist, reported that the essential problem with the TRC was that it did not think more "psychologically."[6] For example, the TRC gave full amnesty to perpetrators who confessed, but it did not give reparations to the victims. The TRC was conducted like a British court, not in a manner sensitive to the people it was intended to serve. Finally, the TRC did not hear the testimonies of "bystanders" to atrocities. Friedman argued that it was because of these shortcomings that the TRC was proving to be a failure. Her evidence was the rising tide of violence in the country, which, she said, showed that the South African people had lost faith in the TRC. I agree with the majority of Friedman's criticisms of the TRC. But I am reluctant to agree that thinking more psychologically would improve the problems that either Friedman or Breytenbach cite. I do not believe that psychology or psychiatry are adequately prepared to understand how the telling and interpreting of history were being put to use by the state. I am concerned that more psychological thinking could come with more liabilities than advantages for documenting histories.

Unfortunately, in documenting histories we cannot sufficiently depend upon mental health and human rights—a field that is actually close in proximity to survivors and their stories. When a historical catastrophe of political violence is approached as a mental health and human rights problem, there often is not a sufficient recognition of being in the presence of history. In particular, the trauma mental health perspective that is commonly applied can be drastically ahistorical; it often does not want to recognize or to tell history. Instead, trauma too often sees private lives, or that smaller aspect of experiences that is bounded by the psychopathological. History is backgrounded, which is another way of saying it is not recognized. Trauma mental health has made its mark by extracting the individual from history.[7] When we say, *"It's not that the times are sick. It's that you are,"* history is left out of the equation. The history that trauma mental health often conveys is instead a history of itself as a movement. The field repeats, mantralike, that "we must not forget." What the movement wants others to remember is not survivors' histories, but professionals' claim that trauma is treatable. This is an internalist's history, an embodiment of the trauma mental health movement's own creation myth.

In theory and practice, human rights and humanitarian interventions often do not employ a historical approach that can be brought to testimonies. The human rights field is primarily committed to implementing a global system of principles, laws, monitoring, and enforcement. The burgeoning discourse on humanitarian interventions is focused on building theory and practice concerning why, when, where, and how one state is justified in taking military and civil actions that cross the sovereignty of another state.[8] Human rights and humanitarian interventions are far more interested in either managing history or in rendering a more manageable history than in wading into the messy histories presented by survivors' testimonies.

I recognize that the arguments of both Breytenbach and Friedman come from a moral position; they both claim that it is not right for the state to neglect or manipulate the historical truths of survivors' stories. I agree with that position. The histories produced by survivors should not be severed from the everyday realities, needs, and beliefs of survivors' lives and communities. But to advance the testimonies' role in documenting historical truths, we need more than moral positioning. We need to learn from detailed descriptions of alternatives such as the local approaches being used in Rwanda. We also need to learn from literary principles of narration that can facilitate methods of documentation.[9]

To better address historical truth, testimony needs a new conceptual basis for linking trauma, narrative, and history. I know of no theoretical work that has addressed this head-on, although some scholars and writers provide helpful starting points. Cultural anthropologists such as Veena Das have critiqued the "judicial or media-oriented confessional models" of knowledge of political violence and have advanced the role of ethnography in documenting histories through longer-term and community-oriented methods.[10] From the realm of literature come formulations of far deeper troubles than institutional incapacity. In *On the Natural History of Destruction*, W. G. Sebald investigated the failure of an entire generation of Germans to acknowledge the experience of having endured the Allied air campaign by practicing acts of "pre-conscious self-censorship."[11] Sebald wrote: "There was a tacit agreement, equally binding on everyone, that the true state of material and moral ruin in which the country found itself was not to be described."[12] In postwar Germany, no publicly sanctioned moral space existed to share those memories. In *Regarding the Pain of Others*, Susan Sontag wrote of a human shortcoming that creates obstacles between testimony and history: "Our failure is one of imagination, of empathy." Although Sontag prized the visual, she also acknowledged the necessity of the narrative in "making us understand" and in "thinking."[13] Gary Saul Morson, on the other hand, is suspicious of the narrowing effects of narratives on multiplicity, such as "the need for coherence, the demands of readability" (*CP* 157).

Once again, I turned to Bakhtin because I believed that his ideas about the narrative would provide some helpful concepts for reconceiving testimony work in relation to documenting historical truths.


## Unfinalizability

Bakhtin used the word *nezavershenmost* or "unfinalizability" to denote "genuinely new, openness, potentiality, freedom, and creativity" (*FHY* 37).[14] Unfinalizability was a core value for Bakhtin, about which he wrote: "Nothing conclusive has yet taken place in the world, the ultimate word of the world and about the world has not yet been spoken, the world is open and free, everything is still in the future and will always be in the future" (*PDP* 166).

Bakhtin applied unfinalizability in his writings on literature, ethics, and history. For example, the major characters in Dostoevsky's novels are unfinalizable, in the sense that they are not completed either by the author's authority or by some totalizing theory. To Bakhtin, Dostoevsky's characters possess an "inner unfinalizability, their capacity to outgrow, as it were, from within, and to render untrue any externalizing and finalizing definition of them" (*PDP* 59).

Unfinalizability implies that the self has an obligation to strive toward an open future. Caryl Emerson wrote: "With Bakhtin's help, it seemed, one could get outside any disaster and analyze it" (*FHY* 17). Along these same lines, previously I interpreted Bakhtin's dictum that "catastrophe is not finalization" to mean that even the survivors of political violence cannot be fully defined by the truths of an event of political violence. However, unfinalizability still does tie survivors to the historical realities that mark their lives, and it respects their ties to others to whom their lives are linked. Both givers and receivers of testimony have to work within a given historical reality, and they have to tell or interpret histories within particular moral communities.

Unfinalizability has important implications for how history itself is conceptualized. According to Morson, Bakhtin believed that historicity required unfinalizability (*NF* 43). Morson wrote: "History is not history unless particular experience is meaningful, actions are responsible, results are partially unexpected, and the lives of people, both individually and in groups, are surprising" (*NF* 44). This sense of large, unruly history anchored in the messiness of everyday lives is contrary to the historical views of mental health and human rights, which wants history backgrounded and predictable. Producing this unfinalized history not only depends on survivors' testimonies, but also needs testimonies that are themselves unfinalized narratives.

One of testimony's most important characteristics and greatest strengths is that it often embodies the unfinalizability of survivors' experiences of historical events. For example, unfinalizability is present when survivors' accounts reflect that they often did not know what had happened, or what would happen in the future (as opposed to saying that they knew all along). It is possible that they did not believe that violence would occur in the first place; and it is likely that even now as they speak they still do not know what the future will bring. Testimonies are often replete with moments of unpredictability and surprise. Survivors may have believed that they would be safe, or they may have believed that they were going to perish, but then it didn't turn out that way. Listening to testimonies, it is sometimes hard to believe that there could be any genuine telling, given the proliferation of unplanned starting points, unanticipated turns of events, and unexpected outcomes.

Unfinalizability in testimonies and history is necessary because unfinalizability is linked with hope. In the act of giving testimony, survivors are expressing hope that articulating their terrifying and dismal experiences can yield some new meanings, understandings, obligations, or relationships that will be beneficial to those who receive their histories. There is nothing that they can do to change the events that have already happened; but through testimony, they may change how those past events continue to be known and what meanings, responsibilities, and choices are associated with them. Through testimonies, survivors (individuals and groups) can also reassert their sense of identity by claiming that although marked by events, they still have voices and perspectives that are uniquely their own. Emerson's description of the unfinalized expressed this sense of hope: "In an unfinalized world, everything (even a bad thing) can change (even if only a little)—and in the process, it gives birth to something new" (FHY 37). This something new that testimony produces belongs not only to the self but to the discourse in a local community; it may also carry a moral and historical weight that has the potential to enter into other broader discourses, in their society or globally.

When the unfinalizability of testimonies is diminished by the institutions that oversee acquiring survivors' testimonies and composing histories, then the possibility of something new emerging from their histories is also diminished. The more institutionalized the telling of history, the less room for the surprises that survivors' stories can bring. This problem can be found across disciplines. There may be one dominant historical narrative to which others are either forced or expected to converge. There may be a legalistic focus on "just the facts," which leaves little room for ambivalence, uncertainty, and the unexpected. There may be a clinical preoccupation with traumatic memory that restricts the range of emotional or cognitive responses that are allowed by survivors in their narratives. Or there may be a journalistic presentation of one-dimensional caricatures of heroic survivors or pathetic victims. All such efforts to render survivors as predictable, knowable, and more easily manageable tend to lessen the unfinalizability of the histories that they tell.

On the other hand, the unfinalizability of survivors' histories is perhaps one of the most challenging demands that testimony places upon both its tellers and its listeners. Unfinalizability in testimonies requires responses from receivers and interpreters that help to organize testimonies into a coherent historical narrative. Unfinalizability also poses the risk that through telling, things may get worse in ways that cannot be predicted. Testimonies may teach some the wrong moral lessons. Furthermore, the notion of unfinalizability may make testimony more vulnerable to distortions, exaggerations, and outright lies. Bakhtin's ideas about the narrative are not very good in addressing these untruths. When certainty or closure is desired, which is often the case in situations of political violence, the unfinalizability of history in survivors' testimonies is difficult and often unwanted. Yet all that being said, when the unfinalizability in survivors' testimonies is rejected, the possibility of a more genuine telling of history is thereby also diminished.

In addition to recognizing and nurturing unfinalizability in narratives, Bakhtin offered several concepts that suggest other ways to engage with history through survivors' testimonies, including ideas focusing on time.

## Heterochrony

Heterochrony is an open modeling of time in narratives, inspired by Bakhtin and investigated in the books of two of his disciples. One is Michael André Bernstein, whose book *Foregone Conclusions: Against Apocalyptic History* critiqued the prevalent tendencies of narrating the Holocaust in literature.[15] Bernstein contended that the narrative strategies by which Holocaust stories were often told utilized false notions of historical causality. Bernstein was against "a triumphalist, unidirectional view of history in which whatever has perished is condemned because it has been found wanting by some irresistible historico-logical dynamic."[16] He contrasted those who write the Holocaust as "apocalyptic history" with those who write "history blind to the future."[17] The former present history as a fateful process toward an inevitable conclusion, whereas the latter's view of history contains multiple contingencies and multiple possibilities. Bernstein condemned the narrative strategies of an apocalyptic history and championed those writers whose narratives promote more open views of time, history, and human experience. Why is it, Bernstein argued, that attempts to narrate the "unimaginable" often fall back upon the most limited of rhetorical strategies (e.g., we should have known that *x* would happen) for narrating history?[18] The effect is to diminish both the true horror of the catastrophe as well as the range of human responses in its wake. Shouldn't the givers and the receivers of that history, Bernstein implied, have more say in deciding whether the unimaginable was inevitable or not?

Gary Saul Morson, in a companion book to *Foregone Conclusions* entitled *Narrative and Freedom: The Shadows of Time,* investigated how some literary narratives distorted and closed down historical time, and how some extraordinary novels (*War and Peace* and *The Brothers Karamazov*) created models that conveyed the openness of time. Morson based his theory upon the literary philosophy of Bakhtin, who he claimed was "the most remarkable modern thinker to examine time in narrative" (*NF* 82). According to Morson, Bakhtin believed that a sense of history was not possible without an open sense of time: "He consistently opposed all ways of thinking that reduced the present moment—each present moment—to a simple derivative of what went before" (*CP* 46). In *Narrative and Freedom,* Morson examined time in narratives especially in relation to history. Drawing upon Bakhtin, Dostoevsky, Tolstoy, and other thinkers and writers, Morson examined different ways of representing temporality.

Morson contrasted the "closed temporalities" that he identified as "foreshadowing" and "backshadowing" with an "open sense of temporality" that he called "sideshadowing" (*CP* 5–7). Foreshadowing "robs a present moment of its presentness" because it says that time is unidirectional and that "what will be must be" (*NF* 117). Backshadowing is "foreshadowing after the fact" in that it claims when looking back after an event has transpired that the signs were all there, that the event was inevitable, and that we should have known (*NF* 234). In contrast, sideshadowing "conveys the sense that actual events might just as well not have happened," such that "along with an event, we see its alternatives; with each present, another possible present . . . the ghostly presence of might-have-beens or might-bes" (*NF* 118).

Bernstein's and Morson's investigations of heterochrony may assist in reconceiving testimony and its role in documenting histories. In the narratives of survivors of political violence, survivors may be saying that at multiple points in their odyssey, events might have gone otherwise, for better or worse. Instead of saying that they knew all along what would happen, they can be open to uncertainties that they, and those around them, had to struggle with. Surviving that history meant living with uncertainty. In telling history, there is more to be gained from being open to and examining these alternative histories and the related ambivalence and struggle than there is from shutting them out.

To be more fully historical, testimony narratives may be able to represent the multiple event potentials that are associated with key moments. They may represent that the outcomes of history are not predetermined, but get worked out as time moves along. When history is presented in a more open way, it is far more inviting to the reader's or listener's genuine response. If history is to be a body of living knowledge, then it has to be response-worthy, and an open sense of time is one important element. Morson wrote: "For there to be eventness, there must be alternatives. Eventful events are performed in a world in which there are multiple possibilities, in which some things that could happen do not" (*NF* 22).

Bakhtin's notion of heterochrony challenges the rather ahistorical mentalities that are often brought to bear upon testimony. Although neither Bakhtin, Morson, nor Bernstein directly addressed writings on the psychological consequences of testimony, many of their concerns are warranted here. The discourses of human rights and humanitarian interventions often approach events of political violence as a suddenly erupting "humanitarian crisis" that exists outside of the flow of historical time with its causality and consequences. One event is selected and amplified by observers and raised to the level of public spectacle that makes it look as if other historical events and processes never existed.

The trauma mental health profession's mentality associated with post-traumatic stress disorder encourages a rigid tripartite time sense. It divides time into pretrauma, trauma, and post-trauma. But historical time follows no such rigid plan. Before this trauma was another, and after it will come yet another. Thus, what was pre this trauma may have been post another, and conversely what is post this trauma may be pre yet another. We might be post one trauma and not know it. Even within one trauma, there is much heterogeneity of time course within societies, communities, and families. In addition, critics of PTSD have pointed out that post is often not really post, especially when the person lives in a society which is still experiencing collective traumatization.[19] What is also missing from the PTSD model of time is a genuine vision of the future. The future is far more than post-trauma. For Bakhtin, the sense of the future was crucial, as I will discuss in the following section.

## Historical Emergence

Bakhtin described a particular form of novel writing called "historical emergence" which may help to further elucidate a narrative that would be useful for documenting histories through testimonies. Bakhtin found the narrative form of historical emergence in great novels. He described it as follows: "The most profound novels of emergence, as we have suggested, represent not only individual becoming but also social becoming; and they represent these two processes as irreducible to each other but nevertheless closely linked" (*CP* 409; *SG* 19–25).

What made historical emergence a pinnacle of novelistic form was that it did not focus exclusively on either private life in domestic spaces or on public life in social spaces. Historical emergence gave each of these spaces their due. Most important, historical emergence presented an interactive, dynamic, open process between self and history. The idea of historical emergence was related to the key idea of "threshold," an "extraordinary situation" where "it is impossible to live a biographical life—here one can experience only crisis, make ultimate decisions, die or be reborn" (*DI* 248).

Bakhtin specified that the threshold phenomenon, like the novel of historical emergence, takes place in social spaces:

> The threshold, the foyer, the corridor, the landing, the stairway, its steps, doors opening onto the stairway, gates to front and back yards, and beyond these, the city: squares, streets, facades, taverns, dens, bridges, gutters. This is the space of the novel. And in fact absolutely nothing here ever loses touch with the threshold, there is no interior of drawing rooms, dining rooms, halls, studios, bedrooms, where biographical life unfolds. (*DI* 170)

Recall that the clinical testimony emphasized the importance of interior spaces. Torture took place in a prison. For giving torture testimonies, Inger Agger used her flat's blue room, whereas Dori Laub used the psychiatric consulting room. They made the claim that these kinds of spaces were what makes healing possible. Yet these types of spaces may also have been what kept a sense of history and its eventness out of the testimonies. The spaces where history is made and political violence is experienced are, indeed, out in the squares and the streets, or in the passageways where people happen to meet, and not in the clinicians' chambers. To engage history the testimony must be prepared to enter into the social spaces where history is made and where it is retold, shared, and interpreted. This implies that the spaces of production, but also transmission and response, should be spaces that are equally conducive to the social, historical, and political as well as to the personal.

Historical emergence in novels also depended upon how the future was approached in the narrative. Bakhtin believed that the depiction of the future was the novel's most crucial characteristic. The future must be open, for if it was closed, then its finalizability shadowed the whole narrative, and in turn made it closed. The future was a "zone of proximal development" (FHY 223; CP 411); a place where important decisions were to be made for individuals and for society. Not only were these not finished, nor given, but they were seen as requiring the highest possible degree of human creative response. It was in response to this special depiction of the future that "problems of reality and human potential, problems of freedom and necessity, and the problem of creative initiative rise to their full height" (SG 24).

The future plays a similar role in testimonies and the histories that they tell. When using testimony in order to create a sense of historical emergence, survivors may explore their sense of the future in their lives and in history. They have to face a future that is not given, but is still up for grabs. Those who receive testimonies may assist the survivor attend to this future. Perhaps there is only so much that a receiver can do. The persons who give testimony may have to come with their own sense of an open future. Testimony may not be able to create open futures if it isn't there already, or at least sensed in part. This could mean that young people would be better candidates for testimony than the aged. On the other hand, because youth isn't just for the young, there have to be many older adults who could come to testimony with a sense of open futures. These may be adults who can see through the eyes of their children, or adults who give testimony especially for the younger generations. This sense of the future may come to adults who let themselves be opened up by the very act of giving testimony as they would by singing a song of grace and passion.

Testimonies given in times of historical transition may stimulate survivors and receivers to think more about the future, and may prompt responses that can lead to changes in their historical outlook or consciousness. In the novel of historical emergence, "a person emerges along with the world and he reflects the historical emergence of the world itself" (SG 23; CP 411). In giving testimony, survivors are presented with an opportunity to creatively explore the relationship between selfhood and history. They speak of what has happened to them, how their world has changed and still is changing, how they have changed and are changing, what they now see for themselves and their world. Each survivor, in his or her own humble way, has an opportunity to rewrite history and his or her own self. Those who receive the testimony, like those who read the novel, can partake in this process of historical emergence.

There is a greater chance that the quality of emergence can be present in the testimony if the teller and the receiver imagine catastrophes not just as crisis and loss, but as points of collision both between eras in the personal life and historical eras, and also as points of transition and turbulence toward a future whose outcome is not known. The history that emerges comes with the veracity and legitimacy of lived experience. This history may help the survivor who gave testimony, and those who received it, to emerge from catastrophe with a deeper sense of rootedness and · contingency concerning history.

To write a narrative based on testimonies that is true to Bakhtin's sense of historicity is to face a basic dilemma: How do you finish the unfinalizable? This dilemma, which was inherent to the novel of historical emergence, is also a profound metaphysical challenge: How do you stay true to an openness of historical possibility while needing to complete a text of historical understandings? Bakhtin took different positions on this core problem as it applied to novel writing over his own writing life. I have already discussed several of the strategies that he advocated, including polyphony, active-dialogic understanding, and outsideness.

I would also like to turn to Bakhtin's ideas on the basic requirements of a work of art, as analyzed by Caryl Emerson. If we consider the dilemma of documenting history through testimony as an aesthetic one, then Bakhtin's ideas are useful principles for rethinking what qualities are to be nurtured in the writing of histories from testimonies in order to complete them without finalizing them. Emerson wrote of art: "It must be singular (that is, non-systematizable and unique); answerable ('signed' by its author or beneficiary, responsible); 'participatory' (oriented toward another consciousness, response-worthy); and it must be undertaken in a spirit of 'aesthetic love'" (*FHY* 208).[20]

It is not surprising that many works of literary testimony achieve these aesthetic benchmarks extremely well. It is more surprising that many works of testimony from persons who are not literary artists somehow manage to convey the narrative power of literature. Perhaps that is because the testimonies of survivors of political violence naturally tend toward the artistic principles of unfinalized, heterochronic, historically emergent narratives. But survivors often need help from receivers and interpreters to enable their testimonies to keep these qualities and to become open stories of living history. Survivors need their "aesthetic love." Those who want to use testimonies to document history may need to be reminded to adhere to the principles of unfinalizability, heterochronicity, and historical emergence, not because they necessarily want more aesthetic results, but because these are characteristics that naturally occur in testimonies and because together they comprise an artistic model which may help to deliver more open histories.

## Heroes and Heroic Ideas

Scholarly and media discussions of political violence often present the survivor as a hero. A hero in what sense? Robert Lifton wrote of the survivor as one who is distinguished because he or she knows death. Lifton wrote about the "death imprint," which is "associated not only with pain but also with value—with a special form of knowledge and potential inner growth associated with the sense of having "been there and returned."[21] Veena Das wrote of the special moral position of the victim of political violence.[22] In journalistic accounts, survivors are commonly portrayed as heroes by possessing some special personal qualities that enabled them to survive, or that the experience of survival bestowed upon them (such as faith in the human spirit). The literary scholar Lawrence Langer is one of many who have critiqued abstract hopeful evocations from the mass media as psychologically superficial; Langer claims they ignore the deeper layering of memories and long-term changes in the self that are the true responses to trauma.[23] Equally problematic is the tendency for the heroes of testimony to be known far more for what they are as individuals than for what they are as persons who are participants in local moral communities.

Bakhtin demonstrated other ways to conceive of the survivor as a hero in relation to history that might be helpful for documenting histories through testimonies. Bakhtin's ideas appeared primarily in his analysis of the hero in Dostoevsky's novels. Dostoevsky gave to his heroes the obligations of "self-definition" and "agonizing self-awareness" (PDP 48, 49). Bakhtin wrote: "Dostoevsky sought a hero who would be occupied primarily with the task of becoming conscious, the sort of hero whose life would be concentrated on the pure function of gaining consciousness of himself and the world" (PDP 50).

The hero in Dostoevsky is thoroughly committed to a "discourse about himself and his world" (PDP 53). The world is not a mere background for the journey of an individual, as it is the case in adventure novels. With Dostoevsky, the hero's movement toward understanding his world becomes the focus of the novel. More than that, Dostoevsky places his characters in a turbulent world that exposes heroes to crises and struggles of immense social and historical dimensions. In Dostoevsky's novels, the heroes are "poised on the threshold," and the author "inflicts" a "special sort of moral torture . . . upon his heroes" (PDP 54). Under these difficult conditions, Dostoevsky's historically conscious hero helped Bakhtin to articulate a new philosophy of historicity. Bakhtin wrote:

> The "truth" at which the hero must and indeed ultimately does arrive through clarifying the events to himself, can essentially be for Dostoevsky only the truth of the hero's own consciousness. In the mouth of another person, a word or definition identical in content would take on another meaning and tone, and would no longer be the truth. Only in the form of a confessional self-utterance, Dostoevsky maintained, could the final word about a person be given, a word truly adequate to him. (PDP 55–56)

The survivor giving testimony may aspire to a role similar to that of the hero in Dostoevsky's novel. Survivors have been exposed to adversity from political violence, and may want to tell their story. They may want to tell how these adverse experiences have changed them and their world, as well as to discuss the many other important links between the two story lines. The survivor's testimony may be regarded as what Bakhtin referred to as the "confessional self-utterance" (*PDP* 55–56). To transform their testimony into a veritable confessional self-utterance, survivors may need the help and the cooperation of many receivers and interpreters of testimony down the line. Because a confessional self-utterance, as such, can be difficult to produce and to understand, there is a tendency to fall back upon easier ways of representing and understanding the experience.

Heroes' ideas, and especially their ideas concerning history, were very important to Dostoevsky, in so far as Bakhtin claimed that "Dostoevsky himself became a great artist of the idea" (*PDP* 85). Dostoevsky, however, did not present these ideas as abstractions, nor did he simply stuff ideas into the hero's mouth. "It is not the idea in itself that is the 'hero of Dostoevsky's works' . . . but rather the person born of that idea" (*PDP* 85). To present ideas, including historical understandings, in the polyphonic novel, the writer becomes what Dostoevsky calls "a fantastic stenographer" (*PDP* 56). Bakhtin wrote: "We see the hero in the idea and through the idea, and we see the idea in him and through him" (*PDP* 87).

The author of the polyphonic novel becomes the dedicated observer of the hero's struggle to find the right words and to express his or her ideas through encounters and dialogues with other characters. This implies something important for testimony: namely, that the receiver of testimony is there to help survivors to turn their attention, not strictly to themselves, but to the world around them; noticing what others have said about their experiencing of that history, and then responding to that. In testimony, as in Dostoevsky, the aim is to document not only events, objects, and relationships as one survivor understood them, but also as one survivor understood others to be understanding them. With the help of the receiver, survivors may be able to go there. When multiple testimonies are combined, as in an archives or a testimony project, then the portrait of the diverse world grows thicker and richer if the interpreter comes with a sense of himself or herself as part "fantastic stenographer."

Bakhtin emphasized the relationship of the hero to the idea. Heroes struggle with big ideas of their time. Bakhtin wrote: "It is given to all of Dostoevsky's characters to 'think and seek higher things' "; in each of them there is a "great and unresolved thought" (*PDP* 87).

Survivors in testimony may be preoccupied by great thoughts, and it is the role of the receiver to help the survivor to articulate those thoughts. Bakhtin saw in Dostoevsky the gift "for hearing his epoch as a great dialogue," including "the loud, recognized, reigning voices of the epoch, that is, the reigning dominant ideas (official and unofficial), as well as voices still weak, ideas not yet fully emerged, latent ideas heard as yet by no one but himself, and ideas that were just beginning to ripen, embryos of future worldviews" (*PDP* 90). Because survivors giving testimony most likely belong to the latter group, they often need the active support and guidance of the receiver to help them put their great ideas into words. There is also an important role for interpreting and responding in such a way that discerns the great ideas in testimony. But if the receiver, respondent, or interpreter is too authoritative, then this puts the narrative's polyphonic characteristics at risk. Once again, Bakhtin almost took it for granted that survivors would have great thoughts, given the energizing nature of catastrophe, with its attributes of boundaries and outsideness and unfinalizability. This, of course, may not always be true. Sometimes survivors may have no great idea, or their ideas may be commonplace, objectionable, or wrong.

Testimony may also take a cue from Dostoevsky's polyphonic novels in aiming for dialogic interactions between "discourse about the world" and "confessional discourse about oneself"; between "intersecting consciousnesses"; between "ideas and worldview, which in real life [are] absolutely estranged and deaf to one another"; and between "juxtapose[d] orientations" (PDP 91). The temptations to make testimony all one thing or the other are to be resisted. Regarding Dostoevsky's novels, Bakhtin wrote: "Everything in Dostoevsky's novels tends towards dialogue, toward a dialogic opposition, as if tending towards its center. All else is means; dialogue is the end" (PDP 252). Some survivors may resist this on their own, but receivers should be prepared to assist them by turning their attention, early and often, toward the other sides of whatever boundaries are present, and by promoting interweaving in the narrative. The same goes for those who transmit or interpret the survivors' testimonies. There is a risk of pulling out the one thing that agrees with your purpose or theory and neglecting others, when a fuller view of the heroes and their testimony that lets in more unfinalizability would be a more accurate documentation of the histories of political violence.

## Events Rarely Make You Free

In this chapter, I have presented several of Bakhtin's key ideas to assist in making testimonies that are better able to document more open histories of political violence. These are:

Produce testimonies and give responses that respect the unfinalizability of historical experiences.

Maintain an open sense of historical time in the testimonies.

Approach testimonies as narratives of historical emergence through which survivors may be able to creatively address both themselves and historical becoming.

Regard survivors as heroes of history with heroic ideas so as to facilitate testimonies that express valuable historical meanings.

These ideas are meant to apply to the processes of testimony production, representation, transmission, and interpretation. As principles, they may be refined into methods for guiding the activities of many different persons, from the many sectors and disciplines that engage with testimonies in order to document histories.

I believe that oral historians and ethnographers have come the closest to embracing these concerns, both in particular projects and in theoretical work.[24] Unfortunately, it has been difficult for the majority of practitioners and theoreticians working with historical narratives to access or bridge the many different pockets where testimony work occurs daily. This still remains a challenge. The best way to respond to this challenge is not for oral history, psychiatry, human rights, law, or any other discipline to impose its particular thinking and ways upon others. Bakhtin offers a set of ideas around which individuals who come from many disciplines engaged with testimony and documenting histories may gather in active-dialogic conversation.

It is important to remember that many survivors do not want to document their histories: some not at all, and others not in the ways that I have outlined here. Thus, I am not claiming that documenting histories is for all survivors. Many survivors live under tremendous daily pressures. They need to rebuild their lives, help their families, and contribute to their communities and nations. For some, there is no room to tell their story when there are so many other obligations. Some may be tired of history, and may have retreated into private life. Like Bakhtin, they may talk about history with their friends, but actually giving testimony may not be for them.

Bakhtin is an ironic choice for a person to champion the historical documentation of political violence. As an internal exile in the Soviet Union, he never made a record of what happened to him or what he saw being done to others. Bakhtin did not focus upon documenting the facts of historical events, but instead concentrated on unfinalizable, dialogic, and artistic methods for telling histories. Even then, he tended to minimize the burden of past traumas.

If Bakhtin's optimism came through in his belief in dialogism and the unfinalizability of history, his pessimism came through in his concerns about the ideological and political uses of history. Much of Bakhtin's antipathy toward systematic approaches to history such as Marxism was muted, given that he was exiled for most of his life and was at considerable risk of even further political oppression and abuses. There was, however, one written statement in which Bakhtin did express concern about historical untruths in relation to fascism: "The lie is today's most ever-present form of evil. The word does not know whom it serves. It emerges from the dark and does not know its own roots. Its serious links with terror and violence" (*FHY* 170).

Bakhtin was against lies in historical narratives. But he did not have much to say about lies in personal narratives. Nor did he have anything to say directly about what to do concerning lies. One weakness of testimony, for which Bakhtin had no ready answer, is that as a solitary utterance, it is unprotected against the lie. If people are speaking freely, then they are also free to exaggerate, distort, and lie.

There may be other ways in which Bakhtin's ideas can indirectly address this concern. Through active-dialogic conversation, survivors' statements or misstatements about history should get a response. To be more worthy, those responses should be based upon a rigorous knowledge of the particularities of any given event and its historical, political, social, and cultural contexts. There is no possibility of understanding the historical in testimony if one does not know the history or the culture surrounding that testimony. One cannot assume that history and culture can be simply inferred or otherwise intuited from the individual dialogue. There is no building of a bridge to history if the history is not known; and that includes verifying historical facts. Through this knowing of the history, if survivors make claims that are not true, either unintentionally or intentionally, then in the responses that they earn, through receivers or through other respondents down the line, these untruths should be corrected. Where there has been political violence, there will always be the risk of unproductive "border disputes." Still, I trust in the process of active-dialogic responses to overcome individuals' departures from the truth. Without variance, boundaries, outsideness, tensions, and disputes, there can be no true history.

# Afterword

In a world replete with political violence, universes of testimonies can be found all around the globe. After hearing of another such universe, I wonder how similar and how different are the testimonies over there. I regret that in this book it was possible to explore only a few of these universes. But when I learn about political violence in another place, I try to understand how testimonies are being used there. Have those testimonies been finalized or are they energetic stories of living history? Are the testimonies doing some good?

## Tiananmen Testimonies

In the February 4, 2001, issue of the *New York Times Magazine,* Craig S. Smith, the Shanghai bureau chief of the *New York Times,* authored a concise yet powerful article about testimonies called "Tiananmen's Shadow."[1] The piece was subtitled: "The 1989 massacre still haunts the regime, having ruined the lives of its many victims and their families." I will never forget what happened in Tiananmen Square, but China couldn't be any farther from my world or the universes of testimony in this book.

The immediate provocation for this article was the publication of the "Tiananmen Papers." These supposedly authentic leaked government documents gave a picture of Tiananmen from the perspective of China's Communist leadership.[2] This was the epitome of finalized history. Smith's article came from the other side of Tiananmen Square. It bore kernels of testimony that transmitted a powerful message from the people: survivors and their loved ones can speak of the massacre in their own words.

Using survivors' testimonies as a basis for redressing histories of political violence has been the central focus of this book. Many people in China were hesitant to speak about such controversial matters, but not these men and women. In Smith's article, we read their actual names and see photographs of the witnesses, who speak directly to us from within lives of that history. They gave their testimonies and the journalist transmitted them.

In the Tiananmen article, testimony is a narrative response and an attempt at initiating further dialogue concerning the massacre. Why do persons such as these from China want someone to listen to their stories? Why has the *New York Times* chosen these testimonies to share with its readers? In this book I explored the question of what is being asked of testimony and found that testimonies are wanted to relieve suffering, to create cultures of peace and reconciliation, and to document histories.

The stories from Tiananmen, though brief, indicate that what these persons want is similar to what has been discussed in this book concerning other survivors from other universes.

> Yin Min talks to her dead son's ashes and wants "the Chinese government to acknowledge what happened and the courts to prosecute those responsible."[3] Their admission may give her peace.
>
> Qi Zhiyong wants others to know what he now knows the Chinese Communist Party is capable of doing to its own people. Knowing this may change China.
>
> Zhang Xianling, the mother of a nineteen-year-old boy, wants the film from the camera her son was shooting as he was killed. The truth of his murder must be documented.

Smith let these courageous people from China tell the truth about an event in history that killed their loved ones and nearly crushed their lives. Even though they had lost their children in the square, they spoke because they did not believe that the state's history of the event was final. They spoke because they hoped that some good would come from telling these stories. Their testimonies, like those of so many other survivors, challenge the receivers to hold, at the same moment, both the ruin of an anguished history and the belief in a better future.[4]

Mikhail Bakhtin's dialogic work and related narrative concepts have helped us to rethink survivors' testimonies as histories of political violence that are binding yet unfinalizable. After political violence, testimonies draw energy from the belief that the last word has not yet been spoken. The testimonies from Tiananmen in the *New York Times* offered another word and invited other responses. They are living proof that the history of the massacre in Tiananmen Square is far from finished.

This implies that the receivers of testimonies are obligated not only to the realities of survivors' histories, but also to the survivors' lives and hopes. Because reconciling catastrophe with hope, and the bounded with the unfinalized, are both highly difficult, those who engage with testimonies generally do better testimony work when they operate with intuition and imagination. I turned to literature and artworks of testimony and found examples of testimonies rendered in ways that were open, personal, ethical, innovative, and hopeful. But I also found that intuition and imagination were often in short supply in the disciplines and professionals that manage the narratives of political violence, including the field of mental health and human rights. That is why I called upon Bakhtin. Although Bakhtin has no theory of testimony, his dialogic narrative theory offers a means for bridging intuition and imagination with discipline so as to approach testimony as a story of living history.

## Living Histories

Some critics of testimony have said that testimony itself is not a real thing, but instead is a construction of Western intervenors. They object so strongly to the ways in which testimony has been used and finalized by intervenors that they do not believe it could be anything else. I share many of their concerns about what has gone wrong in testimony work, but I do not believe that the last word has yet been spoken about testimony either. I believe that testimony is real because I see it as a part of living history.[5]

Living history is history that is unfinished because important historical events and processes are still unfolding. The processes and events of history directly pertaining to political violence may still be active. A given event may mean one historical era is ending, and another is just beginning. The experience of political violence may reverberate within a society for generations, and sometimes for centuries.

Living history also means that the telling and understanding of history is open, energetic, and free. This history is not just static documentation, but interactive conversation. The past is never just past, nor is it just one solitary occurrence. It lives in the present and future and is full of variability, heterogeneity, and multiplicity. The future is open and contingent upon the choices of the present. Living history also means that testimony is many kinds of stories, told for multiple purposes, toward different outcomes, in different contexts.

As *living* history, it requires certain conditions in order to persist and flourish. Finalized history is for the historians, but living history requires the engagement of survivors as well as receivers and interpreters such as mental health professionals, humanitarian workers, journalists, lawyers, religious clerics, writers, and artists. Living history needs their special attention—"love," Bakhtin even called it—in order to produce stories with a form that remains open and free. This often requires receivers and responders to go beyond how their disciplines trained them and what their institutions asked them to do, and instead to learn from artistic models.

I believe that Bakhtin's dialogic work can help testimony work because in my opinion Bakhtin recognized the presence of living history and put it in his writings. Whether it comes from Bakhtin, Tiananmen Square, Chile, the Holocaust, Bosnia-Herzegovina, or Kosovo, I believe that once you have been touched by living history, you are immediately suspicious of finalized history. You realize that history should not be regarded as something abstract and dead, but as a central part of people's lives and human development. The stories that survivors share about their lives lived in the presence of history really do have the power to change politics, history, and life itself. There is a newfound sense of obligation to the truths of history and to its hopes and dreams.

> Catastrophe is not finalization. It is the culmination, in collision and struggle, of points of view (of equally privileged consciousnesses, each with its own world). Catastrophe does not give these points of view resolution, but on the contrary reveals their incapability of resolution under earthly conditions (PDP 298).

This book has offered pictures that show testimonies' evolution through different universes over time. I cannot claim to know how and where testimony will evolve next, what new universes it will generate, and how it will function there. Nor can I claim that testimony will always do good. Yet I do know that because testimonies belong to living history, they will continue to change and to harbor hope. A significant part of our obligation to testimony as a living history is to the future of testimony work. We should keep learning in many universes of testimony until survivors' stories bring us closer to doing some good.

# Notes

## Introduction

1. Clifford Krass, "Pinochet Case Reviving Voices of the Tortured," *New York Times*, January 3, 2000, sec. A, p. 1.

2. A. J. Cienfuegos and C. Monelli, "The Testimony of Political Repression as a Therapeutic Instrument," *American Journal of Orthopsychiatry* 53, no. 1 (1983): 43–51; Inger Agger and Soren Jensen, "Testimony as Ritual and Evidence in Psychotherapy for Political Refugees," *Journal of Traumatic Stress* 3, no. 1 (1990): 115–30; Nancy Caro Hollander, *Love in a Time of Hate: Liberation Psychology in Latin America* (New Brunswick, N.J.: Rutgers University Press, 1997).

3. Warren Hoge, "Britain's High Court Supports Move to Release Pinochet," *New York Times*, February 1, 2000, sec. A, p. 8.

4. Martha Minnow, *Between Vengeance and Forgiveness: Facing History After Genocide and Mass Violence* (Boston: Beacon, 1998); Priscilla Hayner, *Unspeakable Truths: Confronting State Terror and Atrocity* (New York: Routledge, 2000).

5. Mary Marshal Clark, "The September 11, 2001, Oral History Narrative and Memory Project: A First Report," *Journal of American History* 89, no. 2 (September 2002): 571–79; Bruce Springsteen, *Songs* (New York: HarperCollins, 2003).

6. Inger Agger's and Soren Jensen's works are cited in the text with abbreviations as follows. BR: Inger Agger, *The Blue Room: Trauma and Testimony Among Refugee Women; A Psychosocial Exploration* (London: Zed Books, 1992). TH: Inger Agger and Soren Jensen, *Trauma and Healing Under State Terrorism* (London: Zed Books, 1996).

7. Lawrence Langer, *Holocaust Testimonies: The Ruins of Memory* (New Haven, Conn., and London: Yale University Press, 1991); Cathy Caruth, *Unclaimed Experience* (Baltimore: Johns Hopkins University Press, 1996).

8. Shoshana Felman and Dori Laub, *Testimony: Crises of Witnessing in Literature, Psychoanalysis, and History* (New York and London: Routledge, 1992). Hereafter abbreviated in text as *T*.

9. *New Shorter Oxford English Dictionary* (Oxford: Clarendon, 1993).

10. Karl Popper, *The Open Universe* (Lanham, Md.: Rowman and Littlefield, 1982), xvii.

11. Ian Hacking, *Mad Travelers: Reflections on the Reality of Transient Mental Illness* (Charlottesville and London: University Press of Virginia, 1998).

12. Joseph Roth, *The Radetzky March* (Woodstock: Overlook, 1932); Joseph Roth, *The Emperor's Tomb* (Woodstock: Overlook, 1950).

13. Some may call my focus "Eurocentric," but this is the world that I know best. I offer it not in the spirit of exclusion, but in the hope that readers may learn and respond from their own worlds.

## Chapter 1

1. Ariel Dorfman, *Death and the Maiden* (New York and London: Penguin Books, 1994). Hereafter abbreviated in text as *DM*.

2. Charles Figley, *Compassion Fatigue: Secondary Traumatic Stress Disorders in Those Who Treat the Traumatized* (New York: Bruner/Mazel, 1995).

3. See, for example, the National Consortium of Torture Treatment Programs (http://ncttp.westside.com/default.view) and the Center for Victims of Torture (http://www.cvt.org/main.php).

4. Yael Danieli, Else Stamatopoulou, and Clarence J. Dias, eds., *The Universal Declaration of Human Rights: Fifty Years and Beyond* (New York: Baywood, 1998); Michael Ignatieff and Amy Gutman, *Human Rights and Politics and Idolatry* (Princeton, N.J.: Princeton University Press, 2003).

5. Hacking, *Mad Travelers*, 69.

6. Pres. William Clinton, letter to Sister Diana Ortiz, June 22, 1998, available at http://www.kurdistan.org/you-can-end-it/prez.html.

7. Sen. Paul Wellstone, http://www.cvt.org/main.php/Newsroom/Archives.

8. Barry S. Levy and Victor W. Sidel, eds., *War and Public Health* (New York and Oxford: Oxford University Press and the American Public Health Association, 1997).

9. In countries of exile, torture testimony is also conducted for asylum hearings, in which the aim is to demonstrate that a person suffered torture and has had severe mental health consequences, and that if they are returned their condition will worsen. But this is not legal in the same criminal sense. See Laurence Kirmayer, "Failures of Imagination: The Refugee's Narrative in Psychiatry," *Anthropology and Medicine* 10, no. 2 (2003): 167–85.

10. Tina Rosenberg, *The Haunted Land: Facing Europe's Ghosts After Communism* (New York: Random House, 1996).

11. Timothy Garton Ash deepens and extends the question by asking: "Whether to remember and treat the past at all, in any of the diverse available ways, or simply to try to forget it, and look to the future; when to address it, if it is to be addressed; who should do it; and finally how?" See Timothy Garton Ash, "Truth after Dictatorship," *New York Review of Books*, February 19, 1998, vol. 45, no. 3: 35–40. See also Timothy Garton Ash, "Central Europe: The Present Past," *New York Review of Books*, July 13, 1995, vol. 42, no. 12: 21–23: and Timothy Garton Ash, "Bosnia in Our Future," *New York Review of Books*, December 21, 1995, vol. 42, no. 20: 27–31.

12. Michael Humphrey, "From Victim to Victimhood: Truth Commissions and Trials as Rituals of Political Transition and Individual Healing," *Australian Journal of Anthropology* 14, no. 2 (August 2003): 171–87.

13. Catherine McKinnon, "Turning Rape into Pornography: Postmodern Genocide," *Ms.* (July–August 1993): 24–30; and Catherine McKinnon, "Crimes of War, Crimes of Peace," in *On Human Rights: The Oxford Amnesty Lectures, 1993,* ed. by S. Lukes et al. (New York: Basic Books, 1993).

## Chapter 2

1. Art Spiegelman's works are cited in the text with abbreviations as follows. *M:* Art Spiegelman, *Maus* (New York: Pantheon Books, 1986). *MII:* Art Spiegelman, *Maus II: And Here My Troubles Began* (New York: Pantheon Books, 1991). *CM:* Art Spiegelman, *The Complete Maus: A Survivor's Tale. Part I: My Father Bleeds History; Part II: From Mauschwitz to the Catskills,* CD-ROM (New York: Voyager, 1994).

2. Art Spiegelman, "Projects," exhibition at the Museum of Modern Art, New York, N.Y., December 17, 1991, to January 28, 1992.

3. Hana Volavkova, *I Never Saw Another Butterfly: Children's Drawings and Poems from Terezin Concentration Camp, 1942–1944* (New York: Shocken Books, 1994).

4. Geoffrey Hartman, *The Longest Shadow: In the Aftermath of the Holocaust* (Bloomington: Indiana University Press, 1996). Hereafter abbreviated in text as *LS.*

5. Dominick LaCapra, *History and Memory After Auschwitz* (Ithaca, N.Y., and London: Cornell University Press, 1998); James Young, *At Memory's Edge: After-Images of the Holocaust in Contemporary Art and Architecture* (New Haven, Conn., and London: Yale University Press, 2002).

6. Czeslaw Milosz, *The Collected Poems, 1931–1987* (New York: Ecco, 1988).

7. Spielberg's video testimony project and Spiegelman's *Maus* are both works in the vast Holocaust documentary genre, many of which explore visual dimensions. This is not to claim that any direct influence was at work between Spielberg and Spiegelman. No information supports such a claim. Spiegelman was encouraged to publish the first *Maus* in good speed, to preempt a film by Spielberg about mice. However, Spiegelman claimed that he was working from a totally different aesthetic from Spielberg (*MC*).

8. Herbert Hirsch, *Genocide and the Politics of Memory: Studying Death to Preserve Life* (Chapel Hill and London: University of North Carolina Press, 1995).

9. Susan Sontag, *Regarding the Pain of Others* (New York: Picador, 2004), 89.

10. Claude Lanzman, "The Obscenity of Understanding: An Evening with Claude Lanzman," in Cathy Caruth, *Trauma: Explorations in Memory* (Baltimore: Johns Hopkins University Press, 1995), 202. See also Claude Lanzman, *Shoah: An Oral History of the Holocaust* (New York: Pantheon, 1985).

11. Stevan Weine, Dolores Vojvoda, Stephen Hartman, and Leslie Hyman, "A Family Survives Genocide," *Psychiatry* 60 (1997): 24–39.

12. Yael Danieli, ed., *Intergenerational Handbook of Multigenerational Legacies of Trauma* (New York and London: Plenum, 1998).

13. Oscar Lewis, *The Children of Sanchez: Autobiography of a Mexican Family* (New York: Random House, 1961), xi–xxxi. See also Oscar Lewis, *Five Families: Mexican Case Studies in the Culture of Poverty* (New York: HarperCollins, 1975).

14. Rubie Watson, ed., *Memory, History, and Opposition* (Santa Fe, N. Mex.: School of American Research, 1994); Catherine Merridale, *Night of Stone: Death and Memory in Twentieth-Century Russia* (New York: Viking, 2000).

15. Daniel Jonah Goldhagen, *Hitler's Willing Executioners: Ordinary Germans and the Holocaust* (New York: Alfred A. Knopf, 1996).

## Chapter 3

1. I say "wartime" in the chapter title because it is a word commonly used by Bosnians to indicate the time period of military aggression and conflict. I don't mean to overlook the fact that the aggression wasn't a classic war per se (troops fighting troops), but was military aggression against civilians (ethnic cleansing of villages, sieges of cities, genocide).

2. Two other films made after the war, the Hollywood film *Welcome to Sarajevo* and the independent Bosnian film *No Man's Land*, incorporated testimony in very different ways.

3. Zlata Filipovic, *Zlata's Diary: A Child's Life in Sarajevo* (New York: Viking, 1994).

4. On August 2, 1993, Zlata wrote: "Some people compare me with Anne Frank. That frightens me. I don't want to suffer her fate" (Filipovic, *Zlata's Diary*, 171).

5. Michael Ignatieff, "Homage to Bosnia," *New York Review of Books*, April 21, 1994, vol. 41, no. 8.

6. Filipovic, *Zlata's Diary*, 167.

7. Whether those young girls living in exile or in Bosnia-Herzegovina would write or tell their stories, and more generally what they did with their memories, would depend on many other factors and processes that were active in *Zlata's Diary* but were not the book's explicit topic. These factors include such issues as the support of parents and community, the value placed upon reading and education, and the nurturing of creative talent.

8. Aleksander Hemon, "A Coin," in *The Question of Bruno* (New York: Vintage Books, 2001), 120. Hereafter abbreviated in text as *QB*.

9. Aleksander Hemon, *Nowhere Man* (New York: Nan A. Talese, 2002).

10. Nader Mousavizadeh, *The Black Book of Bosnia* (New York: Basic Books, 1996), xii.

11. Roy Gutman, *Witness to Genocide* (New York: Macmillan, 1993).

12. Zlatko Dizdarevic, *Sarajevo: A War Journal* (New York: Fromm International, 1993); Zlatko Dizdarevic, *Portraits of Sarajevo* (New York: Fromm International, 1994), 8.

13. Mousavizadeh, *Black Book of Bosnia*, xii.

14. Thomas Cushman and Stjepan G. Mestorivic, eds., *This Time We Knew* (New York and London: New York University Press, 1996).

15. Jean Baudrillard, "No Pity for Sarajevo: The West's Serbianization; When the West Stands in for the Dead," in *This Time We Knew*, ed. Cushman and Mestorivic, 79–89.

16. Zlatko Dizdarevic, "Sarajevo's 700 Days," *New York Times Magazine*, April 10, 1994, sec. 6, p. 36.

17. Dizdarevic, "Sarajevo's 700 Days," 36.

18. Human Rights Watch website, at http://www.hrw.org/about/faq/.

19. Human Rights Watch, *War Crimes in Bosnia-Herzegovina* (New York: Helsinki Watch, 1992); Human Rights Watch, *War Crimes in Bosnia-Herzegovina, Volume II* (New York: Helsinki Watch, 1993).

20. "About HRW," Human Rights Watch website, at http://www.hrw.org/about/whoweare.html.

21. All quotes concerning the ICTY come from its official website, http://www.un.org/icty/.

22. The approach of the United States government to addressing political violence changed with the humanitarian intervention in Kosovo and changed again after the September 11 attack on the United States, which led to military interventions in Afghanistan and Iraq, presumably to stop global terrorism. See J. L. Holzgrefe and Robert O. Keohane, eds., *Humanitarian Intervention* (Cambridge and New York: Cambridge University Press, 2003); Nicholas Wheeler, *Saving Strangers: Humanitarian Intervention in International Society* (Oxford: Oxford University Press, 2000).

23. Tim Judah, *The Serbs: History, Myth and the Destruction of Yugoslavia* (New Haven, Conn., and London: Yale University Press, 1997); Laura Silber and Allen Little, *Yugoslavia: Death of a Nation* (New York: TV Books, 1995); and Stephen Pavlowitch, *The Improbable Survivor: Yugoslavia, 1918–1988* (London: C. Hurst, 1989).

24. See, for example, Alexander Labin Hinton, *Annihilating Difference: The Anthropology of Genocide* (Berkeley: University of California Press, 2002).

25. Quotation from a Bosnian survivor's testimony gathered through the Project on Genocide, Psychiatry, and Witnessing, published in Stevan Weine et al., "Testimony Psychotherapy in Bosnian Refugees: A Pilot Study," *American Journal of Psychiatry* 155 (1998): 1720–26.

26. Regarding cross-cultural notions of healing, Agger described the testimony from the vantage point of Victor Turner's theory of ritual transitions, including mention of the "threshold phase" (*Blue Room*, 115), which brings to mind

Mikhail Bakhtin's idea of the threshold that will be discussed in part 2 of the present volume.

27. For example, we found it in poetry and prose collections by the authors Carolyn Forche and Lawrence Langer; in memoirs of suffering written during communism by Gustav Herling, Czeslaw Milosz, Nadezhda Mandelstam, and Eugenia Ginzburg; and in the writings of "present history" that use a literary documentary narrative approach. See Timothy Garton Ash, *History of the Present: Essays, Sketches, and Dispatches from Europe in the 1990s* (New York: Vintage Books, 1999).

28. James Joyce, *Ulysses* (New York: Modern Library, 1914), 35.

29. Stevan Weine, *When History Is a Nightmare: Lives and Memories of Ethnic Cleansing in Bosnia-Herzegovina* (New Brunswick, N.J., and London: Rutgers University Press, 1999), 10.

30. Ibid., 13.

31. Carl Schmitt, *The Concept of the Political* (Chicago and London: University of Chicago Press, 1996), 49.

32. Weine, *When History Is a Nightmare*, 213–14.

## Chapter 4

1. Ralph Cintron, Stevan Weine, and Ferid Agani, "Exporting Democracy," *Boston Review: A Political and Literary Forum* 28 (December 2003/ January 2004).

2. This and subsequent quotations from testimony interview were conducted through the Project on Genocide, Psychiatry, and Witnessing by either Stevan Weine or Sabina Leuben and Stevan Weine.

3. Czeslaw Milosz, *A Roadside Dog* (New York: Farrar, Straus, Giroux, 1999).

4. James Clifford, *Routes: Travel and Translation in the Late Twentieth Century* (Cambridge, Mass., and London: Harvard University Press, 1997).

5. Anton Berishaj, "Violence Following Violence," *Psychosocial Notebook* 2 (October 2001): 81.

6. Natali Losi, "Beyond the Archives of Memory," *Psychosocial Notebook* 2 (October 2001): 5–14. Hereafter abbreviated in text as "BAM."

7. Ibrahim Rugova, Harillaq Kekezi, and Rexhep Hida, *What the Kosovars Say and Demand* (Tirana: 8 Nentori Publishing House, 1991), 429.

8. This information was provided by Ferid Agani, director of the Department of Strategic Management, of the Kosovar Ministry of Health.

9. Silvia Salvatici, "Memory Telling: Individual and Collective Identities in Post-War Kosovo: The Archives of Memory," *Psychosocial Notebook* 2 (October 2001): 15–52. Hereafter abbreviated in text as "MT."

10. Luisa Passerini, "An Afterthought on a Work in Progress and a Forethought Towards Its Future," *Psychosocial Notebook* 2 (October 2001): 219–26.

11. Passerini, "Afterthought," 224.

12. Enrica Capussoti, "Memory: A Complex Battlefield," *Psychosocial Notebook* 2 (October 2001): 214.

13. Stevan Weine et al., "The TAFES Multi-Family Group Intervention for Kosovar Refugees: A Descriptive Study," *Journal of Nervous and Mental Diseases* 191, no. 2 (2003): 100–107.

## Chapter 5

1. Gary Saul Morson's and Caryl Emerson's books are cited in the text with abbreviations as follows. *NF:* Gary Saul Morson, *Narrative and Freedom: The Shadows of Time* (New Haven, Conn., and London: Yale University Press, 1996). *FHY:* Caryl Emerson, *The First Hundred Years of Mikhail Bakhtin* (Princeton, N.J.: Princeton University Press, 1997). *CP:* Gary Saul Morson and Caryl Emerson, *Mikhail Bakhtin: Creation of a Prosaics* (Palo Alto, Calif.: Stanford University Press, 1991).

2. Ruth Coates, *Christianity in Bakhtin: God and the Exiled Author* (Cambridge: Cambridge University Press, 1999), 87.

3. Mikhail Bakhtin's works are cited in the text with abbreviations as follows. *PDP:* Mikhail Bakhtin, *Problems of Dostoevsky's Poetics,* trans. Caryl Emerson (Minneapolis: University of Minnesota Press, 1984). *SG:* Mikhail Bakhtin, *Speech Genres and Other Late Essays,* trans. Vern McGee (Austin: University of Texas Press, 1986). *DI:* Mikhail Bakhtin, *The Dialogic Imagination: Four Essays,* trans. Caryl Emerson and Michael Holquist (Austin: University of Texas Press, 1981).

4. Valerie Z. Nollan, *Bakhtin's Ethics and Mechanics* (Evanston, Ill., and London: Northwestern University Press, 2004).

## Chapter 6

1. See Gerald Edelman, *Wider Than the Sky: The Phenomenal Gift of Consciousness* (New Haven, Conn., and London: Yale University Press, 2004).

2. Caryl Emerson, personal comment to the author.

3. Dori Laub and Nannette Auerhan, "Knowing and Not Knowing Massive Psychic Trauma: Forms of Traumatic Memory," *International Journal of Psycho-Analysis* 74 (1993): 287–302.

4. Robert Jay Lifton, *The Protean Self: Human Resilience in an Age of Fragmentation* (New York: Basic Books, 1993).

5. Ian Hacking, *Rewriting the Soul: Multiple Personality and the Sciences of Memory* (Princeton, N.J., and Chichester, Eng.: Princeton University Press, 1995); Hacking, *Mad Travelers.*

6. Hacking, *Rewriting the Soul*, 198–220.

7. Stevan Weine, "'A Forgotten History' and Related Risks for Speech Genre Users in Trauma Mental Health: A Commentary," *Journal of Contemporary Psychotherapy* 29, no. 4 (1999): 267–81.

8. Patrick Bracken, *Trauma: Culture, Meaning, and Philosophy* (London and Philadelphia: Whurr, 2002), 210.

9. Judith Herman, *Trauma and Recovery* (New York: Basic Books, 1992).

10. Allen Young, *The Harmony of Illusions: Inventing Post-Traumatic Stress Disorder* (Princeton, N.J.: Princeton University Press, 1995); Michael Humphrey, "From Victim to Victimhood," 171–87.

11. Coates, *Christianity in Bakhtin*, 6–9, 16–17.

12. Morson and Emerson refer to Bakhtin's condemnation of the sin of "theoretism," which "reduce(s) people to the circumstances that produced them, without seeing their genuine freedom to remake themselves and take responsibility for their action" (*Creation of a Prosaics*, 92).

13. Hacking, *Rewriting the Soul*, 210–20.

14. Patrick Bracken has written that the focus upon memory is so highly biased toward individual cognition as to remove persons from cultural, social, and historical contexts.

15. Michael Holquist, *Dialogism: Bakhtin and His World* (New York: Routledge, 1990).

16. A. Kleinman and J. Kleinman, "The Appeal of Experience, the Dismay of Images," *Daedalus* 125, no. 1 (Winter 1996): xi.

17. A. Kleinman, "Moral Experience and Ethical Reflection: Can Ethnography Reconcile Them? 'A Quandary for the New Bioethics,'" *Daedalus*, "Bioethics and Beyond," vol. 128, no. 4 (Fall 1999): 82. Hereafter abbreviated in text as "ME."

18. Pierre Bourdieu et al., *The Weight of the World: Social Suffering in Contemporary Society* (Stanford, Calif.: Stanford University Press, 1993), 3. Hereafter abbreviated in text as *WW*.

19. Veena Das, "The Act of Witnessing: Violence, Poisonous Knowledge, and Subjectivity," in *Violence and Subjectivity*, ed. Veena Das et al. (Berkeley, Los Angeles, and London: University of California Press, 2000).

20. Bakhtin also wrote: "And everything internal gravitates not toward itself but is turned to the outside and dialogized, every internal experience ends up on the boundary, encounters another, and in this tension-filled encounter lies its entire essence" (*Problems of Dostoevsky's Poetics*, 287).

21. Martha Nussbaum, *Poetic Justice: The Literary Imagination and Public Life* (Boston: Beacon, 1995).

22. Robert Coles, *Doing Documentary Work* (New York and Oxford: Oxford University Press, 1997); Robert Coles, *The Call of Stories: Teaching and the Moral Imagination* (Boston: Houghton Mifflin, 1990).

23. Morson wrote: "Read this way, the plots of certain literary works possess great philosophical importance" (*Narrative and Freedom*, 87).

24. Bakhtin wrote: "The idea in Dostoevsky is never cut off from the voice" (*Problems of Dostoevsky's Poetics*, 279).

25. "Unfinalizability" is defined in chapter 8. It is an awkward term, but I chose to use it because it is widely used by Bakhtin and in writings on him.

26. Weine et al., "Testimony Psychotherapy in Bosnian Refugees," 1720–26.


# Chapter 7

1. For example, see Derrick Summerfield, "The Invention of Post-Traumatic Stress Disorder and the Social Usefulness of a Psychiatric Category," *British Medical Journal* 322 (2001): 95–98; and Maurice Eisenbruch, "From Post-Traumatic Stress Disorder to Cultural Bereavement: Diagnosis of Southeast Asian Refugees," *Social Science and Medicine* 33, no. 6 (1991): 673–80.

2. Lawrence Kirmayer, "Confusion of the Senses: Implications of Ethnocultural Variations in Somatoform and Dissociative Disorders for PTSD," in *Ethnocultural Aspects of Posttraumatic Stress Disorder: Issues, Research, and Clinical Applications*, ed. A. J. Marsella et al. (Washington, D.C.: American Psychological Association, 1996).

3. Bracken, *Trauma: Culture, Meaning, and Philosophy*, 209.

4. Ibid., 6

5. Humphrey, "From Victim to Victimhood," 171–87.

6. Stevan Weine, "Against Evil," *Peace and Conflict* 5, no. 4 (1999): 357–64; Ervin Staub, *The Roots of Evil: The Origins of Genocide and Other Group Violence* (Cambridge and New York: Cambridge University Press, 1989).

7. Veena Das et al., *Remaking a World: Violence, Social Suffering, and Recovery* (Berkeley: University of California Press, 2001), 2.

8. Das et al., *Remaking a World*, 26.

9. Ibid., 2.

10. See Edward A. Tiryakian, "The Wild Cards of Modernity," *Daedalus*, "Human Diversity," vol. 126, no. 2 (Spring 1997): 147–82.

11. James Dobbins et al., *America's Role in Nation-Building: From Germany to Iraq* (Santa Monica, Calif.: RAND, 2003).

12. Michael Ignatieff, "State Failure and Nation Building," in *Humanitarian Intervention*, ed. J. L. Holzgrefe and Robert O. Keohane (Cambridge and New York: Cambridge University Press, 2003), 299–321.

13. "Human sciences" has been interpreted by others to mean the humanities as opposed to sciences in the sense of "hard sciences." I am using the term "human sciences" somewhat differently, in a way closer to Bakhtin's own comment that human sciences were "sciences of the spirit" (*Speech Genres*, 161). "Human sciences" is a

key term that speaks not only to the humanities per se, but also for an approach to multidisciplinary scholarship and practice regarding trauma and testimony that includes the social sciences, clinical sciences, humanities, and human services.

14. Bracken, *Trauma: Culture, Meaning, and Philosophy*, 212.

15. Peter Brooks, *Troubling Confessions* (Chicago and London: University of Chicago Press, 2000), 3.

16. Breyten Breytenbach, *Dog Heart: A Memoir* (Harcourt Brace, 1999).

17. Bracken, *Trauma: Culture, Meaning, and Philosophy*, 223–24.

18. Kai Erikson, "Notes on Trauma and Community," in *Trauma: Explorations in Memory*, ed. Caruth, 183–99; A. Kleinman, V. Das, and M. Lock, eds., *Social Suffering* (Berkeley: University of California Press, 1997); Eisenbruch, "Post-Traumatic Stress Disorder," 673–80; Bourdieu et al., *Weight of the World*, 3; Das et al., *Remaking a World*.

19. "Centripetal" and "centrifugal" are important Bakhtinian terms (Morson and Emerson, *Creation of a Prosaics*, 30–35).

20. Bakhtin wrote: "To be means to communicate" (*Problems of Dostoevsky's Poetics*, 87).

21. Susan Sontag, "Regarding the Torture of Others," *New York Times Magazine*, May 23, 2004, sec. 6, p. 25.

22. American Psychiatric Association, *Diagnostic and Statistical Manual of Mental Disorders DSM-III* (Washington, D.C.: American Psychiatric Association, 1984).

23. Pierre Bourdieu, *Practical Reason* (Stanford, Calif.: Stanford University Press, 1998), 1–18.

24. Thomas Kent, "Hermeneutics and Genre: Bakhtin and the Problem of Communicative Interaction," in *Landmark Essays on Bakhtin, Rhetoric, and Writing*, ed. Frank Farmer (Nahwah, N.J.: Hermagon, 1998), 35.

25. Holquist, *Dialogism*.

26. Ibid., 71.

27. Kleinman refers to the "crucial mediatization of violence and trauma in the global moral economy of our times" in Arthur Kleinman, "Forms and Dynamics of Social Violence," in *Violence and Subjectivity*, ed. Das et al., 232. Kleinman continues: "The mediatization of violence and suffering creates a form of inauthentic social experience: witnessing at a distance, a kind of voyeurism in which nothing is acutely at stake for the observer" (232). Bakhtin wrote about "the sentimental-humanistic dematerialization of man, which remains objectified" (*Problems of Dostoevsky's Poetics*, 297).

28. Weine, *When History Is a Nightmare*, 3–4.

29. See the discussion on spectacle, media, and nongovernmental organizations in the section on "Mixed Constitution" in Michael Hardt and Antonio Negri, *Empire* (Cambridge, Mass., and London: Harvard University Press, 2000). See also

Arthur Kleinman, "The Violences of Everyday Life," in *Violence and Subjectivity*, ed. Das et al.

## Chapter 8

1. The official Truth and Reconciliation Commission website is at www.doj .gov.za/trc. See also the Promotion of National Unity and Reconciliation Act. No. 34 of 1995.

2. Jacobus A. du Pisani and Kwang Su-kim, "Establishing the Truth about the Apartheid Past: Historians and the South African Truth and Reconciliation Commission," *African Studies Quarterly* 8, no. 1 (Fall 2004).

3. Breytenbach, *Dog Heart*, 21.

4. Ibid.

5. Jeffrey Rosen, "Pursuing Justice: Perils of the Past," *New York Times*, December 21, 2003, sec. 4, p. 1.

6. Merle Friedman, paper presented at the March 2001 Conference on Refugee Mental Health at the University of New South Wales, Sydney, Australia.

7. See, for example, the previously cited works by Ian Hacking, Patrick Bracken, and Allen Young.

8. Holzgrefe and Keohane, eds., *Humanitarian Intervention;* Wheeler, *Saving Strangers*.

9. Helena Cobban, "The Legacies of Collective Violence," *Boston Review*, April/May 2002; Samantha Power, "Rwanda: The Two Faces of Justice," *New York Review of Books*, January 16, 2003, vol. 50, no. 1; Reuters, "Africa: Rwanda: Traditional Courts for Genocide Cases," *New York Times*, June 25, 2004, Foreign Desk.

10. Das et al., *Remaking a World*, 26.

11. W. G. Sebald, *On the Natural History of Destruction* (New York: Random House, 2003), 10.

12. Sebald, *Natural History of Destruction*, 10.

13. Sontag, *Regarding the Pain of Others*, 8.

14. "Unfinalizability" is an awkward term in English, but because it is the convention in English-language writings on Bakhtin, it is what I use. The most serious potential misunderstanding of "unfinalizability" is that it be construed as a certain and finite labeling of experience. Michael Holquist interprets *nezavershenmost* as "openness" or "unfinishedness" (Bakhtin, *Speech Genres*, xii).

15. Michael André Bernstein, *Foregone Conclusions: Against Apocalyptic History* (Berkeley, Los Angeles, and London: University of California Press, 1994).

16. Bernstein, *Foregone Conclusions*, 3.

17. Ibid., 9–41, 36.

18. For example, in *Foregone Conclusions*, Bernstein wrote: "Especially in the face of catastrophe, there is an urge to surrender to the most extreme foreshadowing imaginable, thereby resisting sideshadowing altogether. We try to make sense of a historical disaster by interpreting it, according to the strictest teleological model, as the climax of a bitter trajectory whose inevitable outcome it must be" (9).

19. David Becker, "The Deficiency of the Concept of Post-Traumatic Stress Disorder When Dealing with Victims of Human Rights Violations," in *Beyond Trauma: Cultural and Social Dynamics*, ed. R. J. Kleber, C. R. Figley, and P. R. Gersons (New York: Plenum, 1995), 99–110.

20. See Ruth Coates's description of love as a theme in Bakhtin. Coates wrote: "In contrast to the essentially negative approach of, say, the cognitive disciplines, which strip away from their object everything that is extraneous to their purpose, creative activity incorporates the whole of its object into the artwork, giving it the 'gift' of form. This requires a fundamentally positive attitude, which Bakhtin describes as love: 'through form I express my love, my affirmation, my acceptance'" (Coates, *Christianity in Bakhtin*, 173).

21. Robert Jay Lifton, *Death in Life* (New York: Touchstone Books, 1976).

22. Das et al., *Remaking a World*, 1–30.

23. Langer, *Holocaust Testimonies*.

24. See, for example, Alessandro Portelli, *The Death of Luigi Trastulli and Other Stories* (Albany: State University of New York Press, 1991); and Alessandro Portelli, *The Battle of Valle Giulia: Oral History and the Art of Dialogue* (Madison and London: University of Wisconsin Press, 1997).

## Afterword

1. Craig Smith, "Tiananmen's Shadow," *New York Times Magazine*, February 4, 2001, sec. 6, p. 52.

2. See *The Tiananmen Papers* (2001), comp. Zhang Liang, ed. Andrew J. Nathan and Perry Link. See also Jonathan Mirsky, "The Truth about Tiananmen," *New York Review of Books*, February 8, 2001, vol. 48, no. 2.

3. Smith, "Tiananmen's Shadow," 52.

4. I do not know what became of these people. Testimonies inexplicably pop up onto the media's screen and then in a heartbeat drop out of our awareness. I sincerely doubt that they either received mental health services or got the justice they sought.

5. I described this "living history" in writings prior to Hilary Clinton publishing her autobiography: Hilary Rodham Clinton, *Living History* (New York: Simon and Schuster, 2003).

# Index

ABC Evening News with Peter Jennings, 54
Afghanistan, 123, 165n22
African slaves in America, xxi
Afrim (young Kosovar man), 76–77
Agger, Inger, xvii, xviii–xix, 20, 23; in Chile,
    9–13, 22, 38, 40, 104, 123; in Denmark
    blue room, 13–16, 17, 21, 32–35, 59, 61,
    66, 149; in former Yugoslavia, 59–62,
    63, 123
Albania, Kosovo refugees in, 74
Amnesty International, 17, 55
Apartheid testimony, xxi, 142
Archives of Memory (Kosovo project), 71,
    79–82, 85–86, 123–24
Ash, Timothy Garton, 23
Auschwitz, 26, 27, 29, 33, 65

Bakhtin, Mikhail, 95–96, 105, 118, 132–40
    passim, 150, 151; and consciousness, 98–
    99, 102–3; and creative understanding,
    120, 130–32; dialogism of, see Dialogue;
    and eventness, 148, (in testimonies)
    135–36, 139; and heterochrony, 141,
    147–49, 151; and historical emergence
    in narrative, 141, 149–51, 154; and
    "human sciences," 92, 119, 124–27, 130–
    31; key ideas of, 154–56; and novel writ-
    ing, 149, (Dostoevsky) 93–103 passim,
    109–14, 116, 137, 145, 152–54; and
    novelistic selfhood, 111–15; and outside-
    ness (of testimony), 120, 132–35, 139,
    154; polyphony, 92, 95, 103–4, 107,
    108–9, 111, 112, 134, (in narrative) 95,
    113–14, 115–18, 154, (in novel) 103,
    112, 153, 154; psychology of, 105–9,
    (psychiatric limits) 97, 100, 104, 109;
    and speech genre, 120, 136–38, 139;
    and threshold phenomenon, 110, 149;

and unfinalizability, 141, 144–46, 151.
    See also Catastrophe; Consciousness;
    Ethics; Heroes; Narratives; Novel
Balkans, the, 37, 51; American (dehistori-
    cized) view of, 50, ("Balkan wars") 55;
    former Yugoslavia, 45, 49, 57, (Chilean
    testimony model used in) 59–62; mental
    health professionals in, xv, 81–82. See also
    Kosovar testimonies
Baudrillard, Jean, 54–55
BBC (British Broadcasting Corporation), 74
Belgrade, 59
Berishaj, Anton, 73
Bernstein, Michael André, 92, 113, 147, 148
Bettelheim, Bruno, 43
"Beyond the Archives of Memory"("BAM")
    (Losi), 79
Blue room as safe space, 37, 38, 41, 61, 66
The Blue Room: Trauma and Testimony Among
    Refugee Women (BR) (Agger), xvii, 13–17,
    21, 31–34 passim, 38, 66
Bosnia-Herzegovina: concentration camps in,
    54; cultural issues (merhamet), 66–68, 70,
    84; ethnic cleansing in, 37, 47–48, 51,
    53–58, 63, 68–69, 77, (civil war vs.)
    60, (Kosovar awareness of) 84; Muslims
    in, see Muslims, Bosnian; refugees from, in
    U.S., xx, 35, 37, 63–65; testimonies from
    wartime, xx, xxi, 47–70, 72, 79, (Chilean
    model) 59–63, (contradictions in) 67–
    68; Western attitude toward, 55–56
Boundaries, 132–34, 139, 154
Bourdieu, Pierre, 107, 108, 128, 132
Bracken, Patrick, 102, 106, 121, 125, 126,
    128
Breytenbach, Breyten, 3, 142–43
Brooks, Peter, 125
"Brotherhood and Unity," 62, 68–69

# About the Author

Stevan Weine is a professor of psychiatry and the director of the International Center on Responses to Catastrophes at the University of Illinois at Chicago. He is the author of *When History Is a Nightmare: Lives and Memories of Ethnic Cleansing in Bosnia-Herzegovina.*